Theoretical Writings

Some titles are not available in North America.

Theoretical Writings

Alain Badiou

Edited and translated by

Ray Brassier and Alberto Toscano

Bloomsbury Academic
An imprint of Bloomsbury Publishing Plc

B L O O M S B U R Y
LONDON · OXFORD · NEW YORK · NEW DELHI · SYDNEY

Bloomsbury Academic

An imprint of Bloomsbury Publishing Plc

50 Bedford Square	1385 Broadway
London	New York
WC1B 3DP	NY 10018
UK	USA

www.bloomsbury.com

BLOOMSBURY and the Diana logo are trademarks of Bloomsbury Publishing Plc

First published by Continuum, 2004

Bloomsbury Revelations edition published 2015

© Ray Brassier and Alberto Toscano 2004, 2015

British Library Cataloguing-in-Publication Data
A catalogue record for this book is available from the British Library.

ISBN: PB: 978-1-4742-3411-5
ePub: 978-1-4742-3412-2
ePDF: 978-1-4742-3413-9

Library of Congress Cataloging-in-Publication Data
A catalog record for this book is available from the Library of Congress.

Series: Bloomsbury Revelations

Typeset by Newgen Knowledge Works (P) Ltd., Chennai, India
Printed and bound in India

Contents

LIST OF SOURCES

'Mathematics and Philosophy: The Grand Style and the Little Style' is translated from an unpublished manuscript; 'Philosophy and Mathematics: Infinity and the End of Romanticism' originally appeared as 'Philosophie et mathématique' in *Conditions* (Paris: Seuil, 1992), pp. 157–78; 'The Question of Being Today' originally appeared as 'La question de l'être aujourd'hui' in *Court traité d'ontologie transitoire* (Paris: Seuil, 1998), pp. 25–38; 'Platonism and Mathematical Ontology' originally appeared in *Court traité d'ontologie transitoire*, pp. 95–119; 'The Being of Number' originally appeared in *Court traité d'ontologie transitoire*, pp. 141–51; 'One, Multiple, Multiplicities' originally appeared as 'Un, multiple, multiplicité(s), in *multitudes* 1 (2000), pp. 195–211; 'Spinoza's Closed Ontology' originally appeared as 'L'ontologie fermée de Spinoza' in *Court traité d'ontologie transitoire*, pp. 73–93; 'The Event as Trans-Being' is a revised and expanded version of 'L'événement comme trans-être' in *Court traité d'ontologie transitoire*, pp. 55–9; 'On Subtraction' originally appeared as 'Conférence sur la soustraction' in *Conditions*, pp. 179–95; 'Truth: Forcing and the Unnameable' originally appeared as 'Vérité: forçage et innomable' in *Conditions*, pp. 196–212; 'Kant's Subtractive Ontology' originally appeared as 'L'ontologie soustractive de Kant' in *Court traité d'ontologie transitoire*, pp. 153–64; 'Eight Theses on the Universal' originally appeared as 'Huit thèses sur l'universel' in *Universel, singulier, sujet*, ed. Jelica Sumic (Paris: Kimé, 2000), pp. 11–20; 'Politics as a Truth Procedure' originally appeared in *Abrégé de métapolitique* (Paris: Seuil, 1998), pp. 155–67; 'Being and Appearance' originally appeared as 'L'être et l'apparaître' in *Court traits d'ontologie transitoire*, pp. 179–200; 'Notes Toward a Thinking of Appearance' is translated from an unpublished manuscript; 'The Transcendental' and 'Hegel and the Whole' are translated from a draft manuscript of *Logiques des mondes* (Paris: Seuil, forthcoming); 'Language, Thought, Poetry' is translated from the author's manuscript, a Portuguese language version has been published in *Para uma Nova Teoria do Sujeito: Conferências Brasileiras* (Rio de Janeiro: Relume-Dumará, 1994), pp. 75–86.

EDITORS' NOTE

The purpose of this volume is to distil the essential lineaments of Alain Badiou's philosophical doctrine. In spite of the plural 'writings' in our title, this is not a reader, an overview or a representative selection. Anyone already acquainted with Badiou's 'English' works, but not familiar with his entire output, could be forgiven for mistaking him for a polemical essayist – gifted, insightful, provocative, but by no means a thinker capable of recasting the existing parameters of philosophical discourse. Those who have reacted sceptically to zealous claims made on his behalf may feel legitimately entitled to their scepticism on the basis of the evidence presented by Badiou's extant and forthcoming English publications (these being, in chronological order: *Manifesto for Philosophy; Deleuze; Ethics; Infinite Thought; Saint Paul; On Beckett; Handbook of Inaesthetics; On Metapolitics*). Notwithstanding the undeniable interest and often striking originality of these works, without an adequate grasp of Badiou's *systematic doctrine*, they can easily be (and indeed have been) treated as works of polemical intervention, pedagogy, popularisation, commentary . . . in short, as works that might elicit enthusiastic assent or virulent rejection, but which fail to command the patient, disciplined engagement solicited by an unprecedented philosophical project. What do we mean by an unprecedented philosophical project? Quite simply, the one laid out in Badiou's *Being and Event* (1988) – a book which may yet turn out to have effected the most profound and far-reaching renewal of the possibilities of philosophy since Heidegger's *Being and Time*, regardless of one's eventual evaluation of the desirability or ultimate worth of such a renewal. Just as one does not have to be a Heideggerean to acknowledge the epochal importance of *Being and Time*, one does not have to accept Badiou's startling claims in order to acknowledge the astonishing depth and scope of the project initiated in *Being and Event*, which is being extended and partially recast in the forthcoming *The Logics of Worlds* (2005).

Theoretical Writings provides a concentrate of this project. Admittedly, it is a book assembled from a wide variety of texts, some published, some unpublished: essays, book chapters, lectures, conference papers, as well as two extracts previewing *The Logics of Worlds*. In spite of the heterogeneity of the sources, and the constraints these inevitably imposed, we have deliberately assembled the material in such a way as to articulate and exhibit the fundamental structure of Badiou's system. Accordingly, *Theoretical Writings* is divided into three distinct sections, each section anchored in the preceding one. Thus the book is explicitly designed to be read in sequential order. Each section unfolds the content and ramifications of a core component of Badiou's doctrine. Section I, *Ontology is Mathematics*, introduces the reader to the grounding gesture behind Badiou's philosophical project, the identification of ontology with mathematics. Section II, *The Subtraction of Truth*, puts forward the link between the fundamental concepts of event, truth and subject as they are articulated onto the ontological doctrine outlined in Section I. Section III, *Logics of Appearance*, outlines the recent development in Badiou of a theory of appearance that seeks to localize the truth-event within the specific consistency, or transcendental logic, of what he calls a world. In conformity with the architectonic just outlined, each section begins with direct treatments of the relevant feature of Badiou's system (ontology and the axiom; subjectivity, subtraction and the event; appearance, logic, world), before going on to elaborate on these features through (1) targeted engagements with key philosophical interlocutors and/or rivals (Deleuze on the status of the multiple; Spinoza on axiomatic ontology; Kant on subtraction and subjectivity; Hegel on totality and appearance), and (2) brief exemplifications of philosophy's engagement with its extra-philosophical conditions (emancipation and universality; the numerical schematization of politics; the relation between language and poetry).

Since we consider Badiou's original material and our arrangement thereof to render any further prefatory remarks a hindrance to the reader's engagement with the work itself, we have chosen to confine our own remarks to a postface, which will try to gauge the consequences and explicate the stakes of Badiou's project vis-à-vis the wider philosophical landscape. Were the reader to encounter intractable difficulties in navigating Badiou's conceptual apparatus, we strongly recommend that he or she refers to what will undoubtedly remain the 'canonical' commentary on Badiou's thought, Peter Hallward's *Badiou: A Subject to Truth* (Minneapolis: Minnesota University Press, 2003), complementing it if needs be with writings from the burgeoning secondary literature.

We have tried to keep editorial interventions to a strict minimum, providing bibliographical references or clarifications wherever we deemed it necessary. All notes in square brackets are ours.

The editors would like to thank Tristan Palmer, who first commissioned this project, Hywel Evans, Veronica Miller and Sarah Douglas at Continuum,

Editors' Note

and Keith Ansell Pearson for providing us with the initial contact. We would also like to express our gratitude to those friends who have contributed, in one way or another, to the conception and production of this volume, whether through ongoing debate or editorial interventions: Jason Barker, Lorenzo Chiesa, John Collins, Oliver Feltham, Peter Hallward, Nina Power and Damian Veal. Most of all, our thanks go to Alain Badiou, whose unstinting generosity and continuous support for this venture over the past three years have proved vital.

R.B., A.T.
London, November 2003

AUTHOR'S PREFACE

Philosophical works come in a peculiar variety of forms. Ultimately, however, they all seem to fall somewhere between two fundamental but opposing tendencies. At one extreme, we find the complete absence of writing and the espousal of oral transmission and critical debate. This is the path chosen by Socrates, the venerable inceptor. At the other extreme, we find the single 'great work', perpetually reworked in solitude. This is basically the case with Schopenhauer and his endlessly revised *The World as Will and Representation*. Between these two extremes, we find the classical alternation between precisely focused essays and vast synoptic treatises. This is the case with Kant, Descartes and many others. But we also encounter the aphoristic approach, much used by Nietzsche, or the carefully orchestrated succession of works dealing with problems in a clearly discernible sequence, as in Bergson. Alternatively, we have an amassing of brief but very dense texts, without any attempt at systematic overview, as is the case with Leibniz; or a disparate series of long, quasi-novelistic works (sometimes involving pseudonyms), like those produced by Kierkegaard and also to a certain extent by Jacques Derrida. We should also note the significant number of works that have acquired a mythical status precisely because they were announced but never finished: for example, Plato's dialogue, *The Philosopher*; Pascal's *Pensées*, the third volume of Marx's *Capital*, part two of Heidegger's *Sein und Zeit*, or Sartre's book on morality. It is also important to note how many 'books' of philosophy are in fact lecture notes, either kept by the lecturer himself and subsequently published (this is the case for a major portion of Heidegger's work, but also for figures like Jules Lagneau, Merleau-Ponty and others), or taken by students (this is the case for almost all the works by Aristotle that have been handed down to us, but also for important parts of Hegel's work, such as his aesthetics and his history of philosophy). Let's round off this brief sketch by remarking that the philosophical corpus seems to encompass every conceivable style of presentation: dramatic dialogue (Plato, Malebranche, Schelling . . .); novelistic narrative (Rousseau, Hölderlin, Nietzsche . . .); mathematical treatises in the Euclidean manner (Descartes, Spinoza . . .); autobiography

(St. Augustine, Kierkegaard . . .); expansive treatises for the purposes of which the author has forged a new conceptual vocabulary (Kant, Fichte, Hegel . . .); poems (Parmenides, Lucretius . . .); as well as many others – basically, anything whatsoever that can be classified as 'writing'.

In other words, it is impossible to provide a clear-cut criterion for what counts as a book of philosophy. Consider then the case of these *Theoretical Writings*: in what sense can this present book really be said to be one of my books? Specifically, one of my books of philosophy? Is it not rather a book by my friends Ray Brassier and Alberto Toscano? After all, they gathered and selected the texts from several different books, which for the most part were not strictly speaking 'works' but rather collections of essays. They decided that these texts merited the adjective 'theoretical'. And they translated them into English, so that the end result can be said not to have existed anywhere prior to this publication.

Basically, I would like above all to thank these two friends, as well as Tristan Palmer from Continuum, who agreed to publish all this work. I would like to thank them because they have provided me, along with other readers, with the opportunity of reading a new, previously unpublished book, apparently authored by someone called 'Alain Badiou' – who is reputed to be none other than myself.

What is the principal interest of this new book? It is, I think, that it provides a new formulation of what can be considered to be the fundamental core of my philosophical doctrine – or 'theory', to adopt the term used in the title of this book. Rather than linger over examples, details, tangential hypotheses, the editors have co-ordinated the sequence of fundamental concepts in such a way as to construct a framework for their articulation. They try to show how, starting from an ontology whose paradigm is mathematical, I am able to propose a new vision of what a *truth* is, along with a new vision of what it is to be the *subject* of such a truth.

This pairing of subject and truth goes back a long way. It is one of the oldest pairings in the entire history of philosophy. Moreover, the idea that the root of this pairing lies in a thinking of pure being, or being qua being, is not exactly new either. But this is the whole point: Ray Brassier and Alberto Toscano are convinced that the way in which I propose to link the three terms being, truth, and subject, is novel and persuasive; perhaps because there are rigorously exacting *conditions* for this linking. In order for being to be thinkable, it has to be considered on the basis of the mathematical theory of multiplicities. In order for a truth to come forth, a hazardous supplementing of being is required, a situated but incalculable event. Lastly, in order for a subject to be constituted, what must be deployed in the situation of this subject is a multiplicity that is anonymous and egalitarian, which is to say, generic.

What these essays, which my two friends have gathered and basically reinvented here, show – at least in my eyes – is that in order for the theoretical triad of being, truth, and subject to hold, it is necessary to think the triad that follows from it – which is to say the triad of the multiple (along with the void), the event (along with its site) and the generic (along with the new forms of knowledge which it allows us to force).

In other words, what we have here is the theoretical core of my philosophy, because this book exhibits, non-deductively, new technical concepts that allow us to transcribe the classical problematic (being, truth, subject) into a conceptual assemblage that is not only modern, but perhaps even 'morethan-modern' (given that the adjective 'postmodern' has been evacuated of all content). These concepts are: mathematical multiplicity, the plurality of infinities, the void as proper name of being, the event as trans-being, fidelity, the subject of enquiries, the generic and forcing. These concepts provide us with the radically new terms required for a reformulation of Heidegger's fundamental question: 'What is it to think?'

But one of the aims of my translator friends is also to explain why my conception of philosophy – and hence my answer to the question about thinking – requires that philosophy remain under the combined guard of the mathematical condition as well as the poetic condition. Generally, the contemporary philosophies that place themselves under the auspices of the poem (e.g. in the wake of Heidegger) differ essentially from those that place themselves under the auspices of the matheme (e.g. the various branches of analytical philosophy). One of the peculiar characteristics of my own project is that it requires both the reference to poetry and a basis in mathematics. It does so, moreover, through a combined critique of the way in which Heidegger uses poetry and the way analytical philosophers use mathematical logic. I believe that this double requirement follows from the fact that at the core of my thinking lies a rational denial of finitude, and the conviction that thinking, our thinking, is essentially tied to the infinite. But the infinite as form of being is mathematical, while the infinite as resource for the power of language is poetic.

For a long time, Ray Brassier and Alberto Toscano hoped the title of this book would be *The Stellar Matheme*. Perhaps this is too esoteric an expression. But it encapsulates what is essential to my thinking. Thought is a 'matheme' insofar as the pure multiple is only thinkable through mathematical inscription. But thought is a 'stellar matheme' in so far as, like the symbol of the star in the poetry of Mallarmé, it constitutes, beyond its own empirical limits, a reserve of eternity.

A.B
Paris, Spring 2003

SECTION I
ONTOLOGY IS MATHEMATICS

CHAPTER 1
MATHEMATICS AND PHILOSOPHY: THE GRAND STYLE AND THE LITTLE STYLE

In order to address the relation between mathematics and philosophy, we must first distinguish between the grand style and the little style.

The little style painstakingly constructs mathematics as an *object* for philosophical scrutiny. I call it 'the little style' because it assigns mathematics a subservient role, as something whose only function seems to consist in helping to perpetuate a well-defined area of philosophical *specialization*. This area of specialization goes by the name 'philosophy of mathematics', where the genitive 'of' is objective. The philosophy of mathematics can in turn be inscribed within an area of specialization that goes by the name 'epistemology and history of science'; an area possessing its own specialized bureaucracy in those academic committees and bodies whose role it is to manage a personnel comprising teachers and researchers.

But in philosophy, specialization invariably gives rise to the little style. In Lacanian terms, we could say that it collapses the discourse of the Master – which is rooted in the master-signifier, the S1 that gives rise to a signifying chain – onto the discourse of the University, that perpetual commentary which is well represented by the second moment of all speech, the S2 which exists by making the Master disappear through the usurpation of commentary.

The little style, which is characteristic of the philosophy and epistemology of mathematics, strives to dissolve the ontological sovereignty of mathematics, its aristocratic self-sufficiency, its unrivalled mastery, by confining its dramatic, almost baffling existence to a stale compartment of academic specialization.

The most telling feature of the little style is the manner in which it exerts its grip upon its object through historicization and classification. We could characterize this object as a neutered mathematics, one which is the exclusive preserve of the little style precisely because it has been created by it.

When the goal is to eliminate a frightening master-signifier, classification and historicization are the hallmarks of a very little style.

Let me straightaway provide a genuinely worthy instance of the little style; in other words, a great example of the little style. I refer to the 'philosophical remarks' that conclude a truly remarkable work entitled *Foundations of Set-Theory*, whose second edition, from which I am quoting here, dates from 1973. I call it great because, among other things, it was written by three firstrate logicians and mathematicians: Abraham Fraenkel, Yehoshua Bar-Hillel and Azriel Levy. This book's concluding philosophical paragraph baldly states that:

> Our first problem regards the ontological status of sets – not of this or the other set, but sets in general. Since sets, as ordinarily understood, are what philosophers call *universals*, our present problem is part of the well-known and amply discussed problem of the *ontological status of universals*.[1]

Let us immediately note three features of this brief paragraph, with which any adept of the little style would unhesitatingly concur.

Firstly, what is at stake is not what mathematics might entail for ontology, but rather the specific ontology of mathematics. In other words, mathematics here simply represents a particular instance of a ready-made philosophical question, rather than something capable of challenging or undermining that question, and still less something capable of providing a paradoxical or dramatic solution for it.

Secondly, what is this ready-made philosophical question? It is actually a question concerning logic, or the capacities of language. In short, the question of universals. Only by way of a preliminary reduction of mathematical problems to logical and linguistic problems does one become able to shoehorn mathematics into the realm of philosophical questioning and transform it into a specialized objective region subsumed by philosophy. This particular move is a fundamental hallmark of the little style.

Thirdly, the philosophical problem is in no sense sparked or provoked by the mathematical problem; it has an independent history and, as the authors remind us, featured prominently in 'the scholastic debates of the middle ages'. It is a classical problem, with regard to which mathematics represents an opportunity for an updated, regional adjustment.

This becomes apparent when we consider the classificatory zeal exhibited by the authors when they come to outline the possible responses to the problem:

> The three main traditional answers to the problem of universals, stemming from medieval discussions, are known as *realism*,

nominalism, and *conceptualism*. We shall not deal here with these lines of thought in their traditional version but only with their modern counterparts known as *Platonism, neo-nominalism*, and *neo-conceptualism* (though we shall mostly omit the prefix 'neo-' since we shall have no opportunity to deal with the older versions). In addition, we shall deal with a fourth attitude which regards the whole problem of the ontological status of universals in general and of sets in particular as a metaphysical pseudo-problem.[2]

Clearly, the philosophical incorporation of mathematics carried out by the little style amounts to a *neo-classical* operation pure and simple. It assumes that mathematics can be treated as a particular area of philosophical concern; that this treatment necessarily proceeds through a consideration of logic and language; that it is entirely compatible with ready-made philosophical categories; and that it leads to a classification of doctrines in terms of proper names.

There is an old technical term in philosophy for this kind of neo-classicist approach: scholasticism.

Where mathematics is concerned, the little style amounts to a regional scholasticism.

We find a perfect example of this regional scholasticism in an intervention by Pascal Engel, Professor at the Sorbonne, in a book called *Mathematical Objectivity*.[3] In the course of a grammatical excursus concerning the status of statements, Engel manages to use no less than twenty-five classificatory syntagms. These are, in their order of appearance in this little jewel of scholasticism: Platonism, ontological realism, nominalism, phenomenalism, reductionism, fictionalism, instrumentalism, ontological antirealism, semantic realism, semantic antirealism, intuitionism, idealism, verificationism, formalism, constructivism, agnosticism, ontological reductionism, ontological inflationism, semantic atomism, holism, logicism, ontological neutralism, conceptualism, empirical realism and conceptual Platonism. Moreover, remarkable though it is, Engel's compulsive labelling in no way exhausts the possible categorial permutations. These are probably infinite, which is why scholasticism is assured of a busy future, even if, in conformity with the scholastic injunction to intellectual 'seriousness', its work is invariably carried out in teams.

Nevertheless, it is possible to sketch a brief survey of modern scholasticism in the company of Fraenkel, Bar-Hillel and Levy. First, they propose definitions for each of the fundamental approaches. Then they cautiously point out that, as we have already seen with Engel, there are all sorts of intermediary positions. Finally, they designate the purest standard-bearers for each of the four positions.

Let's take a closer look.

First, the definitions. In the following passage, the word 'set' is to be understood as designating any mathematical configuration that can be defined in rigorous language:

> A *Platonist* is convinced that corresponding to each well-defined (monadic) condition there exists, in general, a set, or class, which comprises all and only those entities that fulfil this condition and which is an entity in its own right of an ontological status similar to that of its members.
>
> A *neo-nominalist* declares himself unable to understand what other people mean when they are talking about sets unless he is able to interpret their talk as a *façon de parler*. The only language he professes himself to understand is a calculus of individuals, constructed as a first-order theory.
>
> There are authors who are attracted neither by the luscious jungle flora of Platonism nor by the ascetic desert landscape of neo-nominalism. They prefer to live in the well-designed and perspicuous orchards of *neo-conceptualism*. They claim to understand what sets are, though the metaphor they prefer is that of *constructing* (or *inventing*) rather than that of *singling out* (or *discovering*), which is the one cherished by the Platonists . . . [T]hey are not ready to accept axioms or theorems that would force them to admit the existence of sets which are not constructively characterizable.[4]

Thus the Platonist admits the existence of entities that are indifferent to the limits of language and transcend human constructive capacities; the nominalist only admits the existence of verifiable individuals fulfilling a transparent syntactic form; and the conceptualist demands that all existence be subordinated to an effective construction, which is itself dependent upon the existence of entities that are either already evident or constructed.

Church or Gödel can be invoked as uncompromising Platonists; Hilbert or Brouwer as unequivocal conceptualists; and Goodman as a rabid nominalist.

We have yet to mention the approach which remains radically agnostic, the one that always comes in fourth place. Following thesis 1 ('Sets have a real existence as ideal entities independent of the mind'), thesis 2 ('Sets exist only as individual entities validating linguistic expressions'), and thesis 3 ('Sets exist as mental constructions'), comes thesis 4, the supernumerary thesis: 'The question about the way in which sets exist has no meaning outside a given theoretical context':

> The prevalent opinions [i.e. Platonism, nominalism and conceptualism] are caused by a fusion of, and confusion between, two different questions: the one whether certain existential sentences can be proved, or disproved, or shown to be undecidable, *within a given theory*, the other whether this theory as a whole should be accepted.[5]

Carnap, the theoretician most representative of this clarificatory approach, suggests that the first problem, which depends on the resources of the theory in question, is a purely technical one, and that the second problem boils down to a practical issue that can only be decided according to various criteria, which Fraenkel et al. summarize as:

> [L]ikelihood of being consistent, ease of maneuverability, effectiveness in deriving classical analysis, teachability, perhaps possession of standard models, etc.[6]

It is by failing to distinguish between these two questions that one ends up formulating meaningless metaphysical problems such as: 'Are there non-denumerable infinite sets?' – a question that can only lead to irresolvable and ultimately sterile controversies because it mistakenly invokes existence in an absolute rather than merely theory-relative sense.

Clearly then, the little style encompasses all four of these options, and holds sway whether one adopts a realist, linguistic, constructivist or purely relativist stance vis-à-vis the existence of mathematical entities.

But this is because one has already presupposed that philosophy relates to mathematics through a critical examination of its objects, that it is the mode of existence of these objects that has to be interrogated, and that there are ultimately four ways of conceiving of that existence: as intrinsic; as nothing but the correlate of a name; as a mental construction; or as a variable pragmatic correlate.

The grand style is entirely different. It stipulates that mathematics provides a direct illumination of philosophy, rather than the opposite, and that this illumination is carried out through a forced or even violent intervention at the core of these issues.

I will now run through five majestic examples of the grand style: Descartes, Spinoza, Kant, Hegel and Lautréamont.

First example: Descartes, *Regulae ad directionem ingenii*, 'Rules for the Direction of the Mind', Rule II:

> This furnishes us with an evident explanation of the great superiority in certitude of Arithmetic and Geometry to other sciences. The former alone deal with an object so pure and uncomplicated, that they need make no assumptions at all which experience renders uncertain, but wholly consist in the rational deduction of consequences. They are on that account much the easiest and clearest of all, and possess an object such as we require, for in them it is scarce humanly possible for anyone to err except by inadvertence. . . .

> But one conclusion now emerges out of these considerations, viz, not indeed, that Arithmetic and Geometry are the sole sciences to be studied, but only that in our search for the direct road towards truth we should busy ourselves with no object about which we cannot attain a certitude equal to that of the demonstrations of Arithmetic and Geometry.[7]

For Descartes, mathematics clearly provides the paradigm for philosophy, a paradigm of certainty. But it is important not to confuse the latter with a logical paradigm. It is not proof that lies behind the paradigmatic value of mathematics for the philosopher. Rather, it is the absolute simplicity and clarity of the mathematical object.

Second example: Spinoza, appendix to Book One of the *Ethics*, a text dear to Louis Althusser:

> So they maintained it as certain that the judgments of the gods far surpass man's grasp. This alone, of course, would have caused the truth to be hidden from the human race to eternity, if mathematics, which is concerned not with ends, but only with the essences and properties of figures, had not shown men another standard of truth. . . .

> That is why we have such sayings as: 'So many heads, so many attitudes', 'everyone finds his own judgment more than enough', and

'there are as many differences of brains as of palates'. These proverbs show sufficiently that men judge things according to the disposition of their brain, and imagine, rather than understand them. For if men had understood them, the things would at least convince them all, even if they did not attract them all, as the example of mathematics shows.[8]

It would be no exaggeration to say that, for Spinoza, mathematics governs the historial destiny of knowledge, and hence the economy of freedom, or beatitude. Without mathematics, humanity languishes in the night of superstition, which can be summarized by the maxim: there is something we cannot think. To which it is necessary to add that mathematics also teaches us something essential: that whatever is thought truly is immediately shared. Mathematics shows that whatever is understood is radically undivided. To know is to be absolutely and universally convinced.

Third example: Kant, *Critique of Pure Reason*, Preface to the second edition:

In the earliest times to which the history of human reason extends, *mathematics*, among that wonderful people, the Greeks, had already entered upon the sure path of science. But it must not be supposed that it was as easy for mathematics as it was for logic – in which reason has to deal with itself alone – to light upon, or rather construct for itself, that royal road. On the contrary, I believe that it long remained, especially among the Egyptians, in the groping stage, and that the transformation must have been due to a *revolution* brought about by the happy thought of a single man, the experiments which he devised marking out the path upon which the science must enter, and by following which, secure progress throughout all time and in endless expansion is infallibly secured . . .

A new light flashed upon the mind of the first man (be he Thales or some other) who demonstrated the properties of the isosceles triangle. The true method, so he found, was not to inspect what he discerned either in the figure, or in the bare concept of it, and from this, as it were, to read off its properties; but to bring out what was necessarily implied in the concepts that he has himself formed a priori and had put into the figure in the construction by which he presented it to himself.[9]

Thus Kant thinks, firstly, that mathematics secured for itself from its very origin the sure path of a science. Secondly, that the creation of mathematics is tantamount to an absolute historical singularity, a 'revolution' – so much so that its emergence deserves to be singularized: it was due to the felicitous thought of a single man. Nothing could be further from a historicist or culturalist explanation. Thirdly, Kant thinks that, once opened up, the path is infinite, in time as well as in space. This universalism is a concrete universalism because it is the universalism of a trajectory of thought that can always be retraced, irrespective of the time or the place. And fourthly, Kant sees in mathematics something that marks the perpetual rediscovery of its paradigmatic function, the inaugural conception of a type of knowledge that is neither empirical (it is not what can be discerned in the figure), nor formal (it does not consist in the pure, static, identifiable properties of the concept). Thus mathematics paves the way for the critical representation of thinking, which consists in seeing knowledge as an instance of non-empirical production or construction, a sensible construction that is adequate to the constituting a priori. In other words, 'Thales' is the putative name for a revolution that extends to the entirety of philosophy – which is to say that Kant's critical project amounts to an examination of the conditions of possibility that underlie Thales' construction.

Fourth example: Hegel, *Science of Logic*, the lengthy Remark that follows the explication of the infinity of the quantum:

> [I]n a philosophical respect the mathematical infinite is important because underlying it, in fact, is the notion of the genuine infinite and it is far superior to the ordinary so-called *metaphysical infinite* on which are based the objections to the mathematical infinite. . . .
>
> It is worthwhile considering more closely the mathematical concept of the infinite together with the most noteworthy of the attempts aimed at justifying its use and eliminating the difficulty with which the method feels itself burdened. The consideration of these justifications and characteristics of the mathematical infinite which I shall undertake at some length in this Remark will at the same time throw the best light on the nature of the true Notion itself and show how this latter was vaguely present as a basis for those procedures.[10]

The decisive point here is that, for Hegel, mathematics and philosophical speculation share a fundamental concept: the concept of the infinite. More particularly, the destitution of the metaphysical concept of infinity – in other words, the destitution of classical theology – is initially undertaken through the determination of the mathematical concept of the infinite. Hegel obviously has in mind the creation of the differential and integral calculus during the seventeenth and eighteenth centuries. He wants to show how the true (i.e. dialectical) conception of the infinite makes its historical appearance under the auspices of mathematics. His method is remarkable: it consists in examining the contradictory labour of the Notion in so far as the latter can be seen to be at work within the mathematical text itself. The Notion is both active and manifest, it ruins the transcendent theological concept of the infinite, but it is not yet the conscious knowledge of its own activity. Unlike the metaphysical infinite, the mathematical infinite is the same as the good infinite of the dialectic. But it is the same only according to the difference whereby it does not yet know itself *as* the same. In this instance, as in Plato or in my own work, philosophy's role consists in informing mathematics of its own speculative grandeur. In Hegel, this takes the form of a detailed examination of what he refers to as the 'justifications and characteristics' of the mathematical concept of the infinite; an examination which, for him, consists in carrying out a meticulous analysis of the ideas of Euler and Lagrange. Through this analysis, one sees how the mathematical conception of the infinite, which for Hegel is still hampered by 'the difficulty with which the method feels itself burdened', harbours within itself the affirmative resource of a genuinely absolute conception of quantity.

It seems fitting that we should conclude this survey of the grand style with a figure who straddles the margin between philosophy and the poem: Isidore Ducasse, aka the Comte de Lautréamont. Like Rimbaud and Nietzsche, Lautréamont, using the post-Romantic name 'Maldoror', wants to bring about a denaturing of man, a transmigration of his essence, a positive becoming-monster. In other words, he wants to carry out an ontological deregulation of all the categories of humanism. Mathematics plays a crucial auxiliary role in this task. Here is a passage from Book II of *Maldoror*:

O rigorous mathematics, I have not forgotten you since your wise lessons, sweeter than honey, filtered into my heart like a refreshing wave. Instinctively, from the cradle, I had longed to drink from your source, older than the sun, and I continue to tread the sacred sanctuary of your solemn temple, I, the most faithful of your devotees. There was a vagueness in my mind, something thick as smoke; but I managed to mount the steps which lead to your altar, and you drove away this dark veil, as the wind blows the draught-board. You replaced it with excessive coldness, consummate prudence and implacable logic. . . . Arithmetic! Algebra! Geometry! Awe-inspiring trinity! Luminous triangle! He who has not known you is a fool! He would deserve the ordeals of the greatest tortures; for there is blind disdain in his ignorant indifference . . . But you, concise mathematics, by the rigorous sequence of your unshakeable propositions and the constancy of your iron rules, give to the dazzled eyes a powerful reflection of that supreme truth whose imprint can be seen in the order of the universe. . . . Your modest pyramids will last longer than the pyramids of Egypt, those anthills raised by stupidity and slavery. And at the end of all the centuries you will stand on the ruins of time, with your cabbalistic ciphers, your laconic equations and your sculpted lines, on the avenging right of the Almighty, whereas the stars will plunge despairingly, like whirlwinds in the eternity of horrible and universal night, and grimacing mankind will think of settling its accounts at the Last Judgment. Thank you for the countless services you have done me. Thank you for the alien qualities with which you enriched my intellect. Without you in my struggle against man I would perhaps have been defeated.[11]

This is an arresting text. It develops around mathematics a kind of icy consecration, fairly reminiscent of the dialectical significance of the great Mallarméan symbols: the star, 'cold from forgetfulness and obsolescence';[12] the mirror, 'frozen in [its] frame';[13] the tomb, 'the solid sepulchre wherein all things harmful lie';[14] and the 'hard lake haunted beneath the ice by the transparent glaciers of flights never flown'.[15] All of which seems to evoke a glacial anti-humanism. But in Lautréamont, the 'excessive coldness' of mathematics is coupled with a monumental aspect, a sort of Masonic symbolism of eternity: the 'luminous triangle', the 'constancy of iron rules', the pyramid . . . Just as Nietzsche wished to surpass Christ and announce the advent of Dionysus by having Zarathustra speak in the language of the Gospels ('in truth', 'I say unto you', etc.), Lautréamont, by coupling Masonic esotericism with Old Testament language, wants to delineate the monstrous becoming to which an exhausted, defiled mankind is destined. In this regard, mathematics, which is divided into algebra, arithmetic and geometry – i.e. 'laconic equations', 'cabbalistic ciphers' and 'sculpted lines' – renders an indispensable service: it imposes on us a kind of implacable eternity which directly challenges the humanist conception of man. Mathematics is, in effect, 'older than the sun' and will remain intact 'on the ruins of time'. Mathematics is the discipline and the severity, the immutability and the image of 'that supreme truth'. This is only a short step away from saying that mathematics inscribes being as such; a step which, as you know, I have taken. But for Lautréamont, mathematics is something even better: it is what furnishes the intellect with 'alien qualities'. This is an essential point: there is no intrinsic harmony between mathematics and the human intellect. The exercise of mathematics, the lessons – 'sweeter than honey' – that it teaches, is the exercise of an alteration, an estrangement of intelligence. And it is first and foremost through this resource of strangeness that mathematical eternity subverts ordinary thinking. Here we have the profound reason why, without mathematics, without the infection of conventional thinking by mathematics, Maldoror would not have prevailed in his fundamental struggle against humanist man, in his struggle to bring forth the free monster beyond humanity of which man is capable.

On all these points, from glacial anti-humanism to the trans-human advent of truths, I think I may well be Isidore Ducasse's one and only genuine disciple. Why then do I call myself a Platonist rather than a Ducassean or a son of Maldoror?

Because Plato says exactly the same thing.

Like Isidore Ducasse, Plato claims that mathematics undoes doxa and defeats the sophist. Without mathematics there could never arise, beyond existing humanity, those philosopher-kings who represent the overman's allegorical name in the conceptual city erected by Plato. If there is to be any chance of seeing these philosopher-kings appear, the young must be taught arithmetic, plane geometry, solid geometry and astronomy for at least ten years. For Plato, what is admirable about mathematics is not just that, as is well known, it sets its sights on pure essences, on the idea as such, but also that its utility can be explicated in terms of the only pragmatics of any worth for a man who has risen beyond man, which is to say, in terms of war. Consider for example this passage from *The Republic*, Book 7, 525c (which I have taken the liberty to retranslate):

Socrates: So our overman must be both philosopher and soldier?
Glaucon: Of course.
Socrates: Then a law must be passed – immediately.
Glaucon: A law? Why a law, in God's name? What law?
Socrates: A law stipulating the teaching of higher arithmetic, you dullard. But we'll have trouble.
Glaucon: Trouble? Why?
Socrates: Take a young fellow who wants to become admiral of the fleet,

or minister, or president, or something of that ilk. A young hotshot straight out of the LSE or Yale. Do you imagine he'll be rushing to enrol at the institute of higher arithmetic? We'll have some serious convincing to do, let me tell you.

Glaucon: I can't imagine what we're going to tell him.

Socrates: The truth. Something harsh. For example: 'My dear fellow, if you want to become minister or admiral, first you have to stop being such an agreeable young man, a common yuppie. Take numbers, for instance, do you know what numbers are? I'm not talking about what you need to know to carry out your petty little business transactions, or count whatever it is you're flogging on the market! I'm talking about number in so far as you contemplate it in its eternal essence through the sheer power of your yuppie intellect, which I promise to de-yuppify! Number such as it exists in war, in the terrible reckoning of weapons and corpses. But above all, number as what brings about a complete upheaval in thinking, as what erases approximation and becoming to make way for being as such, as well as its truth.'

Glaucon: After hearing your little speech, I think our yuppie friend will run like hell, scared out of his wits.

This is what I mean by the grand style: arithmetic as an instance of stellar and warlike inhumanity!

It should come as no surprise, then, that today we see mathematics being attacked systematically from all sides. Just as politics is being systematically attacked in the name of economic and state management; or art systematically attacked in the name of cultural relativity; or love systematically attacked in the name of a pragmatics of sex. The little style of epistemological specialization is merely an unwitting pawn in this attack. So we have no choice: if we are to defend ourselves – 'we' who speak on behalf of philosophy itself and of the supplementary step it can and must take – we have to find the new terms required for the grand style.

But let us first recapitulate the teaching of our admirable predecessors.

It is obvious that for each of them, the confrontation with mathematics is an absolutely indispensable condition for philosophy as such; a condition that is at once descriptively external and prescriptively immanent for philosophy. This holds even where there are enormous divergences as to what constitutes the fundamental project of philosophy. For Plato, it consists in creating a new conception of politics. For Descartes, in enlarging the scope of absolute certainty to encompass the essential questions of life. For

Spinoza, in attaining the intellectual love of God. For Kant, in knowing exactly where to draw the line between faith and knowledge. For Hegel, in showing the becoming-subject of the absolute. For Lautréamont, in disfiguring and overcoming humanist man. But in each case, it is a question of giving thanks to 'rigorous mathematics'. It doesn't matter whether philosophy is conceived of as a rationalism tied to transcendence, as it is from Descartes to Lacan; as a vitalist immanentism, as it is from Spinoza to Deleuze; as pious criticism, as it is from Kant to Ricoeur; as a dialectic of the absolute, as it is from Hegel to Mao Zedong; or an aestheticist creationism, as it is from Lautréamont to Nietzsche. For the founders of each of these lineages, it still remains the case that the cold radicality of mathematics is the necessary exercise through which is forged a thinking subject adequate to the transformations he will be forced to undergo.

Exactly the same holds in my case. I have assigned philosophy the task of constructing thought's embrace of its own time, of refracting newborn truths through the unique prism of concepts. Philosophy must intensify and gather together, under the aegis of systematic thinking, not just what its time imagines itself to be, but what its time is – albeit unknowingly – capable of. And in order to do this, I too had to laboriously set down my own lengthy 'thank you' to rigorous mathematics.

Let me put it as bluntly as possible: if there is no grand style in the way philosophy relates to mathematics, then there is no grand style in philosophy full stop.

In 1973, Lacan, using a 'we' that, for all its imperiousness, included both psychoanalysts and psychoanalysis, declared: 'Mathematical formalization is our goal, our ideal.'[16] Using the same rhetoric, and a 'we' that now includes both philosophers and philosophy, I say: 'Mathematics is our obligation, our alteration.'

*　*　*

None of the partisans of the grand style ever believed that the philosophical identification of mathematics had to proceed by way of a logicizing or linguistic reduction. Suffice it to say that for Descartes, it is the intuitive clarity of ideas that founds the mathematical paradigm, not the automatic character of the deductive process, which is merely the uninteresting, scholastic aspect of mathematics. Similarly, for Kant, the historial destiny of mathematics as construction of the concept in intuition constitutes a revolution that is entirely independent of the destiny of logic, which is already complete and has simply been treading water since the time of its founder, Aristotle. Hegel examines the foundation of a concept, that of the infinite, and disregards the apparel of proof. And although Lautréamont certainly appreciates the iron necessity of the deductive process and the coherence of figures, what is most important for him in mathematics is its icy discipline and power of eternal survival. As for Spinoza, he sees salvation as residing in the ontology that underlies mathematics, which is to say, in a conception of being shorn of every appeal to meaning or purpose, and prizing only the cohesiveness of consequences.

There is not a single mention of language in all this.

Let us be blunt and remark in passing that, in this regard, Wittgenstein, despite the cunning of his sterilized loquacity and despite the undeniable formal beauty of the *Tractatus* – without doubt one of the masterpieces of anti-philosophy – must be counted among the architects of the little style, whose principle he sets out with his customary brutality. Thus, in proposition 6.21 of the *Tractatus*, he declares: 'A proposition of mathematics does not express a thought.'[17] Or worse still, in his *Remarks on the Foundations of Mathematics*, we find this sort of trite pragmatism, which is very fashionable nowadays:

> I should like to ask something like: 'Does every calculation lead you to something useful? In that case, you have avoided contradiction. And if it does not lead you to anything useful then what difference does it make if you run into a contradiction?'[18]

We can forgive Wittgenstein. But not those who shelter behind his aesthetic cunning (whose entire impetus is ethical, i.e. religious) the better to adopt the little style once and for all and (vainly) try to throw to the modern lions of indifference those determined to remain faithful to the grand style.

In any case, our maxim is: *philosophy must enter into logic via mathematics, not into mathematics via logic.*

In my work this translates into: mathematics is the science of being qua being. Logic pertains to the coherence of appearance. And if the study of appearance also mobilizes certain areas of mathematics, this is simply because, following an insight formalized by Hegel but which actually goes back to Plato, it is of the essence of being to appear. This is what maintains the form of all appearing within a mathematizable transcendental order. But here, once again, transcendental logic, which is a part of mathematics tied to contemporary sheaf theory, holds sway over formal or linguistic logic, which is ultimately no more than a superficial translation of the former.

Reiterating the 'we' I used earlier, I will say: Mathematics teaches us about what *must* be said concerning what *is*; not about what it is *permissible* to say concerning what we *think* there is.

*   *   *

Mathematics provides philosophy with a weapon, a fearsome machine of thought, a catapult aimed at the bastions of ignorance, superstition and mental servitude. It is not a docile grammatical region. For Plato, mathematics is what allows us to break free from the sophistical dictatorship of linguistic immediacy. For Lautréamont, it is what releases us from the moribund figure of the human. For Spinoza, it is what breaks with superstition. But you have read their texts. Some today would have us believe that mathematics itself is relative, prejudiced and inconsistent, needlessly aristocratic, or alternately, subservient to technology. You should be aware that this propaganda is trying to undermine what has always been most implacably opposed to spiritualist approximation and gaudy scepticism, the sickly allies of flamboyant nihilism. For the truth is that mathematics does not understand the meaning of the claim 'I cannot know'. The mathematical realm does not acknowledge the existence of spiritualist categories such as those of the unthinkable and the unthought, supposedly exceeding the meagre resources of human reason; or of those sceptical categories which claim we cannot ever provide a definitive solution to a problem or a definitive answer to a serious question.

The other sciences are not so reliable in this regard. Quentin Meillassoux has convincingly argued that physics provides no bulwark against spiritualist (which is to say obscurantist) speculation, and biology – that wild empiricism disguised as science – even less so. Only in mathematics can one unequivocally maintain that if thought can formulate a problem, it can and will solve it, regardless of how long it takes. For it is also in mathematics that the maxim 'Keep going!', the only maxim required in ethics, has the greatest weight. How else are we to explain the fact that the solution to a problem formulated by Fermat more than three centuries ago can be discovered today? Or that today's mathematicians are still actively engaged in proving or disproving conjectures first proposed by the Greeks more than two thousand years ago? There can be no doubt that mathematics conceived in the grand style is warlike, polemical, fearsome. And it is by donning the contemporary matheme like a coat of armour that I have undertaken, alone at first, to undo the disastrous consequences of philosophy's 'linguistic turn';

to demarcate philosophy from phenomenological religiosity; to re-found the metaphysical triad of being, event and subject; to take a stand against poetic prophesying; to identify generic multiplicities as the ontological form of the true; to assign a place to Lacanian formalism; and, more recently, to articulate the logic of appearing.

Let's say that, as far as we're concerned, mathematics is always more or less equivalent to the bulldozer with which we remove the rubble that prevents us from constructing new edifices in the open air.

The principal difficulty probably resides in the assumption that mathematical competence requires years of initiation. Whence the temptation, for the philosophical demagogue, either to ignore mathematics altogether or act as if the most primitive rudiments are enough in order to understand what is going on there. In this regard, Kant set a very bad example by encouraging generations of philosophers to believe that they could grasp the essence of mathematical judgement through a single example like 7 + 5 = 12. This is a bit like someone saying that one can grasp the relation between philosophy and poetry by reciting:

Humpty Dumpty sat on the wall,
Humpty Dumpty had a great fall.
All the king's horses and all the king's men
Couldn't put Humpty together again!

After all, this is just a bunch of verses, just as 7 + 5 = 12 is just a bunch of numbers.

It is striking that, whether one considers a philosophical text written in the little style or one written in the grand style, no justification whatsoever seems to be required for quoting poetry, but no-one would ever dream of quoting a piece of mathematical reasoning. No-one seems to consider it acceptable to dispense with Hölderlin or Rimbaud or Pessoa in favour of Humpty Dumpty, or to ditch Wagner for Julio Iglesias. But as soon as it is a question of mathematics, the reader either simply loses interest or immediately associates it with the little style, which is to say, with epistemology, the history of science, specialization.

This was not Plato's point of view, nor that of any of the great philosophers. Plato very often quotes poetry, but he also quotes theorems, ones which are probably deemed relatively easy by today's standards, but were certainly demanding when Plato was writing: thus, in the *Meno* for instance, the construction of the square whose surface is double that of a given square.

I claim the right to quote instances of mathematical reasoning, provided they are appropriate to the philosophical theses in the context of which they are being inscribed, and the knowledge required for understanding them has already been made available to the reader. Give us an example, I hear you say. But I'm not going to give you an example of an example, because I've already provided hundreds of real examples, integrated into the movement of thought. So I will mention two of these movements instead: the presentation of Dedekind's doctrine of number in Chapter 4 of *Number and Numbers*,[19] and the consideration of the point of excess in Meditation 7 of *Being and Event*.[20] Consult them, read them, using the reminders, cross-references and the glossary I have provided in each book. And anyone who still claims not to understand should write to me telling me *exactly* what it is they don't understand – otherwise, I fear, we're simply dealing with excuses for the reader's laziness. Philosophers are able to understand a fragment by Anaximander, an elegy by Rilke, a seminar on the real by Lacan, but not the 2,500-year-old proof that there are an infinity of prime numbers. This is an unacceptable, anti-philosophical state of affairs; one which only serves the interests of the partisans of the little style.

I have spoken of bulldozers and rubble. Which contemporary ruins do I have in mind? I think Hegel saw it before anyone else: ultimately, mathematics proposes a new concept of the infinite. And on the basis of this concept, it allows for an immanentization of the infinite, separating it from the One of theology. Hegel also saw that the algebraists of his time, like Euler and Lagrange, had not quite grasped this: it is only with Baron Cauchy that the thorny issue of the limit of a series is finally settled, and not until Cantor that light is finally thrown on the august question of the actual infinite. Hegel thought this confusion was due to the fact that the 'true' concept of the infinite belonged to speculation, so that mathematics was merely its unconscious bearer, its unwitting midwife. The truth is that the mathematical revolution – the rendering explicit of what had always been implicit within mathematics since the time of the Greeks, which is to say, the thorough-going rationalization of the infinite – was yet to come, and in a sense will always be yet to come, since we still do not know how to effect a reasonable 'forcing' of the kind of infinity proper to the continuum. Nevertheless, we do know why mathematics radically subverts both empiricist moderation and elegant scepticism: mathematics teaches us that there is no reason whatsoever to confine thinking within the ambit of finitude. With mathematics we know that, as Hegel would have said, the infinite is nearby.

Yet someone might object: 'Well then, since we already know the result, why not just be satisfied with it and leave it at that? Why continue with the arid labour of familiarizing ourselves with new axioms, unprecedented proofs, difficult concepts and inconceivably abstract theories?' Because the infinite, such as mathematics renders it amenable to the philosophical will, is not a fixed and irreversible acquisition. The historicity of mathematics is nothing but the labour of the infinite, its ongoing and unpredictable re-exposition. A revolution, whether French or Bolshevik, cannot exhaust the formal concept of emancipation, even though it presents its real; similarly, the mathematical avatars of the thought of the infinite do not exhaust the speculative concept of infinite thought. The confrontation with mathematics must constantly be reconstituted because the idea of the infinite only manifests itself through the moving surface of its mathematical reconfigurations. This is all the more essential given that our ideas of the finite, and hence of the philosophical virtualities latent in finitude, become retroactively displaced and reinvigorated through those crises, revolutions and changes of heart that affect the mathematical schema of the infinite. The latter is a moving front, a struggle as silent as it is relentless, where nothing – no more there than elsewhere – announces the advent of perpetual peace.

What do the following notions have in common as regards their subtlest consequences for thinking: the infinity of prime numbers as conceived by the Greeks, the fact that a function tends toward infinity, the infinitely small in non-standard analysis, regular or singular infinite cardinals, the existence of a number-object in a topos, the way in which an operator grasps and projects an untotalizable collection of algebraic structures onto a family of sets – not to mention hundreds of other theoretical formulations, concepts, models and determinations? Probably something that has to do with the fact that the infinite is the intimate law of thought, its naturally anti-natural medium. But in another regard, they have nothing at all in common. Nothing that would allow one merely to reiterate and maintain a simplified, allusive relation with mathematics. This is because, in the words of my late friend Gilles Chatelet, the mathematical elaboration of thought is not of the order of a mere linear unfolding or straightforward logical consequence. It comprises decisive but previously unknown gestures.[21] One must begin again, because mathematics is always beginning again and transforming its abstract panoply of concepts. One has to begin studying, writing and understanding again that which is in fact the hardest thing in the world to understand and whose abstraction is the most insolent, because the philosophical struggle against the alliance of finitude and obscurantism will only be rekindled through this recommencement.

This is why Mallarmé was wrong on at least one point. Like every great poet, Mallarmé was engaged in a tacit rivalry with mathematics. He was trying to show that a densely imagistic poetic line, when articulated within the bare cadences of thinking, comprises as much if not more truth than the extra-linguistic inscription of the matheme. This is why he could write, in a sketch for *Igitur*:

Infinity is born of chance, which you have denied. You, expired mathematicians – I, absolute projection. Should end in Infinity.[22]

The idea is clear: Mallarmé accuses mathematicians of denying chance and thereby of fixing the infinite in the hereditary rigidity of calculation. In *Igitur*, that rigidity is symbolized by the family. Whence the poetic, anti-mathematical operation which, Mallarmé believes, binds infinity to chance and is symbolized by the dice-throw. Once the dice have been cast, and regardless of the results, 'infinity escapes the family'.[23] This is why the mathematicians expire, and the abstract conception of the infinite along with them, in favour of that impersonal absolute now represented by the hero.

But what Mallarmé has failed to see is how the operations through which mathematics has reconfigured the conception of the infinite are constantly affirming chance through the contingency of their recommencement. It is up to philosophy to gather together or conjoin the poetic affirmation of infinity drawn metaphorically from chance, and the mathematical construction of the infinite, drawn formally from an axiomatic intuition. As a result, the injunction to mathematical beauty intersects with the injunction to poetic truth. And vice versa.

There is a very brief poem by Álvaro De Campos, one of the heteronyms used by Fernando Pessoa. De Campos is a scientist and engineer and his poem succinctly summarizes everything I have been saying. You should be able to memorize it right away. Here it is:

Newton's binomial is as beautiful as the Venus de Milo.
The truth is few people notice it.[24]

Style – grand style – simply consists in noticing it.

CHAPTER 2
PHILOSOPHY AND MATHEMATICS: INFINITY AND THE END OF ROMANTICISM

What does the title 'philosophy and mathematics' imply about the relation between these two disciplines? Does it indicate a difference? An influence? A boundary? Or perhaps an indifference? For me it implies none of these. I understand it as implying an identification of the modalities according to which mathematics, ever since its Greek inception, has been a *condition* for philosophy; an identification of the figures that have historically entangled mathematics in the determination of the space proper to philosophy.

From a purely descriptive perspective, three of these modalities or figures can be distinguished:

- Operating from the perspective of philosophy, the first modality sees in mathematics an approximation, or preliminary pedagogy, for questions that are otherwise the province of philosophy. One acknowledges in mathematics a certain aptitude for thinking 'first principles', or for knowledge of being and truth; an aptitude that becomes fully realized in philosophy. We will call this the *ontological* modality of the relation between philosophy and mathematics.

- The second modality is the one that treats mathematics as a regional discipline, an area of cognition in general. Philosophy then sets out to examine what grounds this regional character of mathematics. It will both classify mathematics within a table of forms of knowledge, and reflect on the guarantees (of truth or correctness) for the discipline that has been so classified. We will call this the *epistemological* modality.

- Finally, the third modality posits that mathematics is entirely disconnected from the questions, or questioning, proper to philosophy. According to this vision of things, mathematics is a register of language games, a formal type, or a singular grammar. In any case, mathematics does not *think* anything. In its most radical form, this orientation subsumes mathematics within a generalized technics that carries out an unthinking manipulation of being, a levelling of being as pure *standing-reserve*. We will call this modality the *critical* modality, because it accomplishes a critical disjunction between the realm proper to mathematics on the one hand, and that of thinking as what is at stake in philosophy on the other.

The question I would like to ask is the following: how do things stand today as far as the articulation of these three modalities is concerned? How are we to *situate* philosophy's mathematical condition from the perspective of philosophy? And the thesis I wish to uphold takes the form of a gesture whereby mathematics is to be *re-entangled* into philosophy's innermost structure; a structure from which it has, in actuality, been excluded.[1] What is required today is a new conditioning of philosophy by mathematics, a conditioning which we are doubly late in putting into place: both late with respect to what mathematics itself indicates, and late with respect to the minimal requirements necessary for the continuation of philosophy. What is ultimately at stake here can be formulated in terms of the following question, which weighs upon us and threatens to exhaust us: can we be delivered, *finally* delivered, from our subjection to Romanticism?

1. The disjunction of mathematics as philosophically constitutive of Romanticism

Up to and including Kant, mathematics and philosophy were reciprocally entangled, to the extent that Kant himself (following Descartes, Leibniz, Spinoza, and many others) still sees in the mythic name of Thales a common origin for mathematics and knowledge in general. For all these philosophers, it is absolutely clear that mathematics alone allowed the inaugural break with superstition and ignorance. Mathematics is for them that singular form of thinking which has *interrupted the sovereignty of myth*. We owe to it the first form of self-sufficient thinking, independent of any sacred posture of enunciation; in other words, the first form of entirely secularized thinking.

But the philosophy of Romanticism – and Hegel is decisive in this regard – carried out an almost complete disentanglement of philosophy and mathematics. It shaped the conviction that philosophy can and must deploy a thinking that does not at any moment internalize mathematics as condition for that deployment. I maintain that this disentanglement can be identified as the Romantic speculative gesture par excellence; to the point that it retroactively determined the Classical age of philosophy as one in which the philosophical text continued to be intrinsically conditioned by mathematics in various ways.

The positivist and empiricist approaches, which have been highly influential during the last two centuries, merely invert the Romantic speculative gesture. The claim that science constitutes the one and only paradigm for the positivity of knowledge can be made only from within the completed disentanglement of philosophy and the sciences. The anti-philosophical verdict returned by the various forms of positivism overturns the anti-scientific verdict returned by the various forms of Romantic philosophy, but fails to interrogate its initial premise. It is striking that Heidegger and Carnap disagree about everything, except the idea that it is incumbent upon us to inhabit and activate the end of metaphysics. This is because for both Heidegger and Carnap, the name 'metaphysics' designates the Classical era of philosophy, the era in which mathematics and philosophy were still reciprocally entangled in a general representation of the operations of thought. Carnap wants to *purify* the scientific operation, while Heidegger wishes to *oppose* to science – in which he perceives the nihilist manifestation of metaphysics – a path of thinking modelled on poetry. In this sense, both remain heirs to the Romantic gesture of disentanglement, albeit in different registers.

This perspective sheds light on the way in which various forms of positivism and empiricism – as well as that refined form of sophistry represented by Wittgenstein – remain incapable of identifying mathematics *as a type of thinking*, even at a time when any attempt to characterize it as something else (as a game, a grammar, etc.) constitutes an affront to the available evidence as well as to the sensibility of every mathematician. Essentially, both logical positivism and Anglo-American linguistic sophistry claim – but without the Romantic force that would accompany a lucid awareness of their claim – that science is a technique for which mathematics provides the grammar, or that mathematics is a game and the only important thing is to identify its rule. Whatever the case may be, mathematics does not think. The only major difference between the Romantic founders of what I would call the second modern era (the first being the Classical one) and the positivists or modern sophists, is that the former preserve the ideal of thinking (in art, or philosophy), while the latter only admit forms of knowledge.

A significant aspect of the issue is that, for a great sophist like Wittgenstein, it is pointless to *enter into* mathematics. Wittgenstein, more casual in this respect than Hegel, proposes merely to 'brush up against' mathematics, to cast an eye upon it from afar, the way an artist might gaze upon some chess players:

> The philosopher must twist and turn about so as to pass by the mathematical problems, and not run up against one – which would have to be solved before he could go further.
>
> His labour in philosophy is as it were an idleness in mathematics.
>
> It is not that a new building has to be erected, or that a new bridge has to be built, but that the geography *as it now is*, has to be described.[2]

But the trouble is that mathematics, which is an exemplary *discipline* of thought, does not lend itself to any kind of description and is not representable in terms of the cartographic metaphor of a country to which one could pay a quick visit. And in any case, it is impossible to be lazy in mathematics. It is possibly the only kind of thinking in which the slightest lapse in concentration entails the disappearance, pure and simple, of what is being thought about. Whence the fact that Wittgenstein is continuously speaking of something *other* than mathematics. He speaks of the impression he has of it from afar and, more profoundly, of its symptomatic role in his own itinerary. But this descriptive and symptomatological treatment takes it for granted that philosophy can keep mathematics at a distance. This is exactly the standard effect that the Romantic gesture of disentanglement seeks to achieve.

What is the crucial presupposition for the gesture whereby Hegel and his successors managed to effect this long-lasting disjunction between mathematics on the one hand and philosophical discourse on the other? In my opinion, this presupposition is that of *historicism*, which is to say, the temporalization of the concept. It was the newfound certainty that infinite or true being could only be apprehended through its own temporality that led the Romantics to depose mathematics from its localization as a condition for philosophy. Thus the ideal and atemporal character of mathematical thinking figured as the central argument in this deposition. Romantic speculation opposes time and life as temporal ecstasis to the abstract and empty eternity of mathematics. If time is the 'existence of the concept', then mathematics is unworthy of that concept.

It could also be said that German Romantic philosophy, which produced the philosophical means and the techniques of thought required for historicism, established the idea that the genuine infinite only manifests itself as a horizonal structure *for the historicity of the finitude of existence*. But both the representation of the limit as a horizon and the theme of finitude are entirely foreign to mathematics, whose own concept of the limit is that of a present-point and whose thinking requires the presupposition of the infinity of its site. For historicism, of which Romanticism is the philosopheme, mathematics, which links the infinite to the bounded power of the letter and whose very acts repeal any invocation of time, could no longer be accorded a paradigmatic status, whether it be with regard to certainty or with regard to truth.

We will here call 'Romantic' any disposition of thinking which determines the infinite within the Open, or as horizonal correlate for a historicity of finitude. Today in particular, what essentially subsists of Romanticism is the theme of finitude. To re-intricate mathematics and philosophy is also, and perhaps above all, to have done with finitude, which is the principal contemporary residue of the Romantic speculative gesture.

2. Romanticism continues to be the site for our thinking today, and this continuation renders the theme of the death of God ineffectual

The question of mathematics, and of its localization by philosophy, has the singular merit of providing us with a profound insight into the nature of our own time. Beyond the claims – not so much heroic as empty – about an 'irreducible modernity', a 'novelty still needing to be thought', the persistence of the disjunction between mathematics and philosophy seems to indicate that Romanticism's historicist core continues to function as the fundamental horizon for our thinking. The Romantic gesture still holds sway over us insofar as the infinite continues to function as a horizonal correlative and opening for the historicity of finitude. Our modernity is Romantic to the extent that it remains caught up in the temporal identification of the concept. As a result, mathematics is here represented as a condition for philosophy only from the standpoint of a radical disjunctive gesture, which persists in opposing the historical life of thought and the concept to the empty and formal eternity of mathematics.

Basically, if one considers the status ascribed to poetry and mathematics by Plato, one sees how, ever since Romanticism, they have swapped places as conditions. Plato wanted to banish poets and only allow geometers access to philosophy. Today, it is the poem that lies at the heart of the philosophical disposition and the matheme that is excluded from it. In our time, it is mathematics which, although acknowledged in its scientific (i.e. technical) aspect, is left to languish in a condition of exile and neglect by philosophers. Mathematics has been reduced to a grammatical shell wherein sophists can pursue their linguistic exercises, or to a morose area of specialization for cobwebbed epistemologists. Meanwhile, the aura of the poem – seemingly since Nietzsche, but actually since Hegel – glows ever brighter. Nothing illuminates contemporary philosophy's fundamental anti-Platonism more vividly than its patent reversal of the Platonic system of conditions for philosophy.

But if this is the case, then the question that concerns us here has nothing to do with postmodernism. For the modern epoch comprises two periods, the Classical and the Romantic, and our question regards post-romanticism. How can we get out of Romanticism without lapsing into a neoclassical reaction? This is the real problem, one whose genuine pertinence becomes apparent once we start to see how, behind the theme of 'the end of the avant-gardes', the postmodern merely dissimulates a classical–romantic eclecticism. If we wish for a more precise formulation of this particular problem, an examination of the link between philosophy and mathematics is the only valid path I know of. It is the only standpoint from which one has a chance of cutting straight to the heart of the matter, which is nothing other than the critique of finitude.

That this critique is urgently required is confirmed by the spectacle – also very Romantic – of the increasing collusion between philosophy (or what passes for philosophy) and religions of all kinds, since the collapse of Marxist politics. Can we really be surprised at so-and-so's rabbinical Judaism, or so-and-so's conversion to Islam, or another's thinly veiled Christian devotion, given that everything we hear boils down to this: that we are 'consigned to finitude' and are '*essentially* mortal'? When it comes to crushing the infamy of superstition, it has always been necessary to invoke the solid secular eternity of the sciences. But how can this be done *within philosophy* if the disentanglement of mathematics and philosophy leaves behind Presence and the Sacred as the only things that make our being-mortal bearable?

The truth is that this disentanglement defuses the Nietzschean proclamation of the death of God. We do not possess the wherewithal to be atheists so long as the theme of finitude governs our thinking.

In the deployment of the Romantic figure, the infinite, which becomes the Open as site for the temporalization of finitude, remains beholden to the One because it remains beholden to history. As long as finitude remains the ultimate determination of existence, God abides. He abides as that whose disappearance continues to hold sway over us, in the form of the abandonment, the dereliction, or the leaving-behind of Being.

There is a very tenacious and profound link between the disentanglement of mathematics and philosophy and the preservation, in the inverted or diverted form of finitude, of a non-appropriable or unnameable horizon of immortal divinity. 'Only a God can save us', Heidegger courageously proclaims, but once mathematics has been deposed, even those without his courage continue to maintain a tacit God through the lack of being engendered by our co-extensiveness with time.

Descartes was more of an atheist than we are, because eternity was not something he lacked. Little by little, a generalized historicism is smothering us beneath a disgusting veneer of sanctification.

When it comes to the effectiveness, if not the proclamation of the death of God, the contemporary quandary in which we find outselves is a function of the fact that philosophy's neglect of mathematical thinking delivers the infinite, through the medium of history, over to a new avatar of the One.

Only by relating the infinite back to a neutral banality, by inscribing eternity in the matheme alone, by simultaneously abandoning historicism and finitude, does it become possible to think within a radically deconsecrated realm. Henceforth, the finite, which continues to be in thrall to an ethical *aura* and to be grasped in the pathos of mortal-being, must only be conceived of as a truth's differential incision within the banal fabric of infinity.

The contemporary prerequisite for a desecration of thought – which, it is all too apparent, remains to be accomplished – resides in a complete dismantling of the historicist schema. The infinite must be submitted to the matheme's simple and transparent deductive chains, subtracted from all jurisdiction by the One, stripped of its horizonal function as the correlate of finitude and released from the metaphor of the Open.

And it is at this point, in which thought is subjected to extreme tension, that mathematics summons us. Our imperative consists in forging a new modality for the entanglement of mathematics and philosophy, a modality through which the Romantic gesture that continues to govern us will be terminated.

Mathematics has shown that it has the resources to deploy a perfectly precise conception of the infinite as indifferent multiplicity. This 'indifferentiation' of the infinite, its post-Cantorian treatment as mere number, the pluralization of its concept (there are an infinity of different infinities) – all this has rendered the infinite banal; it has terminated the pregnant latency of finitude and allowed us to realize that every situation (ourselves included) is infinite. And it is this evental capacity proper to mathematical thought that finally enjoins us to link it to the philosophical proposition.

It is in this sense that I have invoked a 'Platonism of the multiple' as a programme for philosophy today.

The use of the term 'Platonism' is a provocation, or banner, through which to proclaim the closure of the Romantic gesture and the necessity of declaring once more: 'May no-one who is not a geometer enter here' – once it has been acknowledged that the non-geometer remains in thrall to the tenets of Romantic disjunction and the pathos of finitude.

The use of the term 'multiple' indicates that the infinite must be understood as indifferent multiplicity, as the pure material of being.

The conjunction of these two terms proclaims that the death of God can be rendered operative without privation, that the infinite can be untethered from the One, that historicism is terminated, and that eternity can be regained within time without the need for consecration.

In order to inaugurate such a programme, we will have to look back toward the history of the question. I shall punctuate this history at the two extremities of its arch: at one extreme stands Plato, who exiles the poem and promotes the matheme; while at the other stands Hegel, who invents the Romantic gesture in philosophy and is the thinker of the abasement of mathematics.

3. Plato carries out a philosophical deployment of mathematics at the frontier between thought and the freedom of thought

Plato is obviously the one who deployed a fundamental entanglement of mathematics and philosophy in all its ramifications. He produced a matrix for conditioning in which the three modalities of the mathematics/philosophy relation with which I began are already implicitly contained.

We will use Book 6 of *The Republic* as our point of reference. This text is canonical for our question because it contains an account of the relations between mathematics and the dialectic.

Let us examine the following passage from it. Socrates asks Glaucon, his interlocutor, if he has understood him correctly. In order to check, he invites him to provide a synopsis of the preceding discussion. Having reiterated, as is customary, that this is all very difficult, that he is not sure whether he has properly understood, and so on, Glaucon carries on and his synopsis meets with Socrates' approval:

> The theorizing concerning being and the intelligible which is sustained by the science [*épistémè*] of the dialectic is clearer than that sustained by what are known as the sciences [*techné*]. It is certainly the case that those who theorize according to these sciences, which have hypotheses as their principles, are obliged to proceed discursively rather than empirically. But because their intuiting remains dependent on these hypotheses and has no means of accessing the principle, they do not seem to you to possess the intellection of what they theorize, which nevertheless, in so far as it is illuminated by the principle, concerns the intelligibility of the entity. It seems to me you characterize the procedure of geometers and their ilk as discursive [*dianoia*], which is not how you characterize intellection. This discursiveness lies midway between [*metaxu*] opinion [*doxa*] and intellect [*nous*].[3]

In examining what is of significance for us in this text – i.e. the relation of conjunction/disjunction between mathematics and philosophy – I will proceed by delineating the four fundamental characteristics that structure the matrix for every conceivable relation between these two dispositions of thought.

1. For Plato, mathematics is a condition for thinking or theorizing in general because it constitutes a break with *doxa* or opinion. This much is familiar. But what needs to be emphasized is that mathematics *is the only point of rupture with* doxa *that is given as existing, or constituted.* The existence of mathematics is ultimately what constitutes its absolute singularity. Everything else that exists remains prisoner to opinion, but not mathematics. So the effective, historical, independent existence of mathematics provides a paradigm for the *possibility* of breaking with opinion.

    Of course, there is dialectical conversion, which for Plato is a superior form of breaking with *doxa*. But no one can say whether dialectical conversion, which is the essence of the philosophical disposition, *exists*. It is held up as a proposal or project, rather than as something actually existing. Dialectics is a programme, or initiation, while mathematics is an existing, available procedure. Dialectical conversion is the (eventual) point at which the Platonic text touches the real. But the only point of external support for the break with *doxa* – in the form of something that already exists – is constituted by mathematics and mathematics alone.

Having said this, the singularity of mathematics constantly and unfailingly provokes opinion, which is the reign of the *doxa*. Whence the constant broadsides against the 'abstract' or 'inhuman' nature of mathematics. Whenever one seeks a real, existing basis for a thinking that breaks with every form of opinion, one can always resort to mathematics. Ultimately, this singularity proper to mathematics is consensual, because everyone recognizes there isn't – and cannot be – such a thing as mathematical opinion (which is not to rule out the existence of opinions, generally unfavourable, *about* mathematics – quite the contrary). Mathematics exhibits – and therein lies its 'aristocratic' aspect – an irremediable discontinuity with regard to every sort of immediacy proper to *doxa*.

Conversely, it may legitimately be assumed that every negative opinion about mathematics constitutes, whether explicitly or implicitly, a defence of the rights of opinion, a plea for the immediate sovereignty of *doxa*. Romanticism, I believe, is guilty of this sin. As historicism, it has no choice but to turn the opinions of an era into the truth of that era. Temporalization submerges the concept in the immediacy of historicized representations. The Romantic project implies the ousting of mathematics, because one of its effects is *to render philosophy homogeneous with the historical power of opinion*. Philosophy as the conceptual capture of 'the spirit of the times' cannot encompass an atemporal break with the regime of established discourses.

Yet it is precisely this ability to effect a real break with the circulating immediacy of *doxa* that Plato prizes in the mathematical capacity.

2. Having noted what Plato admires about mathematics, it is necessary to address the twists in his argument. What Plato sets out to explain to us is that, however radical it may seem, the mathematical break with opinion is limited because it represents *a forced* break. Those who practise the mathematical sciences are 'forced' to proceed according to the intelligible, rather than according to the sensible or to *doxa*. They are forced – this implies that their break with opinion is, to some extent, involuntary, unapparent to itself, and above all devoid of freedom.

That mathematics is hypothetical, that it makes use of axioms it cannot legitimate, is an outward sign of what could be called its forced commandeering of the intelligible. The mathematical rupture is carried out under the constraint of deductive chains that are themselves dependent upon a fixed point which is stipulated in authoritarian fashion.

There is something implicitly violent about Plato's conception of mathematics, something which opposes it to the contemplative serenity of the dialectic. Mathematics does not ground thinking itself in the sovereign freedom of its proper disposition. Plato believes, or experiments with the possibility, as do I, that every break with opinion, every founding discontinuity of thought can and probably must resort to mathematics, but also that there is something obscure and violent in that recourse.

The philosophical localization of mathematics conjoins (a) the permanent paradigmatic availability of a discontinuity, (b) a grounding of thought outside opinion, *and* (c) a forced obscurity that cannot be appropriated or illuminated from within mathematics itself.

3. Since the mathematical break, which has the advantage of being supported by a historical real ('mathematicians and mathematical statements exist'), also has the disadvantage of being obscure and forced, the elucidation of this break with opinion requires *a second break*. For Plato, this second break, which traverses the ineluctable opacity of the first, is constituted by the access to a principle, whose name is 'dialectics'. In the philosophical apparatus proper to Plato, this gives rise to an opposition between the hypothesis (that which is presupposed or assumed in an authoritarian gesture) and the principle (that which is at once originary, a beginning, and illuminatingly authoritative, a command).

Ultimately, dialectics or philosophy is the light shed by a second break on the obscurity of the first, whose point of contact with the real is mathematics. If we can succeed in illuminating the hypothesis by the principle, then *even in mathematics* we shall enjoy thought's freedom or mobility with regard to its own break with opinion.

Although mathematics genuinely encapsulates the discontinuity with *doxa*, only philosophy can allow thought to establish itself in such a way as to assert the principle of this discontinuity. Philosophy suspends the violence of the mathematical break. It establishes a peace of the discontinuous.

4. Consequently, mathematics is *metaxu*: its topology, the site of its thinking, situates it in an intermediary position. This theme will prove hugely influential throughout Classical philosophy (which maintains the Platonic entanglement of philosophy and mathematics). Mathematics will always be simultaneously eminent (on account of its readily available capacity for breaking with the immediacy of opinions) and insufficient (on account of the constrictive character which its own obscure violence imposes upon it). Thus, mathematics will be a truth that *fails to achieve the form of wisdom*.

It seems at first glance – and this is usually as far as the analysis goes – that mathematics is *metaxu* because it breaks with opinion without attaining the serenity of the principle. In this sense, mathematics is located between opinion and intellection, or between the immediacy of *doxa* and the unconditioned principle sought by the dialectic. More fundamentally perhaps, we will say that mathematics amounts to an in-between in thinking as such; that it intimates a gap which lies even beyond the break with opinion. This gap is the one between the general requirement of discontinuity and the illumination of this requirement.

But every elucidation of discontinuity serves to establish the idea of a continuity. If mathematics is animated by an obscure violence, it is because the only thing that makes it superior to opinion is its discontinuity. Dialectics, which grasps the intelligible *as a whole*, rather than just the discontinuous edge that separates the intelligible from the sensible, integrates mathematics into a higher continuity. The position of mathematics as *metaxu* represents, in a certain sense, the in-between for the thinking of the discontinuous and the continuous. Mathematics emerges at the point where what demands to be thought is, on the one hand, the relation between that which is violently discontinuous within thought as such, and on the other, the sovereign freedom that illuminates and incorporates this very violence.

Mathematics is the in-between of truth and the freedom of truth. It is the truth that is still bound by unfreedom, yet which is required by the violent gesture through which the immediate is repudiated. Mathematics belongs to truth, but to a constrained form of it. Above and beyond this constrained figure of truth stands its free figure which elucidates discontinuity: philosophy.

For centuries, this positioning of mathematics at the precise point where truth and the freedom of truth enter into relation proved to be of determining historical importance as far the entanglement of mathematics and philosophy is concerned.

Mathematics is paradigmatic, because it cannot be subordinated to the regime of opinion. But the fact that this insubordination entails an impossibility also means that mathematics is incapable of shedding light on its own paradigmatic status. That philosophy is obliged to *ground* mathematics always signifies it must name and think the 'paradigmatic' nature of the paradigm, establish the illumination of the continuous at the moment of discontinuity, at the point where all mathematics has to offer is its blind, stubborn inability to propose anything other than the intelligible, and the break.

From this moment on, Classical philosophy will continually oscillate between the acknowledgement of the salutary function of mathematics with respect to the destiny of truth (this is the ontological mode of conditioning), and the obligation to ground the essence of that function *elsewhere*, which is to say, in philosophy (this is the epistemological mode). The centre of gravity for this oscillation can be captured in the following terms: mathematics is too violently true to be free, or it is too violently free (i.e. discontinuous) to be absolutely true.

4. Hegel deposes mathematics because he initiates a rivalry between it and philosophy with regard to the same concept, that of the infinite

Hegel discusses the relation between philosophy and mathematics in a detailed and technically informed manner in the massive Remark that follows the account of the infinity of the quantum in *The Science of Logic*. Although Hegel's conceptual methodology is far removed from Plato's, we only have to look at a few extracts to see that the movement of oscillation initiated by the Greeks (mathematics produces a break, but does not illuminate it) continues to govern Hegel's text:

But in a philosophical perspective the mathematical infinite is important because underlying it, in fact, is the notion of the genuine infinite and it is far superior to the ordinary so-called *metaphysical infinite* on which are based the objections to the mathematical infinite . . .

It is worthwhile considering more closely the mathematical concept of the infinite together with the most noteworthy of the attempts aimed at justifying its use and eliminating the difficulty with which the method feels itself burdened. The consideration of these justifications and characteristics of the mathematical infinite which I shall undertake at some length in this Remark will at the same time throw the best light on the nature of the true Notion itself and show how this latter was vaguely present as a basis for those procedures.[4]

The four characteristics we highlighted in Plato's text are all basically present in Hegel's analytical programme.

1. The mathematical concept of the infinite was historically decisive in the break with the ordinary metaphysical concept of the infinite. Since in his doctrine every break is a sublation or overcoming (*Aufhebung*), Hegel means to tell us that the mathematical concept of the infinite effectively sublates the metaphysical concept of the infinite, which is to say, the concept of the infinite in dogmatic theology.

   It is in any case entirely legitimate to consider 'metaphysics' as indicating a zone of opinion or *doxa* within philosophy itself, one which Hegel declares to be untrue (since it does not possess the true concept of the infinite). As in Plato, mathematics constitutes a positive break with the untrue concept of dogmatic opinion. Mathematics has the efficacy proper to a sublating-break with regard to the question of the infinite.

2. Nevertheless, this break is blind; it is not illuminated by its own operation. At the very beginning of his Remark Hegel says this:

   > The mathematical infinite has a twofold interest. On the one hand its introduction into mathematics has led to an expansion of the science and to important results; but on the other hand it is remarkable that mathematics has not yet succeeded in justifying its use of this infinite by the Notion. . . .[5]

   It is fair to say that we re-encounter here the Platonic theme: we recognize in this success, in these 'important results', the force of existence proper to mathematics, the fully deployed availability of a break. But this success is immediately balanced by the absence of justification, and hence by an essential obscurity.

A little later, Hegel will state that 'Success does not justify by itself the style of procedure.'[6] The existence of a mathematics of the infinite has all the real force of a genuine success. Nevertheless, one criterion stands higher than success: that of 'the style of procedure' used to accomplish it. Only philosophy can elucidate this style. But was not 'dialectics' in Plato's sense already a question of style? Of the style of thinking?

3. Thus just as for Plato the access to principle, which calls for the dialectical procedure, must sublate the violent use of hypotheses, similarly for Hegel a concept of the genuine infinite must sublate and ground the mathematical concept, which is endowed only with its own success.

4. Lastly, as far as the concept of the infinite is concerned, mathematics finds itself in an intermediary or mediating position: it is *metaxu*.

   • On the one hand, mathematics is paradigmatic for this particular concept because it 'throws the best light on the nature of the true Notion itself'.

   • But on the other, it is still necessary to 'justify its use and eliminate difficulties' – something that mathematics is incapable of doing. The philosopher assumes his traditional role as a kind of mechanic for mathematics: mathematics works, but since it doesn't know why it works, it needs to be taken apart and checked. It's almost certain the engine will need replacing. This is because mathematics lies between the metaphysical or dogmatic concept of the infinite, which modernity characterizes as a mere concept of opinion, and its true concept, which dialectics alone (in Hegel's sense) is capable of conceiving.

But if the four characteristics that singularized the mathematics/ philosophy pair in Plato turn up again in Hegel, what has changed? Why does the Hegelian text, which provides the 'technical' foundation for the Romantic gesture of disentanglement, effect a philosophical abasement of mathematics, when the Platonic text, on the contrary, guaranteed its paradigmatic value for centuries? Why does this major Remark, which is informed, attentive and *still* learned (a learnedness that Nietzsche and Heidegger would later dispense with) function as an abandoning of mathematics, rather than as a new positive form of its entanglement with philosophy? Why do we feel, or know, that after Hegel's assiduousness, our era's Romantic dive into the temporalization of the concept will abandon mathematics to the specialists?

Well, what has changed is that, for Hegel, the centre of gravity of mathematics, and the reason why it is deserving of philosophical examination, must be represented *as a concept*, the concept of the infinite, rather than as a domain of objects.

Mathematics for Plato means geometry and arithmetic, the objects of which are figures and numbers. That is why he is able to designate these types of thinking, or 'sciences', with the word *technè*, understood as an activity of thought whose object is determined in advance. The break with opinion is localizable; the domain in which it is exercised singular.

Hegel does not understand mathematics as the singular thought that pertains to a specific domain of objects, but rather as the determination of a concept, and even, one could say, as the determination of that which is the Romantic concept above all others: the infinite.

The consequences of this seemingly innocuous displacement are incalculable. For Plato, the fact that mathematics restricted itself to a realm of objects, that it dealt in figures and numbers rather than constituting a generic concept devoid of objects, determined mathematics as a figure of thought that was always singular, as a particular realm or procedure which did not need to rival the overarching ambition of philosophy.

But because Hegel posits that the paradigmatic essence of mathematics is tied to one of the central concepts of philosophy itself (i.e. the concept of the infinite), he has no choice but to transform the invariably singular relation of entanglement between philosophy and mathematics into a relation of rivalry before the tribunal of Truth. Moreover, since the true concept of the infinite is the philosophical one, and this concept contains and grounds whatever is acceptable in its mathematical counterpart, philosophy ultimately proclaims the uselessness of the mathematical concept as far as thinking is concerned.

It is certainly the case that the thinkers of the Classical era already considered mathematics as a partially useless activity, since it merely dealt with objects that did not have much 'worth', such as figures. But this depreciation, which operated indirectly through an evaluation of the singular objects of mathematics, did not call into question the extent of the mathematical break with opinion. It merely indicated its local character. The uselessness attributed to mathematics remained relative, since once thinking was established within the narrow realm of the objects in question, it remained absolutely true that the break with *doxa* enjoyed paradigmatic worth.

Hegel turns this judgement of the extrinsic uselessness of mathematics into a judgement of its *intrinsic* uselessness. Once instructed by philosophy as to the true concept of the infinite, we see that its mathematical concept is no more than a crude, dispensable stage on the way to the former. This is the price to be paid for the temporalization of the concept: everything which has been sieved and sublated is henceforth *dead* for thought. For Plato, by way of contrast, mathematics and dialectics are two relations that can be juxtaposed, albeit hierarchically, in an eternal configuration of being.

If Romantic philosophy after Hegel was able to carry out a radical disentanglement of mathematics from philosophy, this is because it proclaimed that philosophy dealt with *the same thing* as mathematics. The Romantic gesture is based on an identification, not a differentiation. In the realm of the concept of the infinite, Hegelian philosophy claims to constitute a superior mathematics, which is to say, a mathematics that has sublated, overtaken, or left behind its own restricted mathematicity and produced the ultimate philosopheme of its concept.

5. The re-entanglement of mathematics and philosophy aims at a dissolution of the Romantic concept of finitude and at the establishment of an evental philosophy of truth

In the final analysis, we can say that what is at stake in the complete disjunction of philosophy and mathematics carried out by the Romantic gesture is *the localization of the infinite*.

Romantic philosophy localizes the infinite in the temporalization of the concept as a historial envelopment of finitude.

At the same time, in what is henceforth its own parallel but separate and isolated development, mathematics localizes *a plurality of infinites* in the indifference of the pure multiple. It has processed the actual infinite via the banality of cardinal number. It has neutralized and completely deconsecrated the infinite, subtracting it from the metaphorical register of the tendency, the horizon, becoming. It has torn it from the realm of the One in order to disseminate it – whether as infinitely small or infinitely large – in the *aura*-free typology of multiplicities. By initiating a thinking in which the infinite is irrevocably separated from every instance of the One, mathematics has, in its own domain, successfully consummated the death of God.

Mathematics now treats the finite as a special case whose concept is derived from that of the infinite. The infinite is no longer that sacred exception coordinating an excess over the finite, or a negation, a sublation of finitude. For contemporary mathematics, it is the infinite that admits of a simple, positive definition, since it represents the ordinary form of multiplicities, while it is the finite that is deduced from the infinite by means of negation or limitation. If one places philosophy under the condition of such a mathematics, it becomes impossible to maintain the discourse of the pathos of finitude. 'We' are infinite, like every multiple-situation, and the finite is a lacunal abstraction. Death itself merely inscribes us within the natural form of infinite being-multiple, that of the limit ordinal, which punctuates the recapitulation of our infinity in a pure, external 'dying'.

This is where we find ourselves. On one hand, the ethical pathos of finitude, which operates under the banner of death, presupposes the infinite through temporalization, and cannot dispense with all those sacred, precarious and defensive representations concerning the promise of a God who would come to cauterize the indifferent wound which the world inflicts on the Romantic trembling of the Open. On the other, an ontology of indifferent multiplicity that can withstand the disjunction and abasement brought about by Hegel; one that secularizes and disperses the infinite, grasps us humans in terms of this dispersion, and advances the prospect of a world evacuated of every tutelary figure of the One.

The gap between these two options configures the site of our initial question, which concerned the possibility of an exit from Romanticism, a genuine post-romanticism, the decomposition of the theme of finitude, and the bracing acceptance of the infinity of every situation. The re-entanglement of mathematics and philosophy is the operation that must be carried out by whoever wants to terminate the power of myths, whatever they may be. This includes the myth of errancy and the Law, the myth of the immemorial, and even – for, as Hegel would say, it is the style of procedure that counts – the myth of the painful absence of myth.

In order for thought to carry out the decisive rupture with Romanticism (and the question is also political, because there have been historicist, and hence Romantic, elements in revolutionary politics), we cannot do without the recourse – which will perhaps once again be blind, possibly stamped with a certain constraint or violence – to the injunctions of mathematics. We philosophers, whose duty consists in thinking this time of ours beyond that which has led to its devastation, must subject ourselves to the condition of mathematics.

It is clear that the statement in terms of which I propose to re-entangle mathematics and philosophy cannot be characterized by the caution proper to the epistemological modality. It is imperative to cut straight to the ontological destiny of mathematics. Thus the statement will initially declare: there is nothing but infinite multiplicity, which in turn presents infinite multiplicity, and the one and only halting point in this presentation presents nothing. Ultimately, this halting point is the void, not the One. God is dead at the heart of presentation.

But since mathematics patently has a century's head start in the secularization of the infinite, and since the only available conception of multiplicity as infinitely weaving the void of its own inconsistency is what mathematics since Cantor claims to be its own site, we shall also make the provocative and therapeutic claim that mathematics *is* ontology in the strict sense, which is to say, the infinite development of what can be said of being qua being.

Finally, if the traversal and suspension of historicism, including Heidegger's historial framework, is carried out by siding with Cantor and Dedekind against Hegel as regards the dialectic of finite and infinite, and if the statement 'mathematics is ontology' today succeeds in putting philosophy under condition, the question that concerns us becomes the following: what happens to truth?

Will it consist in a dialectic, as it did for Plato and Hegel? Will there be (but this can no longer be a matter of ontology) a higher, foundational, illuminating mode of intellection, one that will be appropriate to the brutality of such a break? Is there something that *supplements* the multiple indifference of being? These questions belong to another order of enquiry, one that will fuel the continuation of philosophy by going beyond the morose topic of its 'end', in which it has been ensnared by the exhausted Romanticism of finitude. The core of such a philosophical proposition, conditioned by modern mathematics, is to render truths dependent on evental localizations and subtract them from the sophistical tyranny of language.

Whatever the case, it is incumbent on us to put an end to historicism and dismantle all those myths nourished by the temporalization of the concept. In doing so, resorting to mathematics in its courageous, solitary existence will prove necessary, for in banishing every instance of the sacred and the void of every God, mathematics is nothing but the human history of eternity.

CHAPTER 3
THE QUESTION OF BEING TODAY

There is no doubt we are indebted to Heidegger for having yoked philosophy once more to the question of being. We are also indebted to him for giving a name to the era of the forgetting of this question, a forgetting whose history, beginning with Plato, is the history of philosophy as such.

But what, in the final analysis, is the defining characteristic of metaphysics, which Heidegger conceives as the history of the withdrawal of being? We know that the Platonic gesture subordinates *aletheia* to the *idea*: the delineation of the Idea as the singular presence of the thinkable establishes the predominance of the entity over the initial or inaugural movement of the disclosure of being. Unveiling and unconcealment are thereby assigned the function of fixing a presence; but what is probably most important is that this fixation exposes the being of the entity to the power of a count, a counting-as-one. That through which 'what is' is what it is, is also that through which it is one. The paradigm of the thinkable is the unification of a singular entity through the power of the one; it is this paradigm, this normative power of the one, which erases being's coming to itself or withdrawal into itself as *phusis*. The theme of quiddity – the determination of the being of the entity through the unity of its *quid* – is what seals being's entry into a properly metaphysical normative register. In other words, it is what destines being to the predominance of the entity.

Heidegger sums up this movement in a series of notes entitled 'Sketches for a History of Being as Metaphysics':

> The predominance of quiddity brings forth the predominance of the entity itself each time in what it is. The predominance of the entity fixes being as *koinón* (the common) on the basis of the *hen* (the one). The distinctive feature of metaphysics is decided. The one as unifying unity takes on a normative function for the subsequent determination of being.[1]

Thus it is because of the normative function of the one in deciding being that being is reduced to the common, to empty generality, and is forced to endure the metaphysical predominance of the entity.

We can therefore define metaphysics as the commandeering of being by the one. The most appropriate synthetic maxim for metaphysics is Leibniz's, which establishes the reciprocity between being and the one: 'That which is not *one* being is not a *being*.'

Consequently, the starting point for my speculative claim could be formulated as follows: can one undo this bond between being and the one, break with the one's metaphysical domination of being, without thereby ensnaring oneself in Heidegger's destinal apparatus, without handing thinking over to the unfounded promise of a saving reversal? For in Heidegger himself the characterization of metaphysics as history of being is inseparable from a proclamation whose ultimate expression, it has to be admitted, is that 'only a God can save us'.

Can thinking attain this deliverance – or has thinking in reality always saved itself, by which I mean: delivered itself from the normative power of the one – without it being necessary to resort to prophesying the return of the gods?

In his *Introduction to Metaphysics*, Heidegger declares that 'a darkening of the world comes about on Earth'.[2] He goes on to list the essential components of this darkening: 'the flight of the gods, the destruction of the Earth, the vulgarization of man, the preponderance of the mediocre'.[3] All these themes are coherent with the identification of metaphysics as the exacerbation of the normative power of the one.

Yet although it is philosophical thinking that deploys the normative power of the one, philosophy is also that which, through an originary sundering of its disposition, has always concurrently mobilized the resistance to this power, the subtraction from it. Accordingly, and countering Heidegger, we should declare: the illumination of the world has always accompanied its immemorial darkening. Thus the flight of the gods is also the beneficial event of men's taking-leave of them; the destruction of the Earth is also the conversion that renders it amenable to active thinking; the vulgarization of man is also the egalitarian irruption of the masses onto the stage of history; and the preponderance of the mediocre is also the dense lustre of what Mallarmé called 'restrained action'.

Thus my problem can be formulated as follows: what name can thinking give to its own immemorial attempt to subtract being from the grip of the one? Can we learn to recognize that, although there was Parmenides, there was also Democritus, in whom, through dissemination and recourse to the void, the one is set aside? Can we learn to mobilize those figures who so obviously exempt themselves from Heidegger's destinal apparatus? Figures such as the magnificent Lucretius, in whom the power of the poem, far from maintaining the recourse to the Open in the midst of epochal distress, tries instead to subtract thinking from every return of the gods and firmly establish it within the certitude of the multiple? Lucretius is he who confronts thinking directly with that subtraction from the one constituted by inconsistent infinity, which nothing can envelop:

> Therefore the nature of space and the extent of the deep is so great that neither bright lightnings can traverse it in their course, though they glide onwards through endless tracts of time; nor can they by all their traveling make their journey any the less to go: so widely spreads the great store of space in the universe all around without limit in every direction.[4]

To invent a contemporary fidelity to that which has never been subject to the historial constraint of onto-theology or the commanding power of the one – such has been and remains, my aim.

The initial decision then consists in holding that what is thinkable of being takes the form of radical multiplicity, a multiplicity that is not subordinated to the power of the one, and which, in *Being and Event*, I called the multiple-without-oneness.

But in order to maintain this principle, it is necessary to abide by some very complex requirements.

- First of all, pure multiplicity – the multiplicity deploying the limitless resources of being in so far as it is subtracted from the power of the one – cannot consist in and of itself. Like Lucretius, we must effectively assume that the deployment of the multiple is not constrained by the immanence of a limit. For it is only too obvious that such a constraint would confirm the power of the one as the foundation for the multiple itself.

- Therefore, it is necessary to assume that multiplicity, envisaged as the exposure of being to the thinkable, is not available in the form of a consistent delimitation. Or again: that ontology, if it exists, must be the theory of inconsistent multiplicities as such. This also entails that what is thought within ontology is the multiple shorn of every predicate other than its multiplicity.

- More radically still, a genuinely subtractive science of being qua being must corroborate the powerlessness of the one from within itself. A merely external refutation is insufficient evidence for the multiple's without-oneness. It is the inconsistent composition of the multiple itself which points to the undoing of the one.

In the *Parmenides*, Plato grasped this point in all its patent difficulty by examining the consequences of the following hypothesis: the one is not. This hypothesis is especially interesting as far as Heidegger's determination of the distinctive character of metaphysics is concerned. What does Plato say? First, that if the one is not, it follows that the multiple's immanent alterity gives rise to a process of limitless self-differentiation. This is expressed in the striking formula: *tà alla etera estín*, which could be translated as: the others are Others, with a small 'o' for the first other, and a capital 'O', which I would call Lacanian, for the second. Since the one is not, it follows that the other is Other as absolutely pure multiplicity, intrinsic self-dissemination. This is the hallmark of inconsistent multiplicity.

Next, Plato shows that this inconsistency dissolves any supposed power of the one at its root, including even the power of its withdrawal or non-existence: every apparent exposition of the one immediately reduces it to an infinite multiplicity. I quote:

> For he who considers the matter closely and with acuity, then lacking oneness, since the one is not, each one appears as limitless multiplicity.[5]

What can this mean, if not that, subtracted from the one's metaphysical grip, the multiple cannot be exposed to the thinkable as a multiple composed of ones? It is necessary to posit that the multiple is only ever composed of multiples. Every multiple is a multiple of multiples.

And even if a multiple (an entity) is not a multiple of multiples, it will nevertheless be necessary to push subtraction all the way. We shall refuse to concede that such a multiple is the one, or even composed of ones. It will then, unavoidably, be a multiple of nothing.

For subtraction also consists in this: rather than conceding that if there is no multiple there is the one, we affirm that if there is no multiple, there is nothing. In so doing, we obviously re-encounter Lucretius. Lucretius effectively excludes the possibility that between the void and the multiple compositions of atoms, the one might be attributed to some kind of third principle:

> Therefore besides void and bodies, no third nature can be left self-existing in the sum of things – neither one that can ever at any time come within our senses, nor one that any man can grasp by the reasoning of the mind.[6]

This is what governs Lucretius' critique of those cosmologies subordinated to a unitary principle, such as Heraclitus' Fire. Lucretius clearly sees that to subtract oneself from the fear of the gods requires that beneath the multiple, there be nothing. And that beyond the multiple, there be only the multiple once again.

- Finally, a third consequence of the subtractive commitment consists in excluding the possibility of there being a definition of the multiple. Heideggerean analysis comes to our aid on this point: the genuinely Socratic method of delineating the Idea consists in grasping a definition. The method of definition is opposed to the imperative of the poem precisely to the extent that it establishes the normative power of the one within language itself. The entity will be thought in its being in so far as it is delineated or isolated through the dialectical resource of definition. Definition is the linguistic way of establishing the predominance of the entity.

Yet by claiming to access the multiple-exposition of being from the perspective of a definition, or dialectically, by means of successive delimitations, one is in fact already operating in the ambit of the metaphysical power of the one.

The thinking of the multiple-without-oneness, or of inconsistent multiplicity, cannot therefore proceed by means of definition.

Ontology faces the difficult dilemma of having to set out the thinkable character of the pure multiple without being able to state under what conditions a multiple can be recognized as such. Even this negative requirement cannot be explicitly stated. One cannot, for example, say that thinking is devoted to the multiple and to nothing but the intrinsic multiplicity of the multiple. For this thought itself, because of its recourse to a delimiting norm, would already enter into what Heidegger called the process of the limitation of being. And the one would thereby be reinstated.

Consequently, it is neither possible to define the multiple nor to explain this absence of definition. The truth is that the thinking of the pure multiple must be such as to never mention the word 'multiple' anywhere, whether it be in order to state what it designates, in accordance with the one; or to state, again in accordance the one, what it is powerless to designate.

But what kind of thinking never defines what it thinks and never expounds it as an object? What do you call a thinking which, even in the writing that binds it to the thinkable, refuses to ascribe any kind of name to the thinkable? The answer is obviously *axiomatic* thinking. Axiomatic thinking grasps the disposition of undefined terms. It never encounters either a definition of its terms or a serviceable explanation of what they are not. The primordial statements of such an approach expound the thinkable without thematizing it. No doubt the primitive term or terms are inscribed. But if they are, it is not in the sense of a naming whose referent would need to be represented, but rather in the sense of being laid out in a series wherein the term subsists only through the ordered play of its founding connections.

The most crucial requirement for a subtractive ontology is that its explicit presentation take the form of the axiom, which prescribes without naming, rather than that of the dialectical definition.

It is on the basis of this requirement that it becomes necessary to reinterpret the famous passage in the *Republic* where Plato opposes mathematics to the dialectic.

Let us reread how Glaucon, one of Socrates' interlocutors, summarizes his master's thinking on this point:

> The theorizing concerning being and the intelligible which is sustained by the science [*épistémè*] of the dialectic is clearer than that sustained by what are known as the sciences [*techné*]. It is certainly the case that those who theorize according to these sciences, which have hypotheses as their principles, are obliged to proceed discursively rather than empirically. But because their intuiting remains dependent on these hypotheses and has no means of accessing the principle, they do not seem to you to possess the intellection of what they theorize, which nevertheless, in so far as it is illuminated by the principle, concerns the intelligibility of the entity. It seems to me you characterize the procedure of geometers and their ilk as discursive [*dianoia*], while you do not characterize intellection thus, in so far as that discursiveness is established between [*metaxu*] opinion [*doxa*] and intellect [*nous*].[7]

It is perfectly apparent that for Plato the axiom is precisely what is wrong with mathematics. Why? Because the axiom remains external to the thinkable. Geometers are obliged to proceed discursively precisely because they do not have access to the normative power of the one, whose name is *principle*. What's more, this constraint confirms their exteriority relative to the principal norm of the thinkable. For Plato, once again, the axiom is the bearer of an obscure violence, resulting from the fact that it does not conform to the dialectical and definitional norm of the one. Although thought is certainly present in mathematics and in the axiom, it is not yet as the freedom of thought, which the axiom subordinates to the paradigm or norm of the one.

On this point, my conclusion is obviously the opposite of Plato's. The value of the axiom consists precisely in the fact that it remains subtracted from the normative power of the one. And unlike Plato, I do not regard the axiomatic constraint as a sign that a unifying, grounding illumination is lacking. Rather, I see in it the necessity of the subtractive gesture as such, that is, of the movement whereby thought – albeit at the price of the inexplicit or of the impotence of nominations – tears itself from everything that still ties it to the commonplace, to generality, which is the root of its own metaphysical temptation. And it is in this tearing away that I perceive thought's freedom with regard to its destinal constraint, what could be called its metaphysical tendency.

We could say that once ontology embraces the axiomatic approach or institutes a thinking of pure inconsistent multiplicity, it has to abandon every appeal to principles. And conversely, that every attempt to establish a principle prevents the multiple from being exhibited exclusively in accordance with the immanence of its multiplicity.

Thus we now possess five conditions for any ontology of pure multiplicity as discontinuation of the power of the one; or for any ontology faithful to what, in philosophy itself, has always struggled against its own metaphysical tendency.

1. Ontology is the thinking of inconsistent multiplicity, of multiplicity characterized – without immanent unification – solely in terms of the predicate of its multiplicity.

2. The multiple is radically without-oneness, in that it itself comprises multiples alone. What there is exposes itself to the thinkable in terms of multiples of multiples, in accordance with the strict requirement of the 'there is'. In other words, there are only multiples of multiples.

3. Since there is no immanent limit anchored in the one that could determine multiplicity as such, there is no originary principle of finitude. The multiple can therefore be thought as in-finite. Or even: infinity is another name for multiplicity as such. And since it is also the case that no principle binds the infinite to the one, it is necessary to maintain that there are an infinity of infinites, an infinite dissemination of infinite multiplicities.

4. Even in the exceptional case where it is possible to think a multiple as not being a multiple of multiples, we will not concede the necessity of reintroducing the one. We will say it is a multiple of nothing. And just as with every other multiple, this nothing will remain entirely devoid of consistency.

5. Every effective ontological presentation is necessarily axiomatic.

At this point, enlightened by Cantor's refounding of mathematics, it becomes possible to state: ontology is nothing other than mathematics as such. What's more, this has been the case ever since its Greek origin; even if, from the moment of its inception up until now, as it struggled internally against the metaphysical temptation, mathematics only managed with difficulty, through painful efforts and transformations, to secure for itself the free play of its own conditions.

With Cantor we move from a restricted ontology, in which the multiple is still tied to the metaphysical theme of the representation of objects, numbers and figures, to a general ontology, in which the cornerstone and goal of all mathematics becomes thought's free apprehension of multiplicity as such, and the thinkable is definitively untethered from the restricted dimension of the object.

We can now briefly elucidate how post-Cantorian mathematics becomes in a certain sense equal to its conditions.

1. A set, in Cantor's sense of the word, has no essence besides that of being a multiplicity; it is without external determination because there is nothing to restrict its apprehension with reference to something else; and it is without internal determination because what it gathers as multiple is indifferent.

2. In the version of set-theory established by Zermelo and Fraenkel, there is no other undefined primitive term or possible value for the variables besides that of sets. Thus every element of a set is itself a set. This is the realization of the idea that every multiple is a multiple of multiples, without reference to unities of any kind.

3. Cantor fully acknowledges not only the existence of infinite sets, but the existence of an infinity of such sets. This is an absolutely open infinity, sealed only by the point of impossibility and hence by the real that renders it inconsistent, which amounts to the fact that there cannot be a set of all sets. This is something that was already acknowledged in Lucretius' a-cosmism.

4. There does in fact exist a set of nothing, or a set possessing no multiple as an element. This is the empty set, which is a pure mark and out of which it can be demonstrated that all multiples of multiples are woven. Thus the equivalence of being and the letter is achieved once we have subtracted ourselves from the normative power of the one. Recall Lucretius' powerful anticipation of this point in Book I, verses 910 and following:

    > A small transposition is sufficient for atoms to create igneous or ligneous bodies. Likewise, in the case of words, a slight alteration in the letters allows us to distinguish ligneous from igneous.[8]

    It is in this agency of the letter, to take up Lacan's expression (an agency here constituted by the mark of the void), that the thought of what lets itself be mathematically exhibited as the immemorial figure of being unfolds without-oneness, which is to say, without-metaphysics.

5. What lies at the heart of the presentation of set-theory is simply its body of axioms. The word 'set' plays no part in the theory. Nor does the definition of such a word. This demonstrates how, in its essence, the thought of the pure multiple requires no dialectical principle, and how in this regard the freedom of that thinking which accords with being resides in axiomatic decision, not in the intuition of a norm.

Moreover, since it was subsequently established that Cantor's achievement lay not so much in elaborating a particular theory as in providing the very site for what is mathematically thinkable (the famous 'paradise' evoked by Hilbert), it becomes possible to state by way of retroactive generalization that, ever since the Greek origin of ontology, being has been persistently inscribed through the deployment of pure mathematics. Consequently, thinking has been subtracting itself from the normative power of the one ever since philosophy began. From Plato to Husserl and Wittgenstein, the striking incision which mathematics carries out within philosophy should be interpreted as a singular condition: the condition whereby philosophy experiences a process which is not that of being's subjugation at the hands of the one. Thus under its mathematical condition, philosophy has always been the site of a disparate or divided project. It is true that philosophy exposes the category of truth to the unifying, metaphysical power of the one. But it is also true that philosophy in turn also exposes this power to the subtractive defection of mathematics. Thus every singular philosophy is less an effectuation of metaphysical destiny than an attempt to subtract itself from the latter under the condition of mathematics. The philosophical category of truth results both from a normativity inherited from the Platonic gesture and from grasping the mathematical condition that undoes this norm. This is true even in the case of Plato himself: the gradual multiplication or mixing of the supreme Ideas in the *Sophist* or *Philebus*, like the *reductio ad absurdum* of the theme of the one in the *Parmenides*, indicate the extent to which the choice between definition and axiom, principle and decision, unification and dissemination, remains fluid and indecisive.

More generally, if ontology or what is sayable of being qua being is coextensive with mathematics, what are the tasks of philosophy?

The first one probably consists in philosophy humbling itself, against its own latent wishes, before mathematics by acknowledging that mathematics is in effect the thinking of pure being, of being qua being.

I say against its own latent wishes, for in its actual development philosophy has manifested a stubborn tendency to yield to the sophistical injunction and to claim that although an analysis of mathematics might be necessary to the existence of philosophy, the former cannot lay claim to the rank of genuine thinking. Philosophy is partly responsible for the reduction of mathematics to the status of mere calculation or technique. This is a ruinous image, to which mathematics is reduced by current opinion with the aristocratic complicity of mathematicians themselves, who are all too willing to accept that, in any case, the rabble will never be able to understand their science.

It is therefore incumbent upon philosophy to maintain – as it has very often attempted to, even as it obliterated that very attempt – that mathematics *thinks*.

CHAPTER 4
PLATONISM AND MATHEMATICAL ONTOLOGY

In the introduction to *The Philosophy of Mathematics*, a collection of texts edited by Benacerraf and Putnam, we find the following claim:

> In general, the platonists will be those who consider mathematics as the *discovery* of truths about structures which exist independently of the activity or thought of mathematicians.[1]

This criterion of the exteriority (or transcendence) of mathematical structures (or objects) results in a diagnosis of 'Platonism' for almost all works belonging to the 'philosophy of science'. But this diagnosis is undoubtedly wrong. It is wrong because it presupposes that the 'Platonist' espouses a distinction between internal and external, knowing subject and known 'object'; a distinction which is utterly foreign to the genuine Platonic framework. However firmly established this distinction may be in contemporary epistemology, however fundamental the theme of the objectivity of the object and the subjectivity of the subject may be for it, one cannot but entirely fail to grasp the thought process at work in Plato on the basis of such presuppositions.

First of all, it should be noted that the 'independent existence' of mathematical structures is entirely relative for Plato. What the metaphor of anamnesis designates is precisely that thought is never confronted with 'objectivities' from which it is supposedly separated. The Idea is always already there and would remain unthinkable were one not able to 'activate' it in thought. Furthermore, where mathematical ideas in particular are concerned, the whole aim of the concrete demonstration provided in the *Meno* is to establish their presence even in the least educated, most anonymous instance of thought – that of the slave.

Plato's fundamental concern is to declare the immanent identity, the co-belonging, of the knowing mind and the known, their essential ontological commensurability. If there is a sense in which he remains heir to Parmenides, who declared 'it is the same to think and to be', it is to be found in this declaration. In so far as it touches on being, mathematics intrinsically thinks. By the same token, if mathematics thinks, it accesses being intrinsically. The theme of a knowing subject who has to 'aim' at an external object – a theme whose origins lie in empiricism, even when the putative object is ideal – is entirely ill-suited to the philosophical use to which Plato puts the existence of mathematics.

Moreover, Plato is even less concerned with mathematical structures existing 'in themselves'. There are two reasons for this:

1. 'Ideality' is the general name given to what is thinkable, and is in no way the exclusive province of mathematics. As the old Parmenides points out to the young Socrates, in so far as we think mud or hair, we must acknowledge the idea of mud and the idea of hair. In fact, 'Idea' is the name given to what is thought, in so far as it is thought. The Platonic theme consists precisely in rendering immanence and transcendence indiscernible, in taking up a position in a site of thinking wherein this distinction is inoperative. A mathematical idea is neither subjective ('the activity of the mathematician'), nor objective ('independently existing structures'). In one and the same gesture, it breaks with the sensible and posits the intelligible. In other words, it is an instance of thinking.

2. It is not the status of so-called mathematical 'objects' that Plato is interested in, but the movement of thought, because in the final analysis mathematics is invoked only in order to be contrasted with dialectics. But in the realm of the thinkable, everything is an Idea. Thus it is pointless to look to 'objectivity' to provide a basis for some sort of difference between kinds of thinking. Only the singularity of their respective movements (that of proceeding from hypotheses or of seeking out a principle) allows one to delimit mathematical *dianoia* from dialectical (or philosophical) intellection. The separation of 'objects' is secondary and always obscure. It is an auxiliary categorization 'in being' elaborated on the basis of clues provided by thought.

Finally, only one thing is certain: mathematics thinks (meaning, in the language of Plato, that it constitutes a break with perceptual immediacy), dialectics also thinks, and considered in their protocols, these two thoughts differ.

On this basis, we can attempt to define Plato's inscription of the mathematical condition for 'philosophizing' as follows:

We call Platonic the recognition of mathematics as a form of thinking that is intransitive to perceptual and linguistic experience, and which depends on a decision that makes room for the undecidable and assumes that everything which is consistent exists.

In order to gauge the polemical charge of this 'definition' of Platonism, let us contrast it to the one proposed by Fraenkel and Bar-Hillel in *The Foundations of Set-Theory*:

A *Platonist* is convinced that corresponding to each well-defined (monadic) condition [which is to say, the attribution of a predicate to a variable, in the form $P(x)$] there exists, in general, a set, or class, which comprises all and only those entities that fulfil this condition and which is an entity in its own right of an ontological status similar to that of its members.[2]

I do not believe a Platonist can be convinced of anything of the sort. Plato himself continuously takes pains to show that the correlate of a well-defined concept or proposition can be empty or inconsistent; or that its corresponding 'entity' may necessitate ascribing an exorbitant ontological status to everything invoked in the initial expression. Thus the correlate of the Good, however limpid the definition of its notion, however obvious its practical instantiation, requires an exemption from the status of Idea (the Good is 'beyond' the Idea). The explicit goal of the *Parmenides* is to demonstrate how, in the case of perfectly clear statements such as 'the one is' and 'the one is not', no matter what assumption we make about the correlate of the one and those things that are 'other than one', we come up against a contradiction. Which, after all, is the first example, albeit in a purely philosophical register, of an argument proceeding in terms of absolute undecidability.

Contrary to what Fraenkel and Bar-Hillel declare, I maintain that the undecidable constitutes a crucial category for Platonism, and that we can never know in advance whether there will always exist a thinkable entity corresponding to a well-defined expression. The undecidable testifies to the fact that a Platonist has no confidence whatsoever in the clarity of language when it comes to deciding about existence. In this regard, Zermelo's axiom is Platonist because it refuses to allow the existence and collection of the 'entities' validating a given expression unless they are already given by an existing set. Thought requires a constant and immanent guarantee of being.

The undecidable is the reason behind the aporetic style of the dialogues: the aim is to reach the point of the undecidable precisely in order to show that thought must take a decision with regard to an event of being, that thought is not primarily a description or a construction but a break (with opinion, with experience), and hence a decision.

In this regard, it seems to me that Gödel, whom the 'philosophy of mathematics' continues to class as a 'Platonist', displays a superior acumen.

Consider this passage from the famous text 'What is Cantor's Continuum Problem?':

> However, the question of the objective existence of the objects of mathematical intuition (which, incidentally, is an exact replica of the question of the objective existence of the outer world) is not decisive for the problem under discussion here. The mere psychological fact of the existence of an intuition which is sufficiently clear to produce the axioms of set-theory and an open series of extensions of them suffices to give meaning to the question of the truth or falsity of propositions like Cantor's continuum hypothesis. What, however, perhaps more than anything else, justifies the acceptance of this criterion of truth in set-theory is the fact that continued appeals to mathematical intuition are necessary not only for obtaining unambiguous answers to the questions of transfinite set-theory, but also for the solution of the problems of finitary number theory (of the type of Goldbach's conjecture), where the meaningfulness and unambiguity of the concepts entering into them can hardly be doubted. This follows from the fact that for every axiomatic system there are infinitely many undecidable propositions of this type.[3]

What are the most important features of this 'Platonist' text?

- The word 'intuition' here simply refers to a decision of inventive thought with regard to the intelligibility of the axioms. According to Gödel's own formulation, it refers to the capacity to 'produce the axioms of set-theory', and the existence of such a capacity is purely a 'fact'. Note that the intuitive function does not consist in grasping 'external' entities, but instead involves clearly deciding as to a primary or irreducible proposition. The comprehensive invention of axioms confirms that the mathematical proposition is an instance of thinking, and is consequently what exposes the proposition to truth.

- The question about the 'objective' existence of these supposed objects is explicitly declared to be secondary (it is 'not decisive for the problem under discussion here'). Furthermore, it is in no way peculiar to mathematics, since the existence in question is of the same sort as that of the external world. To see in mathematical existence nothing more, and nothing less, than in existence plain and simple is actually very Platonic: in each and every case, the thinkable (whether it be mud, hair, a triangle, or complex numbers) can be interrogated as to its existence, which is something other than its being. For as far as being is concerned, it is corroborated only through its envelopment in an instance of thought.

- The crucial problem is that of truth. As soon as there is inventive thinking (as attested to by the intelligibility of the axioms), one can 'give meaning to the question of the truth or falsity of propositions' that this thinking legitimates. This meaningfulness derives precisely from the fact that the thinkable, as Idea, necessarily comes into contact with being, as well as from the fact that 'truth' is only ever the name of that through which thinking and being correspond to one another in a single process.

- The infinite and the finite do not indicate a distinction of any momentous importance for thinking. Gödel insists that 'acceptance of [the] criterion of truth' results from the fact that intuition (i.e. the axiomatizing decision) is continually required both in order to decide problems in finitary number theory and to make decisions about problems concerning transfinite sets. Hence the movement of thought, which is the only thing that matters, does not differ essentially whether it deals with the infinite or the finite.

- The undecidable is intrinsically tied to mathematics. Moreover, it does not so much constitute a 'limit' – as is sometimes maintained – as a perpetual incitement to the exercise of inventive intuition. Since every apparatus of mathematical thought, as summarized in a collection of foundational axioms, comprises an element of undecidability, intuition is never useless: mathematics must periodically be redecided.

Finally, I will characterize what is legitimate to call a Platonic philosophical orientation vis-à-vis the modern mathematical condition – and a fortiori, ontology – in terms of three points.

1. Mathematics thinks

I have already developed this assertion at some length, but its importance is such that I would at least like to reiterate it here. Let us recall, by way of example, that Wittgenstein, who is not an ignoramus in these matters, declares that 'A proposition of mathematics does not express a thought' (*Tractatus*, 6.21).[4] Here, with customary radicality, Wittgenstein merely restates a thesis that is central to every variety of empiricism, as well as to all sophistry. It is one which we will never have done refuting.

That mathematics thinks means in particular that it regards the distinction between a knowing subject and a known object as devoid of pertinence. There is a co-ordinated movement of thought, co-extensive with being, which mathematics envelops – a co-extensiveness that Plato called 'Idea'. In this movement, discovery and invention are strictly indiscernible – just like the idea and its *ideatum*.

2. Every instance of thought – and a fortiori mathematics – requires decisions (intuitions) taken from the point of the undecidable (the non-deducible)

The result of this feature is a maximal expansion of the principle of choice as far as the thinkable is concerned: since decision is primary and continuously required, it is pointless to try to reduce it to protocols of construction or externally regulated procedures. On the contrary, the constraints of construction (often and confusingly referred to as 'intuitionist' constraints, which is inappropriate given that the genuine advocate of intuition is the Platonist) should be subordinated to the freedoms of thinking decision. Which is why, as long as the effects engendered in thought are maximal, the Platonist sees no reason to refrain from freely wielding the principle of excluded middle, and consequently resorting to proofs by *reductio ad absurdum*.

3. The sole criterion for mathematical questions of existence is the intelligible consistency of what is thought

Existence here must be considered an intrinsic determination of effective thought in so far as this thought envelops being. Those cases where it does not envelop being invariably register an inconsistency, which it is important not to confuse with an undecidability. In mathematics, being, thought and consistency are one and the same thing.

Several important consequences follow from these features, in terms of which it is possible to recognize the modern Platonist, who is a Platonist of multiple-being.

- First of all, as Gödel points out, when it comes to the so-called 'paradoxes' of the actual infinite, the Platonist's attitude is one of indifference. Since the realm of intelligibility instituted by the infinite seems to pose no specific problem – whether with regard to axiomatic intuition or with regard to demonstrative protocols – the reasons adduced for worrying about intelligibility are always extrinsic, psychological, or empiricist, and deny mathematicians their self-sufficiency *vis-a-vis* to the regime of the thinkable determined by those very same intuitions and protocols.

- Next, the Platonist's desire is for maximal extension in what can be granted existence: the more existences, the better. The Platonist espouses audacity in thought. He disdains restrictions and prohibitions foisted upon him from outside (particularly those originating from timorous philosophemes). So long as the being enveloped by thought prevents thought from lapsing into inconsistency, one can and should proceed boldly in asserting existences. This is how thought pursues a line of intensification.

- Lastly, the Platonist acknowledges a criterion whenever it becomes apparent that a choice is necessary as to the direction in which mathematics will develop. This criterion is precisely that of maximal extension in what can be consistently thought. Thus the Platonist will admit the axiom of choice rather than its negation, because a universe endowed with the axiom of choice is larger and denser in terms of intelligible relations than a universe that refuses to admit it. Conversely, the Platonist will have reservations about admitting the continuum hypothesis, and even more so the hypothesis of constructibility.

For universes regulated in accordance with these hypotheses seem narrow and constrained. The constructible universe is particularly penurious: Rowbottom has shown that if one admits a particular type of large cardinals (Ramsey cardinals), the constructible real numbers become denumerable. For the Platonist, a denumerable continuum seems far too constrictive an intuition. The Platonist's conviction finds reassurance in Rowbottom's theorem, which privileges decided consistencies over controlled constructions.

It then becomes apparent that a 'set-theoretical' decision with regard to mathematics, i.e. an ontological reworking of Cantor's ideas (which, as I have shown, helps elucidate the thinking of being as pure multiplicity), imposes a Platonic orientation of the kind just described. Moreover, this is confirmed by the philosophical choices espoused by Gödel, who is (with Cohen) the greatest of Cantor's heirs.

Set-theory is indeed the prototypical instance of a theory in which (axiomatic) decision prevails over (definitional) construction. Empiricists, along with the twentieth-century partisans of the 'linguistic turn', have not been slow in objecting that the theory cannot even define or elucidate its central concept; that of the set. To this accusation a Platonist like Gödel will always retort that what counts is axiomatic intuitions, which constitute a space of truth, not the logical definition of primitive relations.

Contrary to the Aristotelian orientation (potentiality as a primary singularization of substance) and the Leibnizian orientation (logical possibility as a 'claim to being'), set-theory knows only actual multiplicity. The idea that actuality is the effective form of being, and that possibility or potentiality are fictions, is a profoundly Platonic motif. Nothing is more significant in this regard than the set-theoretical treatment of the concept of function. What seems to be a dynamic operator, often manifested in terms of spatial – i.e. physical – schemata (if $y = f(x)$, one will say that y 'varies' as a function of the variations of x, etc.), is, in the set-theoretical framework, treated strictly as an actual multiple: the multiple-being of the function is the graph, which is to say a set whose elements are ordered pairs of the (x, y) type, and any allusion to dynamics or 'variation' is eliminated.

Similarly, the concept of limit, imbued as it is with the experience of becoming, of tending-toward, of asymptotic movement, is reduced to the immanent characterization of a type of multiplicity. Thus in order to be identified, a limit ordinal does not need to be represented as that toward which the succession of ordinals of which it is the limit 'tends', simply because it *is* that succession as such (the elements of that succession are what define it as a set). The transfinite ordinal $\aleph_0$, which comes 'after' the natural whole numbers, is nothing other than the set of all natural whole numbers.

In each and every case, set-theory demonstrates its indisputable derivation from Platonic genius by thinking virtuality as actuality: there is only one kind of being, the Idea (or in this instance, the set). Thus there is no actualization, because every actualization presupposes the existence of more than one register of existence (at least two: potentiality and act).

Furthermore, set-theory conforms to the principle of existential maximality. Ever since Cantor, its aim has been to go beyond all previous limitations, all criteria for 'reasonable' existence (criteria which are in its eyes extrinsic). The admission of increasingly huge cardinals (inaccessible, Mahlo, measurable, compact, supercompact, enormous, etc.) is intrinsic to its natural genius. But so too is the admission of infinitesimals of all sorts, in accordance with the theory of surreal numbers. Furthermore, this approach deploys more and more complex and saturated 'levels' of being; an ontological hierarchy (the cumulative hierarchy) that, in conformity with an intuition which this time is of Neo-platonic inspiration, is such that its (inconsistent) 'totality' is always consistently reflected in one of its levels, in the following sense: if a statement is valid 'for the universe as a whole' (in other words, if the quantifiers are taken in an unlimited sense, so that 'for every x' really does mean 'for any set whatsoever in the universe as a whole'), then there exists a set in which that statement is valid (the quantifiers this time being taken as 'relativized' to the set in question). Which means that this set, considered as a 'restricted universe', reflects the universal value of the statement, localizes it.

This theorem of reflection tells us that what can be said with regard to 'limitless' being can also always be said in a determinate site. Or that every statement prescribes the possibility of a localization. One will recognize here the Platonic theme of the intelligible localization of all rational pronouncements – which is the very thing Heidegger criticizes as the Idea's 'segmentation' of being's 'unconcealment' or natural presencing.

More fundamentally, set-theory's Platonic vocation entails consequences for three of the constitutive categories in any philosophical ontology: difference, the primitive name of being, and the undecidable.

For Plato, difference is governed by the Idea of the Other. But according to the way this idea is presented in the *Sophist*, it necessarily implies an intelligible localization of difference. It is to the extent that an idea 'participates' in the Other, that it can be said to be different from another.

Thus there is a localizable evaluation of difference: that of the proper modality according to which an idea, even though it is 'the same as itself', participates in the Other as other idea. In set-theory, this point is taken up through the axiom of extensionality: if a set differs from another, it is because there exists at least one element which belongs to one but not the other. This 'at least one' localizes the difference and prohibits purely global differences. There is always one point of difference (just as for Plato an idea is not other than another 'in itself', but only in so far as it participates in the Other). This is a crucial trait, particularly because it undermines the appeal (whether Aristotelian or Deleuzean) to the qualitative and to global, natural difference. In the Platonic style favoured by the set-theoretical approach, alterity can always be reduced to punctual differences, and difference can always be specified in a uniform, elementary fashion.

In set-theory, the void, the empty set, is the primitive name of being. The entire hierarchy is rooted in it. There is a certain sense in which it alone 'is'. And the logic of difference implies that the void is unique. For it cannot differ from another, since it contains no element (no local point) through which this difference could be verified. This combination of primitive naming through the absolutely simple (or the in-different, which is the status of the One in the *Parmenides*) and founding uniqueness is indubitably Platonic: the existence of what this primitive name designates must be axiomatically decided, just as – and this is the upshot of the aporias in the *Parmenides* – it is pointless to try to deduce the existence (or non-existence) of the One: it is necessary to decide, and then assume the consequences.

Finally, as we have known ever since Cohen's theorem, the continuum hypothesis is intrinsically undecidable. Many believe this signals the veritable ruin of the project of set-theory, or points to the 'fragmentation' of what was intended as a unified construction. I have said enough by now to make it clear that my own point of view is diametrically opposed to this verdict: the undecidability of the continuum hypothesis marks the effective completion of set-theory as a Platonic orientation. It indicates the point of flight, the aporia, the immanent errancy, wherein thought is experienced as a groundless confrontation with the undecidable, or – to use Gödel's vocabulary – as a continuous recourse to intuition, which is to say, to decision.

Antiqualitative localization of difference, uniqueness of existence through a primitive naming, intrinsic experience of the undecidable: these are the features through which set-theory can be grasped by philosophy from the perspective of a theory of truth, over and above a mere logic of forms.

CHAPTER 5
THE BEING OF NUMBER

Euclid's definitions show how in the Greek conception of number, the being of number is entirely dependent upon the metaphysical aporias of the one. Number, according to Definition 2 of Book 7 of Euclid, is 'a multiplicity composed of units'. And a unit, according to Definition 1 of the same book, is 'that on the basis of which each of the things that exist is called one'. Ultimately, the being of number is the multiple reduced to the pure combinatorial legislation of the one.

The exhaustion and eventual collapse of this conception of the being of number in terms of the procession of the one ushers the thinking of being into the modern era. This collapse is due to a combination of three factors: the appearance of the Arab zero, the infinitesimal calculus, and the crisis of the metaphysical ideality of the one. The first factor, zero, introduces neutrality and emptiness at the heart of the conception of number. The second, the infinite, either goes beyond the combinatorial and heads toward topology, or appends the numerical position of a limit onto mere succession. The third, the obsolescence of the one, necessitates an attempt to think number directly as pure multiplicity or multiple-without-oneness.

What initially ensues from all this is a kind of anarchic dissemination of the concept of number. The disciplinary syntagm known as 'number theory' bears witness to this: ultimately, it comprises vast amounts of pure algebra, as well as particularly sophisticated aspects of complex analysis. Equally symptomatic is the heterogeneity in the introductory procedures used for the different kinds of classical number: axiomatic for natural whole numbers, structural for the ordinals, algebraic for negative as well as rational numbers, topological for real numbers, and largely geometrical for complex numbers. Lastly, this dissemination can also be seen in the non-categorial character of the formal systems used to capture number. Because they admit non-classical models, these systems open up the fertile path of non-standard analysis, thereby rendering infinite (or infinitesimal) numbers respectable once again.

The difficulty for philosophy, whose aim is to reveal how the conception of number harbours an active thinking of being, is that today, unlike in the Greek era, there no longer seems to be a unified definition of number. What concept could simultaneously encompass the discrete nature of the wholes, the density of the rationals, the swarming of the infinitesimals, not to mention the transfinite numbering of Cantor's ordinals? In what sense is it possible for the philosopher to relate all these back to a single concept, all the while maintaining and intensifying the concept's cognitive power as well as its singular inventiveness? Let's try to clarify this confusion by starting from the ordinary uses of the word number.

What do we mean by 'number'? What is entailed by our uses of the term and the representations associated with those uses?

First of all, by 'number' we understand an instance of measure. At the most elementary level, number serves to distinguish between the less and the more, the large and the small. It provides a discrete distribution of data. Thus one of the principal requirements for any species of number is that it provide a structure of order.

Secondly, a number is a figure of calculation. We count with numbers. To count means to add, subtract, multiply, divide. Thus we will require of a species of number that these operations be practicable or well-defined within it. Technically, this means that a species of number must be capable of being identified algebraically. The completed summary of this identification is the algebraic field structure, wherein all operations are possible.

Thirdly, number must be a figure of consistency. This means that its two characteristics, order and calculation, must obey rules of compatibility. For example, we expect the addition of two clearly positive numbers to be bigger than each of these numbers, or the division of a positive number by a number greater than one to yield a result smaller than the number with which we started. These are the 'linguistic' requirements for the idea of number, in so far as it expresses the reciprocity of order and calculation. Technically, this will be expressed as follows: the adequate figure in which a species of number is inscribed is that of the ordered field.

If, in light of all this, we want a definition of number to subsume all its species, this means it must determine what I will call the 'ordered macro-field' wherein all the species of number may be situated.

This is precisely the result of the definition put forward by the great mathematician Conway, under the paradoxical name of 'surreal numbers'.

In the general framework of set-theory, this definition specifies a configuration in which a total order is defined, and in which addition, subtraction, multiplication and division are universally possible. Note that this configuration or macro-field of numbers includes the ordinals, the whole naturals, the ring of positive and negative wholes, the field of rationals and the field of reals, along with all their known structural determinations. But also note that it includes an infinity of as yet unnamed species of numbers, particularly infinitesimals, or numbers located between two adjacent and disconnected classes of reals, as well as all sorts of infinite numbers, besides cardinals and ordinals. I speak of a macro-field because it is not a set. That is why I called it a configuration. It is a class in its own right. This is obvious, because it contains all the ordinals, which already do not constitute a set. Invoking once more an intrinsic characteristic of multiple-being, we will say that the concept of number designates an inconsistent multiplicity – but add that the species of numbers carve out consistent numerical situations within this inconsistency, which constitutes their being. Thus the field of real numbers consists; it is a set. But its identification as field of numbers comes down to its being an internal consistency in the inconsistency of the site of number; in other words, a sub-field of the numerical macro-field.

We could therefore say that the apparent anarchy or concept-less multiplicity of the species of numbers resulted from the fact that, up until now, they were effectuated in their operations but not located in their being. The macro-field provides us with the inconsistent generic site wherein numerical consistencies co-exist. Henceforth, it becomes legitimate to conceive of these multiplicities as pertaining to a single concept, that of Number.

The being of Number as such, which is that aspect of number which thinks being, is ultimately given in the definition of the macro-field as inconsistent site of being for the consistency of numbers.

Thus, we will use the term 'Number' (capitalized) to refer to every entity that belongs to the macro-body. And we will use the term 'numbers' (lower case) to designate the diversity of species, or the immanent consistencies whose site is fixed by the inconsistency of Number.

What then is the definition of a Number?

This definition is admirably simple: a Number is a set with two members, an ordered pair, comprising an ordinal and a part of that ordinal, in that order. Accordingly, we will denote a Number as (α, X), where X is a part of the ordinal α, or $X \subseteq \alpha$.

It might be objected that this definition is circular, since it makes use of ordinals, which we have declared to be numbers, and which therefore already figure in the macro-field.

But in reality it is possible to provide an initial definition of ordinals in a purely structural fashion, without resorting to any numerical category whatsoever, not even (despite their name) to the idea of order. Von Neumann defines an ordinal as a transitive set all of whose members are also transitive. But transitivity is an ontological property: it simply means that all the elements of a set are also parts of that set, or that given $\alpha \in \beta$, you also have $\alpha \subseteq \beta$. This maximal correlation between belonging (or element) and inclusion (or part) endows transitive sets with a specific sort of ontological stability; one which I regard as peculiar to *natural* being.[1] It is this natural stability of ordinals, this immanent homogeneity, which makes of them the primordial material of Number.

What is striking about the definition of Number – the ordered pairing of an ordinal and a part of that ordinal – is the instance of the pair. In order to define Number, it is necessary to install oneself in the realm of the two. Number is not a simple mark. There is an essential duplicity to Number. Why this duplicity?

Because Number is an ontological gesture – to use the vocabulary of Gilles Châtelet[2] – and the double marking is a trace of this gesture. On the one hand, you have a stable, homogeneous mark: the ordinal. On the other, a mark that, in a certain sense, has been torn from the former; an indeterminate part that, on the whole, does not conserve any immanent stability and can be discontinuous, dismembered, and devoid of any concept – because there is nothing more errant than the notion of the 'part' of a set.

Thus the numerical movement is, in a certain sense, the forced, unbalanced, inventive sampling of an incalculable part of that which, by itself, possesses all the attributes of order and internal solidity.

This is why, as a philosopher, I have renamed the two components of Number. I have called the ordinal the *material* of Number, in order to evoke that donation of stability and of a powerful but almost indifferent internal architecture. And I have called the part of the ordinal the *form* of the Number, not to evoke a harmony or essence but rather to designate that which, as in certain effects achieved by contemporary art, is inventively extracted from a still legible backdrop of matter. Or that which, by extracting a sample of unforeseeable, almost lightning-like discontinuity from matter, allows an unalterable material density to be glimpsed as though through the gaps left by that extraction.

Thus a Number is entirely determined by the coupling of an ordinal material and a form carved out from that material. It is the duplicity constituted by a dense figure of multiple-being and a lawless gesture of carving out that traverses that density.

What is remarkable is that this simple starting point allows one to establish all the properties of order and calculation required from that which is supposed to provide the ontological correlate for the word 'Number'.

This is done by proving – here lies the technical aspect of the matter – that the universe of Numbers is completely ordered, and that one can define a field-structure within it, which means adding, multiplying, subtracting and dividing. One thereby accomplishes the construction of an ordered macro-field, the site for the ontological identification of everything that falls under the concept of number.

One can then go on to show that all the familiar species of number are in fact consistencies carved out from this site: natural whole numbers, relative numbers, rational numbers and real numbers are all sub-species of the macro-field or numbers that can be identified within the ontological site of Number.

But aside from these historical examples, there are many other strange and as yet unidentified or unnameable entities swarming under the concept of Number.

Here are two examples:

1. We are accustomed to considering finite negative numbers. But the idea of a negative of the infinite is certainly more unusual. Nevertheless, within the macro-field of Numbers, there is no difficulty in defining the negative of an ordinal, whether finite or infinite.

2. It can demonstrated that, within the macro-field which identifies the site of Number, the real numbers include all the Numbers whose matter is the first infinite ordinal, i.e. ω_0, and whose form is infinite. What can we say about those Numbers whose material is an infinite ordinal greater than ω_0? Well, we can say that, generally speaking, these are Numbers that we have yet to study and that remain as yet unnamed. They make up an infinitely infinite reservoir of Numbers belonging to an open future in which the ontological forms of numericality will be investigated. This testifies to the fact that those numbers with which we are familiar merely make up a tiny fraction of what being harbours under the concept of Number. In other words, the ontological prescription latent in the concept of Number infinitely exceeds the actual historical determination of known and named numerical consistencies. The word 'Number' harbours a greater share of being than anything mathematics has hitherto been

able to circumscribe or capture through the toils of its consistent constructions.

In fact, in each of its segments, even in those that seem miniscule from the point of view of our intellect, the macro-field of Numbers is populated by an infinite infinity of Numbers. In this respect it probably provides the best possible image for the universe as described by Leibniz in paragraph 67 of the *Monadology*: 'Each portion of matter may be conceived as a garden full of plants, and as a pond full of fish. But every branch of each plant, every member of each animal, and every drop of their liquid parts is itself likewise a similar garden or pond.'[3] Each miniscule section in the macro-field of Numbers may be conceived as the site for an infinity of species of Numbers, and each species in turn – as well as every miniscule section of that species – as a similar site or infinity.

What can we conclude from all this?

That Number is neither a trait of the concept (Frege), nor an operational fiction (Peano), nor an empirico-linguistic datum (the vulgar conception), nor a constitutive or transcendental category (Kronecker, or even Kant), nor a grammar or language game (Wittgenstein), nor even an abstraction from our idea of order. Number is a form of multiple-being. More precisely, the numbers we manipulate represent a miniscule sample of being's infinite abundance when it comes to species of Number.

Basically, a Number is a form torn from a stable, homogeneous multiple-material, a material whose concept is that of the ordinal, in the intrinsic sense ascribed to the latter by von Neumann.

Number is neither an object, nor an objectivity. It is a gesture in being. Before all objectivity, before all bound presentation, in the unbound eternity of its being, Number makes itself available to thought as a form carved-out within the maximal stability of the multiple. It is ciphered through the correspondence between this stability and the often un-predicable result of the gesture. The name of Number is the duplicitous trace of the components of the numerical gesture.

Number is the site of being qua being for the manipulable numericality of the species of number. Number, capital 'N', 'ek-sists' in numbers, lower-case and plural, as the latency of their being.

What's remarkable is that we have any access at all to this latency, to Number as such, even if this access points to an excess: the excess of being over knowledge. This excess becomes apparent in the innumerable expanse of Numbers relative to our knowledge of how to structure these into presentations of the species of numbers. That mathematics allows us to at least gesture toward this excess, to access it, confirms the potency of the discipline's ontological vocation.

In the case of the concept of Number as in the case of every other concept, the history of mathematics is precisely the necessarily interminable history of the relation between the inconsistency of multiple-being and the consistency which our finite thought is able to carve out from this inconsistency.

As far as Number and numbers are concerned, the task can only consist in pursuing and ramifying the deployment of their concept. Number (capitalized) pertains exclusively to mathematics as soon as it's a question of thinking its various species and situating these within the macro-field which is their ontological site. Philosophy declares that Number belongs exclusively to mathematics and points to those instances where it manifests itself as a resource of being within the confines of a particular situation: the ontological or mathematical situation.

Where the thinking of Number is concerned, we must abandon not only Frege's approach but also the respective approaches of Peano, Russell and Wittgenstein. The project started by Dedekind and Cantor must be radicalized, exceeded, pushed to the point of its dissolution.

There is no deduction of Number, but no induction of it either. Language and perceptual experience prove to be inoperative guides where Number is concerned. It is simply a question of being faithful to whatever portion of the inconsistent excess of being, to which our thought occasionally binds itself, comes to be inscribed as a consistent historical trace in the simultaneously interminable and eternal movement of mathematical transformation.

CHAPTER 6
ONE, MULTIPLE, MULTIPLICITIES[1]

1. I thought that my *Deleuze* had made its point perfectly clearly. But since it seems I was mistaken and I am being asked to restate my argument, allow me to reiterate why I consider the work of Gilles Deleuze to be of exceptional importance. Deleuze conceded nothing to the hegemonic theme of the end of philosophy, whether in its pathetic version, which ties it to the destiny of Being, or its bland one, which binds it to the logic of judgement. Thus, Deleuze was neither hermeneutic nor analytic – this is already a lot. He courageously set out to construct a modern metaphysics, for which he devised an altogether original genealogy, a genealogy in which philosophy and the history of philosophy are indiscernible.

Deleuze frequented the more incontestable cognitive productions of our time, and of some others besides, treating them as so many inaugural 'cases' for his speculative will. In so doing, he displayed a degree of discernment and acumen unparalleled among his contemporaries, especially where prose, cinema, certain aspects of science and political experimentation are concerned. For Deleuze really was a progressive, a reserved rebel, an ironic supporter of the most radical movements. That is why he also opposed the *nouveaux philosophes* and remained faithful to his vision of Marxism, making no concessions to the flaccid restoration of morality and 'democratic debate'. These are rare virtues indeed.

Moreover, Deleuze was the first to properly grasp that a contemporary metaphysics must consist in a theory of multiplicities and an embrace of singularities. He linked this requirement to the necessity of critiquing the thornier forms of transcendence. He saw that only by positing the univocity of being can we have done with the perennially religious nature of the interpretation of meaning. He clearly articulated the conviction that the truth of univocal being can only be grasped by thinking its evental advent.

This bold programme is one which I also espouse. Obviously, I do not think Deleuze successfully accomplished it; or rather, I believe he gave it an inflection which led it in a direction opposite to the one I think it should take. Otherwise, I would have rallied to his concepts and orientations of thought.

Our quarrel can be formulated in a number of ways. We could approach it by way of some novel questions such as, for example: how is it that, for Deleuze, politics is not an autonomous form of thought, a singular section of chaos, one that differs from art, science and philosophy? This point alone bears witness to our divergence, and there is a sense in which everything can be said to follow from it. But the simplest thing is to start from what separates us, *at the point of greatest proximity*: the requirements for a metaphysics of the multiple. For it is on this issue that my critics were most vocal in their protests. Or rather, not so much vocal as muffled, given the way they choked on the quasi-mystical thesis of the One. It seems these critics read my fundamental claims (about the One, asceticism or univocity), but failed to examine either their composition or the specifics of my argument.

But are these critics *really* preoccupied with the Eternal Return, or Relation, or the Virtual, or the Fold? I am not so sure. For it seems that they believe, unlike their Master, that all this can be debated in haughty ignorance of their opponent's doctrine. Thus we see them resort to the setting up of elaborate trials for misrepresentation. But such trials can only be superficial or incorrect, given that they invoke what academics have written about Deleuze's works on Spinoza or Nietzsche. Even if my critics intended to show – as they should, in conformity with the doctrine of free indirect discourse that they've inherited – that my claims about Deleuze conformed to the theses of my book *Being and Event*, it would still be necessary, as Deleuze himself at least attempted, to encapsulate the singularity of that work. We would then have something a little broader and a little better than a defence and illustration of textual orthodoxy. We would be getting nearer to the inherent philosophical tension that characterizes our turn of the century.

Nothing could be more pointless than to argue, for example, that the opposition between the One and the Multiple is 'static' and then, as though unveiling the latest theoretical innovation, to try to counter this with a third concept – such as that of 'multiplicities', for instance – which is supposed to nourish the unimaginable 'wealth' of the movement of thought, the experience of immanence, the quality of the virtual, or the infinite speed of intuition. I consider this vitalist terrorism – whose hallowed version was provided by Nietzsche, and whose polite bourgeois version, as Guy Lardreau rightly notes, derives from Bergson – to be puerile.

First of all, because it presupposes the consensual nature of the very norm that needs to be examined and established, to wit, that movement is superior to immobility, life superior to the concept, time to space, affirmation to negation, difference to identity, and so on. In these latent 'certainties', which command the peremptory metaphorical style of Deleuze's vitalist and anti-categorical exegeses, there is a kind of speculative demagogy whose entire strength lies in addressing itself to each and everyone's animal disquiet, to our confused desires, to everything that makes us scurry about blindly on the desolate surface of the earth.

Second, and most importantly, my appraisal is based on the fact that no 'interesting' philosophy (to use Deleuze's own normative vocabulary), no matter how abruptly conceptual and anti-empiricist, has ever been content simply to adopt inherited categorical oppositions, and that in this respect vitalist philosophies cannot lay claim to any kind of singularity. Plato institutes simultaneous proceedings against multiple-becoming (in the *Theaetetus*) and the immobile-One (in the *Parmenides*); proceedings whose radicality has yet to be outdone. The notion that thought should always establish itself beyond categorical oppositions, thereby delineating an unprecedented diagonal, is constitutive of philosophy itself. The whole question consists in knowing what value to ascribe to the operators of this diagonal trajectory, and in identifying the unknown resource to which they summon thought.

In this regard, to state of a philosophical framework – as I did in detail – that the conceptual diagonal it invents beyond the categorical opposition of the One and the Multiple is subordinated to a renewed intuition of the power of the One (as is manifestly the case for the Stoics, for Spinoza, for Nietzsche, for Bergson and for Deleuze) is by no means a 'critique' which one should hasten to 'refute' in order to maintain some sort of orthodoxy concerning the diagonal invention itself. All these philosophies, through operations of great complexity to which it is important to do justice case by case, maintain that the effective intuition of the One (which may take the name of 'All' or 'Whole', 'Substance', 'Life', 'the Body without Organs' or 'Chaos') is that of its immanent creative power, or of the eternal return of its differentiating power as such. Thus, in conformity with Spinoza's maxim, the stakes of philosophy consist in adequately thinking the greatest possible number of particular things (this is the 'empiricist' aspect in Deleuze – the disjunctive syntheses or the 'small circuit'), *in order to* adequately think Substance, or the One (which is the 'transcendental' aspect – Relation or the 'great circuit'). It is to the precise degree that such stakes are present that these apparatuses of thought are philosophies. Otherwise, they would be no more than more or less lively phenomenologies, vainly and indefinitely recommenced. Which is what, as far as I can see, the majority of their disciples intend to reduce them to.

Since we are dealing with philosophy (and I believe I was among the first, if not the first, to have treated Deleuze as a philosopher), only those who remain trapped by the subjective constraint of allegiance or academicism believe that in order to say something about it repetition is required. *Truly* to speak about a philosophy means evaluating, within a set-up that is itself inventive, or consigned to its own power, the diagonal operators that a metaphysical apparatus proposes to us. Consequently, it is not a question of knowing whether 'multiplicities' is a term that endures beyond the categorical opposition between the One (as transcendence) and the Multiple (as empirical givenness). This is trivially obvious in the context of Deleuze's metaphysical project. What needs to be evaluated with regard to the promise harboured by the concept of multiplicity – which is oriented towards a vital intuition of the One and a thinking fidelity to 'powerful inorganic life' or the impersonal – is the intrinsic density of this concept, and whether a thinking whose own movement comes from elsewhere is capable of sustaining the philosophical announcement borne by the concept of multiplicity.

Now, in my view the construction of this concept is marked (and this indicates its overtly Bergsonian lineage) by a preliminary deconstruction of the concept of *set*. Deleuze's didactic of multiplicities is from beginning to end a polemic against sets, just as the qualitative content of the intuition of duration in Bergson is only identifiable on the basis of the discredit that must attach to the purely spatial quantitative value of chronological time (on this crucial issue I cannot register any kind of caesura between *Difference and Repetition* and the more detailed philosophical texts to be found in the two volumes on cinema).

On this basis, I'd like to sketch the demonstration of three theses:

a. What Deleuze calls 'set' – in contradistinction to which he identifies multiplicities – does nothing but repeat the traditional determinations of external, or analytical, multiplicity, effectively ignoring the extraordinary immanent dialectic which this concept has undergone at the hands of mathematics ever since the end of the nineteenth century. From this point of view, the experiential construction of multiplicities is anachronistic, because it is pre-Cantorian.

b. As for the density of the concept of multiplicities, it remains inferior – even in its qualitative determinations – to the concept of Multiple that can be extracted from the contemporary history of sets.

c. This lag (one of whose symptoms is an 'impoverished' interpretation of Riemann), makes it impossible to subtract multiplicities from their equivocal absorption into the One, or to achieve the univocal determination of a multiple-without-oneness, such as I have developed in my own doctrine.

2. The specific mode whereby 'multiplicity' lies beyond the categorical opposition of the One and the Multiple is of an intervallic type. By this I mean that, for Deleuze, only the *play in becoming* of at least two disjunctive figures allows us to think a multiplicity. By taking things experientially 'in the middle', every figure of transcendence is rejected. Nevertheless, it is easy to see that this 'middle' is really the element of the categorical opposition itself. For a multiplicity is really that which, in so far as it is grasped by the numerical one, will be called a set, and in so far as it remains 'open' to its own power – or grasped by the vital One – will be called an effective multiplicity. Once it is conceptually reconstructed, multiplicity appears as *suspended between two forms of the One*: on the one hand, the form that relates to counting, number, the set; on the other, the form that relates to life, creation, differentiation. The norm for this tension, the real conceptual operator at work within it, is borrowed from Bergson: multiplicity will be called 'closed' when grasped by the numerical one, and 'open' when grasped by the vital One. Every multiplicity is the joint effectuation of the closed and the open, but its 'veritable' multiple-being lies on the side of the open, just as for Bergson the authentic being of time lies on the side of qualitative duration, or the essence of the dice-throw is to be sought in the single primordial Throw, and not in the numerical result displayed by the immobile dice.

Now, assigning the set to the closed, i.e. to numerical unity, reveals a limited conception of set. This is what lies behind the supposed 'sublation' of the set by the differentiating opening of life. But after Cantor, the set – which is intuited as a multiple of multiples whose only halting point is the void, within which infinite and finite are equivalent, and which guarantees that every multiplicity is immanent and homogeneous – cannot be assigned either to number or to the closed.

I have devoted an entire book (*Number and numbers*)[2] to showing how, far from the set being reducible to number, it is rather number – i.e. an innumerable infinity of kinds of number (for the most part yet to be studied) – which presupposes the prior availability of the ontology of sets for the apprehension of its concept. Number is but a small and particular section of being-multiple such as it is given to thought in the set-theoretical axiomatic, which is really rational ontology itself. Only the unwillingness to accept this point, and the obstinate wish to maintain at all costs and in the face of all evidence, that every set is a number, can explain the very strange text which Deleuze devoted to my book *Being and Event* in *What is Philosophy?*[3] No clearer demonstration could be given of the manner in which the insistence on using the normative logic of the closed and the open as an interpretive filter vis-à-vis a philosophy that takes Cantor as one of its conditions only succeeds in generating confusion.

For the set is the exemplary instance of something that is thinkable only if one dispenses entirely with the opposition between the closed and the open – for the important reason that it is only on the basis of the undetermined concept of set that this opposition can be granted a satisfactory meaning. We could even say that the set is that neutral-multiple which is originarily subtracted from both openness and closure, but which is also capable of sustaining their opposition.

We know in fact that if we take any set, it is possible for us to define numerous topologies relative to it. Now, what is a topology? It is precisely the fixation of a concept of the open (or of the closed). But rather than putting its trust in dynamic intuition, as the vitalist orientation does, with all the paradoxical consequences that I registered in my *Deleuze*, topology operates – as every approach faithful to a principle of immanence must – by determining the relational effects of this opening (or closure). A concept of the open is substantially established once we possess a multiple such that we dwell within it by taking the intersection of two elements, or the union of as many elements as we wish (even an infinity of elements). In other words, the intersection of two opens is an open, and any union whatsoever of opens remains open. As for the closed, it is never anything but the dual of the open, its complement or reverse. Its relational properties are symmetric to those of the open: the union of two closed sets is closed, and the intersection of any number whatsoever of closed sets remains closed. The closed also dwells, according to immanent paths that differ from those of the open.

It is from the point of view of this 'dwelling' alone, of this persistence of the 'there' of a multiple being-there in operationally maintaining its own immanence, that we can elucidate one of the main properties of open sets, which Deleuze (wrongly) identifies with their 'absence of parts', and therefore with their qualitative, or intensive, singularity. This property is that the 'points' of an open are partially inseparate, or not assignable, because *the open is the neighbourhood of each of its points*. It is in this way that an open set topologically provokes a sort of coalescence of that which constitutes it.

That the open points back to a 'dwelling' is not at all paradoxical (there are strong intuitions in Heidegger about this question). If opening, in its very construction, effectuates a localization without an outside (which reiterates the idea that the open qua neighbourhood 'localizes' all of its points), it is because 'open' is an intrinsic determination of the multiple – in other words, because we are indeed dealing with an immanent construction. This not the case with Deleuze, since in his thinking the open is always open to something other than its own effectiveness, namely to the inorganic power of which it is a mobile actualization. For Deleuze, to reduce the open to its internal power of localization would be to turn it into a closed set. Moreover, it is because it must be open to its own being that the vitalist notion of the open is ultimately only thinkable as virtuality. By way of contrast, the set-theoretical or ontological open is entirely contained in the actuality of its own determination, which exhausts it univocally. Ultimately, the topological construction of opens on the basis of a set-theoretical ontology demonstrates that the set, taken as such, is in no way an image of the closed, since it is indifferent to the duality of closed and open. Moreover, it also indicates that when conceived in this manner, the thought of the open manages to remain faithful to a principle of immanence and univocity from which the vitalist notion of multiplicity inevitably deviates – for, regardless of how closed it is, the vitalist multiplicity is obliged to signal equivocally toward the opening of which it is a mode.

3. Someone might object that only the dialectic of the open and the closed – such as provides the basis for the concept of multiplicity (or multiplicities) – can do justice to becoming, to singularities, to creations, to the inexhaustible diversity of sensation and life; that it is truly outrageous to see in it some sort of phenomenological monotony; that the post-Cantorian theory of the pure multiple is incapable of equalling this descriptive capacity; and that the latter in fact harbours identity's categorical revenge on difference.

I believe the opposite to be the case, for at least three reasons:

A. Mathematics has this peculiar trait: it is always richer in surprising determinations than any empirical donation whatsoever. The recurrent theme of the 'abstract poverty' of mathematics when compared to the burgeoning richness of the 'concrete' is an expression of pure *doxa* (and one which, incidentally, was entirely foreign to Deleuze himself). In actual fact, mathematics shows itself perfectly capable both of providing schemas adequate to experience, *and* of frustrating this experience by way of conceptual inventions that no intuition could ever accept.

Take a simple example: the empirical notion of 'grazing' – i.e. the notion of a superficial touch, of a contact which is almost identical with a non-contact, or even of a timid caress – is certainly conceived through the notion of tangency, of the infinitesimal approach toward a point, a notion which, ever since the Greeks, requires an ascetic effort of thinking and is oriented toward the concept of the derivative of a function. Very roughly, one can say that, given the curve that represents a function, if this function can be derived for a value of its argument, there will be a tangent to the curve at the point represented by this value. One can therefore argue that the joint notions of curvature and contact at a single point of this curvature intuitively circulate between the concepts of continuous function (curve) and derivative at a point (tangent). I have chosen this example because it is quite Deleuzean, as well as being one with which Deleuze himself was perfectly familiar. Curvatures, contacts, bifurcations, lines of flight (a tangent touches the curve and flees), differentiation, limit – all these are constants of Deleuze's descriptions. Now consider the discovery, in the nineteenth century, that there exist continuous functions that cannot be derived *at any point*. Try to imagine a continuous curve such that it is impossible for a straight line to 'touch' it at any point . . . Even better: We can demonstrate that these functions, which are subtracted from every empirical intuition, and are therefore strictly speaking unrepresentable, are 'more numerous' than those that have hitherto governed mathematical thinking. This is just a particular case of a general law: everywhere where mathematics is close to experience but follows its own movement, it discovers a 'pathological' case that absolutely challenges the initial intuition. Mathematics then establishes that this pathology is the rule, and that what can be intuited is only an exception. We thereby discover that as the thinking of being qua being, mathematics never ceases to distance itself from its starting point, which is to be found in an available local being or a contingent efficacy.

This means in particular that, in the case of the 'rhizomatic' multiplicities that serve as Deleuze's cases (packs, swarms, roots, interlacings, etc.), the variegated configurations proper to set-theory provide an incomparably richer and more complex resource: they always allow one to go further than could be imagined. For instance, the construction of a generic subset in a partially ordered set not only surpasses in violence, as a case for thought, any empirical rhizomatic schema whatsoever, but, by establishing the conditions for 'neutrality' in a multiple that is both dispersive and coordinated, it actually subsumes the ontology of these schemata. This is why, in elaborating an ontology of the multiple, the *first* rule is follow the conceptual mathematical constructions – which we know can overflow in all directions, no matter what the empirical case, once it is a question of the resources proper to the multiple. This rule, of course, is Platonist: may no one enter here who is not a geometer. To use another example: what zone of experience could offer a ramification of the concept of experience as dense as the one provided by the concept that thinks all the kinds of cardinals: i.e. inaccessible, compact, ineffable, measurable, enormous, Mahlo cardinals, Ramsey cardinals, Rowbottom cardinals, etc? So when we hear someone speak in such an impoverished manner about a trajectory of thought 'at infinite speed', we have to ask: what infinite are you referring to? What is this supposed unity of the infinite, now that we have learned not only that there exist an infinity of different infinites, but that there is an infinitely ramified and complex hierarchy of types of infinity?

I recognize the fact that Deleuze is in no way contemptuous of mathematics, and that the differential calculus and Riemannian spaces provided resources for his philosophical thinking. Indeed, I have even praised him for this. But short of allowing these examples simply to be reprocessed by the crypto-dialectic of the closed and the open, they must be allowed to enter into conflict with the vitalist doctrine of multiplicities.

On this point, the case of Riemann is of considerable significance. Riemann fascinates Deleuze because he brilliantly complexifies the elementary intuition of space, providing Deleuze with a war machine against the unilaterally extensive (or extended) conception proper to the Cartesian or even Kantian notions of space. In effect, Riemann speaks of 'multiply extended' spaces, of varieties of space, thereby anticipating the modern notion of functional space. He validates Deleuze's arguments about the layered character of the plane of immanence and the non-partitive conception of localizations. It is also true that Riemann generalizes the concept of space beyond any empirical intuition in at least three respects: he invites the consideration of n-dimensional spaces, rather than just spaces with a maximum of three dimensions; he tries to think relations of position, form, and neighbouring independently of any metrics, and therefore 'qualitatively', without resorting to number; and he imagines we can have not only elements or points but functions as components of spaces – such that space would be 'populated' by variations rather than entities. In doing so, Riemann opens up an immense domain for 'geometric' method, one which is still being continually explored to this very day. Deleuze's vitalist thought concurs with this multi-dimensional geometrization, this doctrine of local variations, this qualitative localization of territories.

Yet it is perfectly clear that, in order to achieve the programme they had set out, Riemann's awe-inspiring anticipations demanded a speculative framework entirely subtracted from the constraints of empirical intuition. Furthermore, what the 'geometry' in question had to grasp was not empirically attestable configurations (whether bifurcating or folded) but rather neutral multiples, detached in their being from every spatial or temporal connotation – neither closed nor open, but beyond figure, freed from any immediate opposition between the quantitative and the qualitative. That is why these anticipations could only constitute the body of modern mathematics as such once Dedekind and Cantor had succeeded in mathematizing the pure multiple under the auspices of the notion of 'set', thereby wrenching the multiple free from every preliminary figure of the One, subtracting it from those residues of experience still provided by the putative 'objects' of mathematics (numbers and figures), and ultimately allowing it to become the basis in terms of which one could define and study the most paradoxical multi-dimensional configurations – including all those harboured under the name of 'spaces'. By reducing Riemann's thought to the notion of qualitative multiplicities and turning it into the emblem for an anti-Cartesian paradigm, Deleuze overlooks the ontology that underlies Riemann's invention, an ontology which, in a staggering display of inconsistency, Deleuze undermines, submitting it to the undecidable, albeit normative, alternative between the closed and the open.

Riemann in no way represents a passage from the Multiple (as opposed to the One) to multiplicities. Rather, he heralds the passage from what subsists of the empirical power of the One (in the modality of an experience of mathematical 'objects') to the multiple-without-one, which in effect can indifferently welcome numbers, points, functions, figures, or places, since it does not prescribe that of which it is composed. The power of Riemann's thought resides entirely in its *neutralization of difference*. Deleuze's interpretation, which sees in it a mobile complexification of the idea of plane, is not incorrect, but it fails to grasp the true metaphysical determinations proper to the Riemannian paradigm.

B. Deleuze routinely argues that multiplicities, unlike sets, have 'no parts'. This is indeed what, in my view, explains the fact that the opposition between sets and multiplicities takes place under the aegis of the One. Of course, I can see that it is a question of saving qualitative singularity and the vital power that accompanies it, but I do not believe Deleuze's means are adequate for such an aim. As a matter of fact, the opposite is the case: *the immanent excess that 'animates' a set, and which makes it such that the multiple is internally marked by the undecidable, results directly from the fact that it possesses not only elements, but also parts.*

    The failure to distinguish between elements (what the multiple presents, or composes) and parts (that which is, for the multiple, represented by a sub-multiple) constitutes a great weakness in any theory of multiplicities. The statement according to which multiplicities have no parts already indifferentiates the two types of immanence, the two fundamental forms of being-in which set-theory separates when it distinguishes between (elementary) belonging and partitive (inclusion). Now, the *relation* between these two forms is the key to every thinking of the multiple, and to ignore it is inevitably to withdraw philosophy from one of its most exacting contemporary conditions.

    At the end of the nineteenth century, Cantor effectively demonstrated that the power of the set comprising the parts of a given set (i.e. that which sustains the inclusive type of immanence) was necessarily superior to the power of the set itself (i.e. that which sustains the elementary type of immanence). This means that there is an ontological excess of representation over presentation. Thirty years ago, Cohen demonstrated that this excess is *unassignable*. In other words, no measure could be prescribed for this excess, since it is something like an errant excess of the set with respect to itself. That is to say, there is no need to look to the All, the great cosmic animal, or to chaos for the principle of the pure multiple's excess-over-itself: this excess is deducible from an internal non-cohesion between the two types of immanence. Furthermore, there is no need to look to the virtual for the principle of indeterminacy or undecidability that affects every actualisation. Every multiple is indeed *actually* haunted by an excess of power that nothing can give shape to, except for an always aleatory decision which is only given through its effects.

It is certainly the case that experience must, each and every time, redetermine this immanent excess. For example, deciding what to do about the excess of the power of the State (in its political sense) over simple presentation (people's thought) is an essential component of every singular politics: if you decide that the excess is very weak, you prepare an insurrection; if you think that it is very large, you settle on the idea of a 'long march', etc. But these singular determinations are by no means within the reach of philosophical description, since they are internal to the effectuations of truths (political, artistic, etc.). What is philosophical is rather setting aside every kind of speculative empiricism, and assigning the form of these determinations to their generic foundation: the theory of the pure multiple. From this standpoint, the 'concrete' operators of the vitalist type, which finally refer the positivity of the Open to an immanent creationism whose foundation is to be found in the chaotic prodigality of the One, are obstacles, not supports. The concrete is more abstract than the abstract.

C. The wealth of the empirical is correctly treated by Deleuze as a wealth *in problems*. That the relation of the virtual to the actual has as its paradigm the relation between the problem and its solution (rather than between the possible and its realization) in my view represents one of the strengths of the Deleuzean method. But what should follow from this is the falsity of a maxim that Deleuze nevertheless practises and teaches: that we can begin from any concrete case whatsoever, rather than from the 'important' cases, or from the history of the problem. If we consider the notion of problem in its original context, mathematics, it becomes immediately apparent that the consideration of a case taken at random precludes any access to those problems that have power, that is to say, to those problems whose solution matters to the dual becoming of thought and what it thinks. Galois once said that the problem was constituted by reading 'the unknown' into the texts of one's predecessors: it is there that the *deposits* of problems were to be found.

By not following this logic of the unknown, which functions like a strict selection principle for productive forms of thought, empirical prodigality becomes something like an arbitrary and sterile burden. The problem ends up being replaced by *verification* pure and simple. Philosophically speaking, verification is always possible. In my youth, I too belonged to this school: after Sartre, and following the example of the café waiter, the skier, the lesbian, and the black man, I could irrefutably transform any 'concrete' datum whatsoever into a philosopheme. Multiplicities, suspended between the open and the closed, or between the virtual and the actual, can serve this end, just as I was in the habit of using the internalized face-to-face of the in-itself and the for-itself for the same purpose. By way of contrast, set-theoretical multiples can never be subordinated to this end, since their being bound to a delicate axiomatic entails that their rule can never be descriptive. In this regard, we could say that the theory of the multiple becomes all the richer in problems to the extent that, incapable of validating any description, it can only serve as a regulative ideal for prescriptions.

4. What difference is there exactly between saying that a pack of wolves and the subterranean network of a tuber plant are cases of rhizome, and saying that they both partake in the Idea of the rhizome? In what sense are we to take the fact that both Spinoza and Bartleby the scrivener can be compared to Christ? If Foucault's work testifies to the Fold between the visible and the sayable, is this in the same way as the films of Straub or Marguerite Duras, whose singularity is defined in similar terms? Does the term 'layered' designate the same property in Riemann spaces (which belong to a scientific plane of reference) and in a philosophical plane of immanence? If in my book I spoke of a certain monotony in Deleuze's work (which, in my mind, was a kind of Bergsonian tribute: there is, all things considered, a single motivating intuition), it was also in order to avoid directly asking such blunt questions. This is because our interpretive field for the innumerable analogies that populate Deleuze's case studies allows us to relate them back to univocity as a donation of sense that is uniformly deployed on the surface of actualizations – and driven, in a manner identical to the power of Spinozist substance, by the ontological determination of the One-Life. When challenged by those who, on the contrary, do not wish for an ontological postulation of this type and who regard as ironic the question 'Could Deleuze's aim have been that of intuiting the One?' (but what else exactly could a self-proclaimed disciple of Spinoza be concerned with?), my response is to ask them what status they would give to these analogies, especially in light of the fact that the Master expressly declared that analogy ought to be prohibited.

I share with Deleuze the conviction (which I think is political) that every genuine thinking is a thinking of singularities. But since for Deleuze actual multiplicities are always purely formal modalities,[4] and since only the Virtual univocally dispenses sense, I have argued that Deleuze has no way of *thinking* singularity other than by classifying the different ways in which singularity is not ontologically singular; in other words, by classifying the different modes of actualization. After all, this was already the cross borne by Spinozism, whose theory of 'singular things' oscillates between a schematism of causality (a thing is a set of modes producing a single effect) and a schematism of expression (a thing bears witness to the infinite power of substance). Similarly, for Deleuze, singularity oscillates between a classificatory phenomenology of modes of actualization (and virtualization), on the one hand, and an ontology of the virtual, on the other.

I maintain that the 'link' between these two approaches is not compatible with either univocity or immanence. It is this incompatibility that furnishes the clue as to why Deleuze's texts swarm with analogies, which are required in order to determine the descriptive Ideas for which singularities provide the cases.

That these Ideas (Fold, Rhizome, Dice-throw, etc.) aim at configurations in becoming, at differentiations, counter-movements, interlacings, etc., changes nothing. I have always maintained that Deleuzian singularities belong to a regime of actualization or virtualization, and not to one of ideal identity. But the fact that only concrete becomings provide the descriptive models for a schema in no way precludes the latter from being an Idea to which the models are isomorphic. Plato's mythical Parmenides already 'objected' to Socrates that there must indeed be an idea of hair, or of mud. It remains the case that in order to argue that the thinking of singularity requires the intuition of the virtual – which, I am convinced, plays the role of transcendence (or takes the place of descriptive Ideas) – one is obliged to deploy, with ever-renewed virtuosity, an analogical and classificatory vision of this singularity. This is why it is so important to hold steadfastly to the multiple as such – the inconsistent composition of multiples-without-oneness – which identifies the singularity *from within*, in its strict actuality, stretching thought towards the point at which there is no difference between difference and identity. A point where there is singularity because both difference and identity are indifferent to it.

Let me sum up: the attempt to subvert the 'vertical' transcendence of the One through the play of the closed and the open, which deploys multiplicity in the mobile interval between a set (inertia) and an effective multiplicity (line of flight), produces a 'horizontal' or virtual transcendence which, instead of grasping singularity, ignores the intrinsic resource of the multiple, presupposes the chaotic power of the One, and analogizes the modes of actualization. When all is said and done, we are left with what could be defined as a natural mysticism. In order to have done with transcendence, it is necessary to follow the thread of the multiple-without-oneness – impervious to any play of the closed and the open, cancelling any abyss between the finite and the infinite, purely actual, haunted by the internal excess of its parts – whose univocal singularity is ontologically nameable only by a form of writing subtracted from the poetics of natural language. The only power that can be attuned to the power of being is the power of the letter. Only thus can we hope to resolve the problem that defines contemporary thought: what exactly is a universal singularity?

CHAPTER 7
SPINOZA'S CLOSED ONTOLOGY

When a proposition in thought presents itself, outside mathematics, as originally philosophical, it bears on the generality of the 'there is'. It then necessarily invokes three primordial operations.

First, it is necessary to construct and legitimate the name or names for the 'there is', which I do with the term 'pure multiple' and Deleuze does with the term 'life'. Such names are always grasped according to a more or less explicit choice bearing on the kind of hinge, or disconnection, that obtains between the one and the multiple.

Second, it is necessary to deploy the relation or relations on the basis of which one proposes to evaluate the consistency of the 'there is'.

Lastly – and this makes up the complex body of every philosophy of being to the extent that it may be considered as an implicit mathematics – it is necessary to guarantee that the formally intelligible relations 'grasp' or seize whatever is presupposed, or founded, in the names for the 'there is'.

Let me offer two typical yet contrasting examples: the first is poetico-philosophical, the second purely mathematical.

- In Lucretius' enterprise, the 'there is' is presupposed under two names: 'void' and 'atoms'. The only relations are those of collision and connection. What guarantees that the relations grasp the nominal constituents of the 'there is' is an unassignable event: the *clinamen*, or swerve, through which the indifferent trajectories of the atoms enter into relations against the backdrop of the void, in such a way as to compose a world.

- In the mathematical theory of sets, which we have already said marks the fulfilment of mathematics as the thinking of multiple-being, the 'there is' is presupposed under the name of the void alone, in the empty set. The only relation is that of belonging. Relation's grasp of the 'there is' is guaranteed by its forms of efficacy, which are encoded in axioms, specifically in the operational axioms of the theory. This grasp engenders a universe, the cumulative, transfinite hierarchy of sets, on the basis of the void alone.

It may well be that there are only two models of such a grasp, and hence of the operation of thought through which the names of being are co-ordinated by the relation that makes them consist: the evental model, which is that of Lucretius, and the axiomatic model.

Spinoza, who excludes every event by precluding excess, chance and the subject, opts unequivocally for the axiomatic model. From this point of view, the *more geometrico* is crucial. It is not just a form of thought; it is the written trace of an original decision of thinking.

A purely technical examination of the *Ethics* can serve to highlight its powerful simplicity. The 'there is' is indexed to a single name: absolutely infinite Substance, or God. The only relation admitted is that of causality. Relation's grasp of the name is of the order of an immanent effectuation of the 'there is' as such, since, as we know from Book I, Proposition 34: 'God's power is his essence itself.'[1] Which means not only that, in the words of Book I, Proposition 18, 'God is the immanent, not the transitive, cause of all things',[2] but also that this constitutes his identity, as conceived through the causal relation's grasp of substance.

Thus it would seem that we are confronted here with a wholly affirmative, immanent and intrinsic proposition about being. Moreover, it would seem that difference in particular, which is constitutive of the ontology of Lucretius (there is the void *and* atoms), is here absolutely subordinated, that is, nominal. In other words, it is a matter of expression, and in no way compromises the determination of the 'there is' under the aegis of the one. Although we could cite countless other passages, let us, by way of evidence, quote the Scholium to Book II, Proposition 7: 'a mode of extension and the idea of that mode are one and the same thing, but expressed in two ways [*duobus modis expressa*]'.[3]

But obviously this simplicity is merely apparent. In fact, I will show:

- First, that the operations that allow for the naming of the 'there is' are interconnected in a multiple, complex fashion, and that in this interconnection the proof of difference is constantly required.

- Second, that causality is not the unique foundational relation; there are at least three, the other two being what I shall call 'coupling' and 'inclusion'.

- Third, that beneath the unity of the 'there is', Spinoza delineates the negative outline of a type of singularity which is in every way exceptional, whose formal characteristics are those of a subject, and whose Spinozist name is *intellectus*. Following Bernard Pautrat's persuasive arguments, I shall translate *intellectus* as 'intellect'. One has grasped the core of Spinozist ontology when one has understood how this intellect necessitates propositions about being that are in fact *heterogeneous to the explicit propositions*.

In the *Ethics*, as we pointed out above, the 'there is' is named 'God'. But the construction of this name – what Spinoza calls its definition – is extremely complex.

God is '*ens absolute infinite*', a 'being absolutely infinite'.[4] Let us, at the outset, note the requirement of the indeterminate term *ens*, 'being', as the name for a virtual 'there is' whose pre-comprehension relates back to an ontological layer that is, if not deeper, then at least more extensive than the term 'God'. 'Infinite' is obviously the crucial term here, because it functions to determine the indeterminate; it practically functions as the 'there is' for the 'there is'. 'Infinite' is defined as follows (Book I, Definition 6): 'a substance consisting of an infinity of attributes, of which each one expresses an eternal and infinite essence'.[5] The important thing here is that the absoluteness of divine infinity is not qualitative, or itself indeterminate. It refers back to an effectively plural, and hence quantitative, infinity. The index of quantity, or of the fact that the adjective *infinitum* presupposes a denumerable *infinitas*, is that this *infinitas* lets itself be thought according to the 'eachness', the *unumquodque*, of its attributes. It is thus indubitably composed of non-decomposable unities, i.e. the attributes. But then of course the concept of the infinite is covered by the law of difference. Because it is composed of 'eachnesses', the infinity of attributes can be apprehended only through a primordial difference. This entails that every attribute must, in a certain sense, differ absolutely from every other. In other words: the infinity of God, which is what singularizes him as substance and entails that he is the name for the 'there is', is only thinkable under the aegis of the multiple. It is the expressive difference of the attributes that renders this notion of the multiple intelligible.

But what is an attribute? Here is Definition 4, Book I: 'By attribute, I understand what the intellect perceives of a substance, as constituting its essence'.[6] The attribute is the essential identification of a substance by the intellect, *intellectus*. This implies that the existential singularization of God ultimately depends upon the elucidation of (or the basic evidence for) what is meant by *intellectus*.

In the letter of March 1663 to Simon de Vries, Spinoza takes pains to declare that the word 'attribute' does not by itself constitute a naming of the 'there is' in any way essentially distinct from the naming of the latter by substance. Having reiterated the definition of substance he adds: 'I understand the same by attribute, except that it is called attribute in relation to (*respectu*) the intellect, which attributes such and such a definite nature to substance.'[7] Thus the attribute, as well as the multiplicity of attributes through which divine infinity is identified, is a function of the intellect. In the general arrangement of the 'there is', there exists – under the name 'God' – a singular localization, that of the intellect, upon whose point of view or operations depends thought's capacity for rational access to divine infinity, and hence to the 'there is' as such.

It is thus necessary to recognize that the intellect occupies the position of a fold – to take up the central concept in Deleuze's philosophy. Or, using my own terminology, that the intellect is an operator of torsion. It is localizable as an immanent production of God, but is also required to uphold the naming of the 'there is' as God. For only the singular operations of the intellect give meaning to God's existential singularization as *infinite* substance.

I believe this concept of torsion is at once the enigma and the key to the Spinozist approach to being, just as the *clinamen* is the enigma of Lucretius, or the continuum hypothesis the enigma of set-theory.

To think this torsion means asking the following question: how does the Spinozist determination of the 'there is' point back to its internal fold, the intellect? Or, more simply: how is it possible to think the being of intellect, the 'there is intellect', if rational access to the thought of being or the 'there is' itself depends upon the operations of the intellect? Or again: the intellect is operative, but what is the ontological status of its operation?

We will refer to everything required in order to think the being of intellect – the collection of operations responsible for the closure of Spinoza's thinking of being – as Spinoza's implicit ontology. This ontology is that which the thinking of a being of thought presupposes as heterogeneous to the thinking of being.

The guiding thread for the investigation of this implicit ontology is Spinoza's construction and variation of the internal fold, and hence of the concept of *intellectus*.

The initial starting point is thought (*cogitatio*) as an attribute of God. This is what Spinoza calls 'absolute thought', and which he distinguishes from intellect. Thus, in the Demonstration for Book I, Proposition 31 he writes: 'By intellect (as is known through itself) we understand not absolute thought, but only a certain mode of thinking, which mode differs from the others, such as desire, love, and the like.'[8] Although it is that on the basis of which the attributive identifications of substance exist, the intellect itself is clearly a mode of the attribute 'thought'. We will say that as attribute, thought is an absolute exposition of being, and that the intellect is the internal fold of this exposition, the fold from whence exposition in general originates.

In its initial figure, the intellect is obviously infinite. It is necessarily infinite because it provides the basis for the identification of the infinity of the attributes of substance. It is the exemplary instance – and even the only one – of an immediately infinite mode of the attribute thought. The immediate infinite modes are described, without any example of their existence being given, in Book I, Proposition 21: 'All things which follow from the absolute nature of any of God's attributes have always had to exist and be infinite.'[9] In July 1675, a certain Schuller asks Spinoza on behalf of Tschirnhaus to provide examples of 'things which are immediately produced by God'. Spinoza responds by saying that 'in thought', the example is 'absolutely infinite intellect'.[10]

The very concept of infinite mode occupies a paradoxical position in the economy of Spinoza's ontology. It is in fact impossible to decide as to the existence of any of these modes, since they are neither deducible a priori, nor given in finite experience. We could say that the concept of an infinite mode is coherent but existentially undecidable. But the existence of an undecidable can only ever be decided through an act of axiomatic positing. This is clearly what one sees in the case of the infinite intellect when, in the letter to Oldenburg from November 1665, for example, Spinoza writes: 'I maintain (*statuo*) that there is also in Nature an infinite power of thinking.'[11] Thus the infinite intellect has, if not a verifiable or provable existence, at least a status, the status conferred upon it by a '*statuo*'.

As statutorily posited, the infinite intellect provides the basis for a series of intimately interconnected operations.

First of all, it is what provides a measure for the power of God. For what God can (and therefore must) produce as immanent power is precisely everything that the infinite intellect can conceive. Hence Proposition 16 in Book I: 'From the necessity of the divine nature there must follow infinitely many things in infinitely many modes, (i.e., everything which can fall under an infinite intellect).'[12] The infinite intellect provides the modal norm for the extent of modal possibility. All the things that it can intellect – '*omnia quae sub intellectum infinitum cadere possunt*' – are held to exist.

Clearly, no other infinite mode imaginable by us possesses such a capacity for measuring God's power. This holds in particular for the other example of an immediate infinite mode given by Spinoza, movement and rest, which is supposed to be the correlate of infinite intellect on the side of extension. For it is obvious that no *general* prescription about God's power follows from the pure concept of movement and rest.

The reason for this dissymmetry is clear. It derives from the fact that, besides its intrinsic determination as infinite mode of the attribute of thought, infinite intellect presupposes an entirely different determination, one which is extrinsic. For the intellect, whose components are ideas, is equally well determined by *what* it intellects, or by what the idea is an idea *of*. It is thus that the attributes of God, as well as the affections of those attributes, compose (without any restriction whatsoever) what the infinite intellect grasps, understands or comprehends (*comprehendit*). Certainly, God is that in which the intellect, as infinite mode, is situated. That follows from the ontological relation of causality. The intellect is an immanent effect of God. But the intellect is also such that it comprehends God and his attributes; they are the correlates of the ideas that constitute it. For every idea is an 'idea of', it is correlated with an *ideatum*; in other words, the idea has an object. And in this sense the attributes of God and the modes of these attributes are objects of the infinite intellect.

The notion of there being an object for an idea is all the stronger in that Spinoza explicitly states that the object partly singularizes or identifies the idea, particularly with regard to what he calls its 'reality'. Thus in the Scholium to Book II, Proposition 13 he writes: 'We cannot deny that ideas differ among themselves, as the objects themselves do, and that one is more excellent than the other, and contains more reality, just as the object of the one is more excellent than the object of the other and contains more reality.'[13]

Clearly, this presupposes *a second fundamental relation* besides causality, a relation that only has meaning for the intellect and which absolutely singularizes it. For we know that for Spinoza, who never resorts to empiricism, the relation between the idea and its *ideatum*, or the idea and the object of the idea, is entirely distinct from the relation of causal action. This is implicit in Book III, Proposition 2: 'The body cannot determine the mind to thinking, and the mind cannot determine the body to motion, to rest, or to anything else (if there is anything else).'[14] No causal relation between the idea and its object is conceivable because the relation of causality is only applicable from within an attributive identification, whereas – and here lies the entire problem – the object of an idea of the intellect may perfectly well be a mode of an attribute other than thought.

A particular kind of relation is required to straddle the disjunction between attributes in this way, one which cannot be causality. I will call this relation *coupling*. An idea of the intellect is always coupled to an object, which means that a mode of thought is always coupled to another mode, which may belong either to extension, to thought, or to a different attribute entirely.

The power of this relation is attested to by the fact that Spinoza does not hesitate to refer to it as a 'union'. Thus, in the Demonstration for Book II, Proposition 21, he writes: 'We have shown that the mind is united to the body from the fact that the body is the object of the mind (see P12 and 13); and so by the same reasoning the idea of mind must be united with its own object, that is, with the mind itself, in the same way as the mind is united with the body.'[15] This shows that, generally speaking, there is a union between the idea and its object, including instances of union that straddle the disjunction between attributes. It is this union, the radical singularity proper to the operations of the intellect, which I call coupling.

It is obviously necessary to add the proviso that coupling has a norm. An idea can be more or less 'well coupled' to its object. A complete coupling is called truth. This is stated as early as Book I, Axiom 6: 'A true idea must agree with its object [*ideatum*].'[16] Agreement is the norm for coupling and what makes of it a truth. Just like the relation of coupling, this norm of agreement is extrinsic and not, like causality, strictly immanent to attributive determination. In the Explanation of Book II, Definition 4, Spinoza carefully distinguishes agreement as intrinsic norm of truth, which ultimately refers back to causality, from 'what is extrinsic, namely, the agreement between the idea and its object [*ideatum*]'.[17] In the latter instance, agreement refers back to coupling, rather than to causality. What's more, it is clear that, apart from the infinite mode of intellect, in no other instance besides the idea is it necessary for the terms composing an infinite mode to support a relation of coupling. It is certainly not necessary for the other infinite modes, whatever they may be, to comply with the norm of coupling, agreement, whose result is truth.

Like the relation of causality, the relation of coupling implies the existence of an infinite regress. Thus every mode has a cause, which itself has a cause, and so on. Similarly, every idea coupled to its object must be the object of an idea that is coupled to it. This is the famous theme of the idea of the idea, which in the Scholium to Book II, Proposition 21 is examined in terms of the mind as idea of the body and the idea of the mind as idea of the idea. The text subtly weaves together ontological identity and the relation of coupling: '[T]he mind and the body are one and the same individual, which is conceived now under the attribute of thought, now under the attribute of extension. So the idea of the mind and the mind itself are one and the same thing, which is conceived under one and the same attribute, namely, thought. . . . For the idea of the mind, that is, the idea of the idea, is nothing but the form of the idea in so far as this is considered as a mode of thinking without relation to the object.'[18] The 'one and the same thing' seems to obliterate every difference underlying the relation of coupling. Nevertheless, that is not how things stand. For all that identifies the individual is the couple, as grasped by the intellect. As a result, in so far as the idea of the body is coupled to the body by straddling the attributive disjunction, it remains necessarily distinct from the idea of that idea, which is coupled to the latter in a manner immanent to the attribute of thought. In other words, an effect of identity always underlies every relation. It is the same individual that is alternately intellected as body and as mind, and then it is the same mind that is intellected twice. But this identity-effect is only intelligible according to the categories of the intellect, and these are precisely the ones that originate in coupling.

Ultimately, the active structure of infinite intellect is radically singular in a way that proves to be exorbitant relative to the general principles of ontological naming.

- It depends upon the undecidability associated with the infinite modes.

- It measures the total power of God.

- It imposes another relation beside causality: coupling, which undermines the domains of identity.

- At each of its points or ideas, not only does the infinite intellect perpetuate an infinite recurrence in accordance with causality, but also a second one, in accordance with coupling.

As a matter of fact, infinite intellect by itself constitutes an exception to the famous Proposition 7 of Book II: 'The order and connection of ideas is the same as the order and connection of things.'[19] For it is impossible to conceive of (or for the intellect to represent) a structure isomorphic with that of the intellect itself in any attribute other than thought. Consequently, the attribute of thought is not isomorphic with any of the other attributes, not even in terms of the relation of causality alone.

Turning now to the human or finite intellect, things become even more complicated.

The major difficulty is the following: is it possible to conceive of the finite intellect as a modification or affection of the infinite intellect? This is the conception of the finite intellect apparently implied by the relation of causality as a constitutive relation for the immanent determination of the 'there is'. Unfortunately, that cannot be correct. For Book I, Proposition 22 establishes that, 'Whatever follows from some attribute of God in so far as it is modified by a modification which, through the same attribute, exists necessarily and is infinite, must also exist necessarily and be infinite.'[20] To put it concisely, everything that follows from an immediate infinite mode such as the infinite intellect is in turn infinite. Hence the finite intellect cannot be an effect of the infinite intellect. Why then do they have the same name?

In order to resolve this problem, Spinoza proposes – not without some hesitation – a *third* fundamental relation, following those of causality and coupling, which we will call 'inclusion'. Granted, the finite intellect is not an effect of infinite intellect; nevertheless, says Spinoza, it is a *part* of it. This is what the Corollary to Book II, Proposition 11 maintains, albeit without offering either a proof or an elucidation for the concept in question: 'the human mind is a part of the infinite intellect of God'.[21] In actual fact, this hitherto unmentioned relation of inclusion has to do with what, in my opinion, constitutes the greatest impediment for Spinozist ontology: the relation between the infinite and the finite.

That we really are dealing with an instance of inclusion, with a conception in terms of sets, is confirmed by the converse thesis: just as the finite intellect is a part of the infinite intellect, similarly, the infinite intellect is the gathering together, the collection, of finite intellects. Thus, in the Scholium to Book V, Proposition 40 Spinoza writes: '[O]ur mind, in so far as it understands, is an eternal mode of thinking, which is determined by another eternal mode of thinking, and this again by another, and so on, to infinity; so that together, they all constitute God's eternal and infinite intellect.'[22] As the infinite sum of an infinite chain of finite modes, the infinite intellect can be designated as the *limit point* of the finitudes it totalizes. Conversely, the finite intellect constitutes a point of composition for its infinite sum. In this instance, causality is merely an apparent order since it is incapable of leading us out of the finite. For, as is established by Book I, Proposition 28, a finite mode only ever has another finite mode as its cause. Genuine relation is inclusive.

Elsewhere, Spinoza has no qualms when it comes to severely criticizing the undisciplined use of the part/whole relation. But when it comes to the intellect, and in order to justify the use of the same word to designate both human operations and the operations of the internal fold of the attribute of thought, he is left with no other option. Only inclusion can provide a global account for the *being* of the finite intellect.

If we now try to uncover what the *operations* of this intellect consist in, we immediately re-encounter the relation of coupling. The essential motif consists in identifying the human mind through its coupling with the body. One thereby avoids directly invoking the third relation, the relation of inclusion, by remaining at the local level, as it were. The human mind is an idea, hence a finite component of that whose higher modality is the infinite intellect. It is the idea of the body.

The great advantage of this purely local treatment is that it accounts for everything that remains obscure in finite thought. We should recall that there exists a norm for the relation of coupling: agreement. We should also note that if the idea does not agree with the object with which it is coupled, it is obscure, or untrue. Everything obscure in thought will be generated and measured in terms of the norm of agreement. The key to this lies in Book II, Proposition 24: 'The human mind does not involve adequate knowledge of the parts composing the human body.'[23] The same thing is put even more bluntly in the Demonstration for Proposition 19 of the same Book: 'The human mind does not know the human body.'[24]

Note the complexity of this approach: ontologically the mind is an idea, the idea of the body. But this does not mean that it knows its object. For the relation of coupling between the idea and its object admits of degrees; it can be more or less subject to the norm of agreement. All the more so if it is a complex idea, related to the body's multiple composition.

Ultimately, it is by appealing to the third relation, the relation of inclusion, that the ontology of the finite intellect is able to account for all the themes broached in Book V: since we are a part of the infinite intellect, we experience ourselves as eternal. Moreover, it is by appealing to the second relation of coupling that the theory of the operations of this finite intellect is able to illuminate the themes of Books III and IV: we do not immediately have an adequate idea of what our own intellect actually is.

The relation between these two relations is certainly not straightforward. In fact, the difficulty can be formulated as follows: if the finite intellect is defined as an ideal coupling with the body, yet one which is without knowledge of its object, how do we account for the possibility of true ideas? Although the relation of inclusion explains it, the latter is no more than global metaphor. What is the *local* operation of truths?

The problem is not that of knowing how we can have true ideas in the extrinsic sense governed by the norm of agreement, for we experience the fact that we do. The true idea is its own verification, even in those instances where it is validated through coupling, agreement. This famous theme is laid out in the Scholium to Book II, Proposition 43: '[H]ow can a man know that he has an idea that agrees with its object [*ideatum*]? I have just shown, more than sufficiently, that this arises solely from his having an idea which does agree with its object [*ideatum*] – *or* that truth is its own standard.'[25] At this juncture, Spinoza wishes to unify the operational approach that uses coupling with the properly ontological approach that uses inclusion. This much is clear from the continuation of the argument: 'Add to this that our mind, in so far as it perceives things truly, is part of the infinite intellect of God.'[26] Thus, the existence of true ideas is guaranteed at the global level by the finite intellect's inclusion in the infinite intellect, and at the local level, by the self-evident exposition of the agreement of a coupling.

The real problem is: How? How does the finite intellect come to have true ideas, given that it does not even have knowledge of the body-object, of which it is the idea?

The solution to this problem, which is strictly operational since it is not existential, is set out in Propositions 38 to 40 of Book II. These Propositions establish that every idea referring back to a property common to all bodies, or to all ideas, or even to everything that is in so far as it is, is true; and that the ideas that follow from true ideas are also true.

In other words: there is no true knowledge of that singular body of which our mind is the idea. But the finite intellect necessarily has a true idea of what is common to all bodies, and consequently of what is not singular, as soon as it is able to couple with it.

We have true ideas because the finite intellect possesses ideas that are coupled to non-singular objects, in other words, to *common* objects.

Ultimately, veridical reason is woven out of common notions.

We are familiar with Spinoza's incessant polemics against universals and homonyms devoid of being. There is a sense in which his doctrine only admits the existence of singularities as immanent effects of the divine 'there is'. On the other hand, the only admissible proof for the local operation of true ideas rests entirely on common notions, on the generic properties of singularities. The true is generic, even when being is the power of singularities.

Spinoza does not hesitate to insist that 'those notions which are called *common* . . . are the foundations of our deductive capacity'.[27] More decisively still, in the Demonstration for Book II, Proposition 44, Corollary 2, he writes: '[T]he foundations of reason [*fondamenta rationis*] are notions (by P38) which explain those things which are common to all, and which (by P37) do not explain the essence of any singular thing. On that account, they must be conceived without any relation to time, but under a certain species of eternity.'[28]

The objection according to which the third kind of knowledge would have to be essentially distinct from reason, providing us with a 'lateral' (or purely intuitive) access to singularities themselves, does not stand up. The debate is too old and too complex to be broached here. We will confine ourselves to noting that the Preface to Book V identifies, in an entirely general fashion, the 'power of mind' with 'reason': '*de sola mentis, seu rationis potentia agam*', 'I shall treat only of the power of the mind, *or* of reason.'[29] And also that if the third kind of knowledge is truly an 'intuitive science [*scientia intuitiva*]',[30] just as 'the eyes of the mind . . . are the demonstrations themselves',[31] then an 'intuition' carried out through these eyes must consist of an 'immediate' grasp of the proofs, an instantaneous verification of the deductive link between common notions. But this does not release us from the pure universality wherein the true ideas of the infinite intellect reside.

Thus we find ourselves back at the pure axiomatic of eternity from whence we initially set out. For if the realm of the thinkable is gauged – for a finite intellect – through 'that which is common to all', then the latter actually refers to the arrangement of the 'there is', which is to say, to the attributive identification of divine infinity.

This circular closure of Spinozist ontology – a closure mediated by the structures of the intellect – is enacted through a complex schema, which needs to be recapitulated.

1. The path to the identification of the 'there is' under the name 'God' can be accessed only through a pre-comprehension of difference, which in turn provides the basis for the purely extensive conception of divine infinity.

2. The possibility of the extensive conception of divine infinity presupposes – both for the attributes and for the measurement of divine infinity – an internal fold, an irreducible singularity, which is the infinite intellect.

3. The infinite intellect has all the characteristics, if not of a subject, then at least of the subjective modality or the predicative power associated with its effect. As immediate infinite mode, it cannot

be accessed through the usual ways of establishing existence. Thus it remains existentially undecidable. The structure of the infinite intellect requires a relation other than causality, which was the only kind of relation proposed at the outset. This second kind of relation is that of coupling. It has a norm – agreement – which is the gauge of truth. Let us say that as an operation of truth, the operation of the intellect is atypical. Ultimately, coupling 'infinitizes' every point of the intellect, just as causality 'infinitizes' every point of the 'there is'. We could say that the intellect is intrinsically a doubling of the immanent productive power.

Undecidable in terms of its existence; atypical in terms of its operation; eliciting a doubling effect – these are the traits which, in my eyes, identify the intellect as a modality of the subject-effect.

4. In order to be localized, the human or finite intellect (mind) requires in turn a third relation, that of inclusion. Just as the relation of coupling allows for a straddling of the disjunction between different attributes, similarly, the relation of inclusion allows for a straddling of the disjunction between finite and infinite. The intellect is then ontologically determined as the local point of the infinite intellect, which is the recollection of all these finite points. If one is willing to grant that the infinite intellect is the intrinsic modality of the subject-effect, it then becomes possible to say that the human intellect is a localized effect of the subject. Or a subjective differential. Or quite simply: a subject.

5. It is also possible to define the human intellect in terms of coupling. An immediate consequence of this is that the only points of truth are axiomatic and general. The singular is subtracted from every local subjective differential. In other words: the only capacity for truth that a subject, hence the human mind, possesses is that of a mathematics of being, or of being as mathematically conceived. All truth is generic. Alternately: what is thinkable of being is mathematical.

My conclusion is that the *more geometrico* is true thought itself as thinking of being, or of the 'there is'. Being can only be thought *more geometrico*. Conversely, all mathematical thinking is a thinking of being within a finite localization. That is why, in effect, 'the eyes of the mind are the demonstrations themselves'. Without mathematics, we are blind.

This conclusion is, in my opinion, indubitable. God has to be understood as mathematicity itself. The name of the 'there is' is: matheme.

Yet even within Spinoza's text, the ways in which this result is established necessitate opening up a space of thought that is not regulated according to the naming of the 'there is' (this is what I call the operations of closure). The terms constituting this space are: indeterminacy, difference, subject, undecidability, atypicality, coupling, doubling, inclusion, genericity of the true. And a few others as well.

What is lacking is a founding category capable of accounting for this converse or reverse of the mathematical, one that would constitute an exception to, or supplement for, the 'there is'. It is precisely at this juncture that we need to introduce what, in the wake of others, I have called 'the event'. The event is also what grounds time, or rather – event by event – *times*. But Spinoza, who according to his own expression wished to think 'without any relation to time',[32] and who conceived freedom in terms of 'a constant and eternal love of God',[33] wanted no part of it. We could say he wished to think according to the pure elevation of the matheme. In other words, according to the love of the 'there is': an 'intellectual' love which is only ever the intuitive shorthand for a proof, a glance from the eyes of the mind.

Yet other thoughts unfold within the very doubling of this exclusive thinking. These thoughts will accept the mathematics of multiple-being. In this regard, they will be explicitly Spinozist. But they will draw their genuine impetus from the implicit, paradoxical Spinozism outlined above, from the evental torsion wherein, under the name 'intellect', the paradox of the subject surges forth.

These thoughts will practise the elevation of the matheme, but, taking stock of what exceeds or outstrips it, they will no longer consent to giving it divine names.

That is why they will enjoy access to the infinite without being encumbered by finitude. On this point, they will rediscover an inspiration that is more Platonist than Spinozist.

SECTION II
THE SUBTRACTION OF TRUTH

CHAPTER 8
THE EVENT AS TRANS-BEING

If we assume that mathematics is the thinking of being qua being, and if we add that this thinking only comes into effect when, at crucial junctures in the history of mathematics, decisions about the existence of the infinite are at stake, we will then ask: what is the field proper to philosophy?

Of course, we know it is up to philosophy to identify the ontological vocation of mathematics. Save for those rare moments of 'crisis' that we have already mentioned, when the mathematician is struck by fear as he confronts that for which he is responsible (infinite multiples), mathematics thinks being, but is not the thinking of the thought that it is. We could even say that in order to unfold historically as the thinking of being, and due to the difficult separation from the metaphysical power of the One this entails, mathematics had to identify itself as something entirely different from ontology. It is therefore up to philosophy to enunciate and validate this equation: mathematics = ontology. In so doing, philosophy unburdens itself of what appears to be its highest responsibility: it asserts that it is not up to it to think being qua being.

This movement whereby philosophy, by identifying its conditions, purges itself of what is not its responsibility, is one that spans the entire history of philosophy. Philosophy freed, or discharged, itself from physics, from cosmology, from politics, and from many other things. Today, it is important that it frees itself from ontology *stricto sensu*. Yet this is a complex task, since it implies a reflective and non-epistemological traversal of real mathematics. In *Being and Event*, for example, I simultaneously:

- studied the ontological efficacy of the axioms of set theory, via the categories of difference, void, excess, infinite, nature, decision, truth and subject;

- showed how and why ontological thought can effectuate itself without needing to identify itself;

- examined, according to my non-unified vision of the destiny of philosophy, the philosophical connections between axiomatic interpretations: Plato's *Parmenides* on difference and the One,

Aristotle on the void, Hegel on the infinite, Pascal on the decision, Rousseau on the being of truths, etc.

In my view, this kind of work still remains very largely open. The work of Albert Lautman in the 1930s had already demonstrated that every significant and innovative fragment of real mathematics can and must, in so far as it constitutes a living condition, elicit its own ontological identification. I have undertaken this task more recently both with respect to the renewed conception of number proposed by Conway and with regard to the theory of Categories and Topoi.

On the other hand, there is the vast question of that which subtracts itself from ontological determination, the question of that which is *not* being qua being. For the law of subtraction is implacable: if real ontology is set out as mathematics by eluding the norm of the One, it is also necessary, lest one allow this norm to re-establish itself at a global level, that there be a point at which the ontological (i.e. mathematical) field is detotalized or caught in an impasse. I have called this point *the event*. Accordingly, we could also say that, beyond the identification of real ontology, which must be ceaselessly taken up again, philosophy is also, first and foremost, the general theory of the event. That is, the theory of that which subtracts itself from ontological subtraction. Or the theory of the impossible proper to mathematics. We could also say that, in so far as mathematical thinking takes charge of being as such, the theory of the event aims at the determination of a trans-being.

What are the characteristic traits of the event, at least within the register of the thinking of being? What subtracts the sheer 'what happens' from the general determinations of 'what is'?

First of all, it is necessary to point out that as far as its material is concerned, the event is not a miracle. What I mean is that what composes an event is always extracted from a situation, always related back to a singular multiplicity, to its state, to the language connected to it, etc. In fact, if we want to avoid lapsing into an obscurantist theory of creation *ex nihilo*, we must accept that an event is nothing but a part of a given situation, nothing but a *fragment of being*.

I have called this fragment the evental site. There is an event only in so far as there exists a site for it within an effectively deployed situation (a multiple).

Needless to say, a site is not just any fragment of an effective multiplicity. One could say that there is a sort of 'fragility' peculiar to the site, which disposes it to be in some sense 'wrested' from the situation. This fragility can be formulated mathematically: the elements of an evental site are such that none of their own elements belong to the site. It is in fact clear that there are many cases where the elements of the elements of a multiple also belong to the given multiple. The liver cells of a cat, for example, also belong to the vitality of the cat. Cells are alive. This is why the liver is a solid, integrated and organic part of the totality that is the cat. The liver is not an evental site. Inversely, a cell can be considered as a site, because the molecules that compose it are not 'organic' in the same sense as the liver may be said to be organic. A chemically determined molecule is no longer 'alive' in the sense that the cat can be said to be alive. Even if it is 'objectively' a part of the cat, a simple aggregate of molecules is not a vital component in the same sense as the liver. We could say that with this aggregate we have reached the material edge of the cat's vitality. This is why such an aggregate will be said to be 'on the edge of the void'; that is, on the edge of what separates the cat, as a singular multiple-situation, from its pure indistinct being, which is the void proper to life (and the void proper to life, as death shows, is matter).

Therefore, the abstract definition of a site is that it is a part of a situation all of whose elements are on the edge of the void.

The ontological material, the underlying multiplicity, of an event is a site thus defined.

Having said this, we encounter a singular problem, which I believe establishes the dividing line between Deleuze's doctrine and my own. The question is effectively the following: if we grant that the event is what guarantees that everything is not mathematizable, must we or must we not conclude that the multiple is intrinsically heterogeneous? To think that the event is a point of rupture with respect to being does not exonerate us from thinking the being of the event itself, of what I precisely call 'trans-being', and of which I've just said that it is in every instance a site. Beyond the acknowledgement that the material of the event is a site, does trans-being require a theory of the multiple heterogeneous to the one that accounts for being qua being? In my view, Deleuze's position amounts to answering 'yes'. In order to think the evental fold, an originarily duplicitous theory of multiplicities is required, a theory that is heir to Bergson. Extensive and numerical multiplicities must be distinguished from intensive or qualitative multiplicities. An event is always the gap between two heterogeneous multiplicities. What happens produces a fold between extensive segmentation and the intensive continuum.

I, on the contrary, argue that multiplicity is axiomatically homogeneous. Therefore I must account for the being of the event both as a rupture of the law of segmented multiplicities *and* as homogeneous to this law. My argument must pass through a defection of the following axiom: an event is nothing other than a set, or a multiple, whose form is that of a site. But the arising of the event, as a supplementation, subtracts one of the axioms of the multiple, namely the axiom of foundation.

What does the axiom of foundation say? That in every multiple, there is at least one element that 'founds' this multiple, in the following sense: there is an element that has no element in common with the initial multiple. On this point, we can recall the example of the cat. One will say that a cell 'founds' the cat as a living totality, in the precise sense that the cat, conceived in this manner, is composed only of cells. It follows that no element of the cell (no chemical molecule as such) is an element of the cat, since every element of the living multiplicity 'cat' is a cell.

The ontological import of this axiom is clear: the decomposition of a multiplicity always includes a *halting point*. At a given moment, you will come upon an element of the multiplicity whose own composition no longer belongs to this multiplicity. In other words: there is no infinite descent into the constituents of a multiplicity. A multiplicity can certainly be (and generally is) infinite in extension (it possesses an infinity of elements), but it is not infinite 'genealogically', or in depth. The existence of such a halting point stabilizes every multiplicity upon itself, and guarantees that in one point at least it encounters something that is no longer itself.

A crucial consequence of the axiom of foundation is that *no multiple can be an element of itself*. Indeed, it seems clear that no cat is an element of the cat which it is, nor are any of the cat's cells an element of the cell which they are, whilst on the contrary a cell can obviously be an element of the cat.

That this point derives from the axiom of foundation can be readily demonstrated. Let's suppose that a multiple is in fact an element of itself (such that we have M∈M, or multiple M 'belongs' to multiple M). Let's now consider the set that has M as its only element (this set is called the 'singleton' of M and is written {M}). I can affirm that this set (this singleton) is not founded. In actual fact, its only element is M, and since M is an element of M (our initial hypothesis), it follows that all the elements of its elements are still elements.

Thus if we accept the axiom of foundation, we must exclude the possibility that a multiple may be a multiple of itself.

It is on this point that the event departs from the laws of being. In effect, an event is composed of the elements of a site, but also by the event itself, which belongs to itself.

There is nothing strange about this definition. It is obvious, for example, that a reflection upon the French Revolution is an element of the revolution itself, or that the circumstances of an amorous encounter (of a love 'at first sight') are part of this encounter – as is shown, from within an instance of love, by the infinite gloss of which they are the object.

Ultimately, an event is the advent of a situated multiple (there is a site of the event) and is in a position to be its own element. The exact meaning of this formulation is that an event is an unfounded multiple. It is this defection of the foundation that turns it into a pure chance supplement of the multiple-situation for which it is an event, and from which it 'wrests' a site from its founded inclusion.

What happens – and, inasmuch as it happens, goes beyond its multiple-being – is precisely this: a fragment of multiplicity wrested from all inclusion. In a flash, this fragment (a certain modulation in a symphony by Haydn, a particular command in the Paris Commune, a specific anxiety preceding a declaration of love, a unique intuition by Gauss or Galois) affirms its unfoundedness, its pure *advent*, which is intransitive to the place in which 'it' comes. The fragment thereby also affirms its belonging to itself, since this coming can originate from nowhere else.

Consequently, it cannot be said that the event is One. Like everything that is, the event is a multiplicity (its elements are those of the site, plus itself). Nevertheless, this multiplicity surges up as such beyond every count, it fulminates the situation from which it has been wrested as a fragment. This is what has pushed me to say that an eventful multiplicity, qua trans-being, can be declared to be an 'ultra-One'.

We are faced here with an extreme tension, balanced precariously between the multiple on the one hand, and the metaphysical power of the One on the other. It should be clear why the general question that is the object of my dispute with Deleuze, which concerns the status of the event vis-à-vis an ontology of the multiple, and how to avoid reintroducing the power of the One at that point wherein the law of the multiple begins to falter, is the guiding question of all contemporary philosophy. This question is anticipated in Heidegger's shift from *Sein* to *Ereignis*, or – switching registers – in Lacan, where it is entirely invested in the thinking of the analytical act as the eclipse of truth between a supposed and a transmissible knowledge, between interpretation and the matheme. Lacan will find himself obliged to say that though the One is not, the act nevertheless installs the One. But it is also a decisive problem for Nietzsche: if it is a question of breaking the history of the world in two, what, in the affirmative absolute of life, is the thinkable principle that would command such a break? And it's also the central problem for Wittgenstein: how does the act open up our access to the 'mystical element' – i.e., to the ethical and the aesthetic – if meaning is always captive to a proposition, or always the prisoner of grammar?

In all these cases, the latent matrix of the problem is the following: if by 'philosophy' we must understand both the jurisdiction of the One and the conditioned subtraction from this jurisdiction, how can philosophy grasp what happens; what happens *in thought?* Philosophy will always be divided between, on the one hand, the recognition of the event as a supernumerary advent of the One, and on the other, the thought of the being of the event as a simple extension of the multiple. Is truth what comes to being or what unfolds being? We remain divided. The whole point is to maintain, as far as possible, and under the most innovative conditions of thought, that, in any case, truth itself is nothing but a multiplicity. In the twofold sense that both its coming (a truth elicits the advent of a typical multiple, a generic singularity) and its being (there is no Truth, there are only truths, disparate and untotalizable) are multiplicities.

This requires a radical inaugural gesture, which is the hallmark of modern philosophy: to subtract the examination of truths from the mere form of judgement. This always means the following: to decide upon an ontology of multiplicities. Consequently, to remain faithful to Lucretius, telling ourselves that every instant is the one in which:

> From all sides there opens up an infinite space
> When the atoms, innumerable and limitless,
> Turn in every direction in an eternal movement.[1]

Hopefully this clarifies why Deleuze, despite his Stoic inflections, is, like myself, a faithful follower of Lucretius.

CHAPTER 9
ON SUBTRACTION[1]

Since I have been invited before you, for whom silence and speech are the principal concerns, to honour that which subtracts itself from their alternation, it is to Mallarmé I turn to mitigate my solitude.

Thus, by way of an epigraph for my address, I have chosen this fragment from the fourth scholium of *Igitur*:

> I alone – I alone – am going to know the void. You, you return to your amalgam.
>
> I proffer speech, the better to re-immerse it in its own inanity. . . .
>
> This, no doubt, constitutes an act – it is my duty to proclaim it: this madness exists. You were right to manifest it: do not think I am going to re-immerse you in the void.[2]

As far as the compactness of your amalgam is concerned, I come here duty-bound to declare that the madness of subtraction constitutes an act. Better, that it constitutes the paragon of the act, the act of a truth, the one through which I come to know the only thing one may ever know in the element of the real: the void of being as such.

If speech is reimmersed in its inanity by the act of truth, don't think *you* too will thereby be reimmersed; you who retain the reason of the manifest. Rather, we will concur – I through the duty of speech, you through that of rendering my speech manifest – that the folly of an act of truth exists.

Nothing can be granted existence – by which I mean the existence that a truth presupposes at its origin – without undergoing the trial of its subtraction.

It is not easy to subtract. Sub-traction, that which draws under, is too often mixed with ex-traction, that which draws from out of, that which mines and yields the coal of knowledge.

Subtraction is plural. The allegation of lack, of its effect, of its causality, masks operations all of which are irreducible to one another.

These operations are four in number: the undecidable, the indiscernible, the generic, and the unnameable. Four figures delineating the cross of being when it surges forth in the trajectory as well as in the obstacle of a truth. A truth about which it would still be too much to say that it is half-said, since, as we shall see, it is rarely-said, or even almost-not-said, traversed as it is by the incommensurable unbinding between its own infinity and the finitude of the knowledge it pierces.

Let us begin with pure formalism.

Consider a norm for the evaluation of statements, in any given situation of a language. The most common of these norms is the distinction between the veridical statement and the erroneous statement. If the language in question is rigorously partitioned, another norm might be the distinction between provable and falsifiable statements. But for our purposes, it is enough that there be such a norm. The undecidable statement will be the one that subtracts itself from that norm. Consider a statement such that it cannot be inscribed in any of the classes within which the norm of evaluation is supposed to distribute all possible utterances.

The undecidable is thus that which subtracts itself from a supposedly exhaustive classification of statements, realized according to the values ascribed to them by a norm. I am unable to decide any assignable value for this statement, in spite of the fact that the norm of assignation exists only on the assumption of its complete efficacy. The undecidable statement is strictly *valueless*, and this is what constitutes its price, through which it contravenes the laws of classical economy.

Gödel's theorem establishes that in the language situation known as firstorder formalized arithmetic, wherein the norm of evaluation is that of the provable, there exists at least one statement that is undecidable in a precise sense: neither it nor its negation can be proved. Thus, formalized arithmetic does not fall under the aegis of a classical economy of statements.

It has long been customary to relate the undecidability of Gödel's statement to the fact that it takes the form of the liar paradox, of a statement declaring its own indemonstrability – a statement subtracted from the norm simply because it states that it is negatively affected by it. We now know that this link between undecidability and paradox is contingent. In 1977, Jeff Paris and Leo Harrington proved the undecidability of a statement they themselves described not as a paradox, but, I quote, as 'a reasonably natural theorem of a finite combinatorial.'[3] In this instance, subtraction is an intrinsic operation; it is not a consequence of the statement's paradoxical structure vis-à-vis the norm from which it subtracts itself.

Consider now a language situation wherein, as before, there exists a norm of evaluation for statements. Take any two given terms whatsoever, let's say a_1 and a_2. Consider now expressions of that language with places for two terms, such as 'x is bigger than y'; e.g. expressions of the kind $F(x, y)$. We will say that such an expression *discerns* the terms a_1 and a_2 when the value of the statement $F(a_1, a_2)$ differs from the value of the statement $F(a_2, a_1)$.

If, for example, a_1 is effectively bigger than a_2, the expression 'x is bigger than y' discerns a_1 and a_2 since the statement 'a_1 is bigger than a_2' takes the value 'true' whereas the statement 'a_2 is bigger than a_1' takes the value 'false'.

You can see then that an expression discerns two terms if putting one in place of the other and vice versa, i.e., permuting the terms in the expression, changes the value of the statement.

Consequently, two terms are *indiscernible* if, in the language situation in question, there exists no expression to discern them. Thus in a hypothetical language reduced to the single expression 'x is bigger than y', if the two terms a_1 and a_2 are equal then they are indiscernible. For, in effect, the expression 'a_1 is bigger than a_2' bears the value 'false', but so does the expression 'a_2 is bigger than a_1'.

Thus two given terms are said to be indiscernible with respect to a language situation if there is no two-place expression of that language marking their difference through the fact that permuting the terms changes the value of the resulting statement by inscribing them in the places prescribed by the expression.

The indiscernible is what subtracts itself from the marking of difference as effected by evaluating the effects of a permutation. Two terms are indiscernible when you permute them *in vain*. These two terms are two in number only in the pure presentation of their being. There is nothing in language to endow their duality with a differentiating value. They are two, granted, but not so that you could re-mark that they are. Thus the indiscernible subtracts difference as such from all remarking. The indiscernible subtracts the two from duality.

Algebra encountered the question of the indiscernible very early on, beginning with the work of Lagrange.

Let us adopt the mathematical language of polynomial equations with several variables and rational co-efficients. We will then fix the norm of evaluation as follows: if, when we substitute determinate real numbers for the variables, the polynomial cancels itself out, we will say that the value is V_1. If the polynomial does not cancel itself out, we will say that the value is V_2.

Under these conditions, a *discerning expression* is obviously a polynomial with two variables: $P(x, y)$. But it can easily be proved, for example, that the two real numbers +2 and –2 are indiscernible. For every polynomial $P(x, y)$, the value of $P(+2, -2)$ is the same as the value of the polynomial $P(-2, +2)$: if the first (when x takes the value +2 and y – 2) cancels itself out, the second (when x takes the value –2 and y + 2) also cancels itself out. In other words, the principle of differential evaluation fails for every permutation of the two numbers +2 and –2.

Consequently, we should not be surprised that it was under the impetus of the study of permutation groups that Galois came to configure the theoretical space wherein the problem of resolving equations by means of radicals first became intelligible. Galois effectively invented a calculus of the indiscernible. This point harbours considerable conceptual consequences which will be set out in the near future by the contemporary mathematician and thinker René Guitart in a forthcoming book which, it should be noted, makes use of a number of Lacanian categories.[4]

From the foregoing discussion we can retain the following result: whereas the undecidable is subtraction from a norm, the indiscernible is subtraction from a mark.

Consider a language situation where there always exists a norm of evaluation. And consider now a fixed set of terms or objects, let's say the set U. We will call U a universe for the language situation. Now let's take one of U's objects, for instance a_1. And let's take a single-place expression of that language, for instance $F(x)$. If in the place marked by x you put the object a_1 you obtain a statement $F(a_1)$ to which the norm will ascribe a certain value, either true, false, or any other value determined by a principle of evaluation. For example, let a_2 be a fixed object in the universe U. Now, suppose our language situation allows for the expression 'x is bigger than a_2'. If a_1 is actually bigger than a_2, we obtain the value 'true' for the statement 'a_1 is bigger than a_2' – the statement in which a_1 has come to occupy the place marked by x.

Now let's imagine that we take *all* the terms in U which are bigger than a_2. We thereby obtain a subset of U. It is the subset made up of all those objects a which, when substituted for x, give the value 'true' to the statement 'a is bigger than a_2'. We will say that this subset is *constructed* in the universe U through the expression 'x is bigger than a_2'.

Generally, we shall say that a subset of the universe U is constructed by an expression $F(x)$ if that subset is made up exclusively of *all* those terms a belonging to U such that, when put in the place marked by x, they accord the statement F(a) a value fixed in advance – in other words, all those terms such that the expression F(a) is evaluated in the same way.

We will say that a subset of the universe U is *constructible* if there exists in the language an expression F(x) that constructs it.

Thus a generic subset of U is one that *is not* constructible. No expression F(x) in the language is evaluated in the same way by the terms that make up a generic subset. It is clear that a generic subset is subtracted from every identification effected by means of a predicate of the language. No single predicative trait gathers together the terms that make up the generic subset.

Crucially, this means that for every expression F(x) there exist terms in the generic set which, when substituted for x, yield a statement with a certain value, and that there are other terms in the same set which, when substituted for x, yield a statement with a different value. The generic subset is such precisely because, given any expression F(x), it is subtracted from every selection and construction authorized by that expression in the universe U. The generic subset, we might say, contains a little bit of everything, so that no predicate ever collects together all its terms. The generic subset is subtracted from predication *by excess*. The kaleidoscopic character and predicative superabundance of the generic subset are such that nothing dependent upon the power of a statement and the identity of its evaluation is capable of circumscribing it. Language is incapable of constructing its contour or the character of its collection. The generic subset is a pure multiple of the universe, one that is evasive and cannot be grasped through any variety of linguistic construction. It indicates that the power of being proper to the multiple exceeds the aspect of that power that such constructions are capable of fixing according to the unity of an evaluation. More precisely, the generic is that instance of multiple-being which subtracts itself from the power of the One in so far as the latter operates through language.

It is easy to show that for every language endowed with a relation of equality and equipped with disjunction – in other words, for almost every language situation – a generic subset is necessarily infinite.

For let us suppose the opposite, that a generic subset is finite.

Its terms will then make up a finite list, let's say a_1, a_2, and so on up until a_n.

Consider now the expression '$x = a_1$ or $x = a_2$, etc., up to $x = a_n$'. This is an expression of the type F(x) since the terms a_1, a_2, etc., are fixed terms, which consequently do not indicate any 'empty' place. Moreover, it is obvious that the set made up of a_1, a_2 . . . a_n is constructed by this expression, since only these terms can validate an equality of the type '$x_3 = a_j$' when j goes from 1 to n. Accordingly, because it is constructible, this finite set cannot be generic.

Thus the generic is that subtraction from the predicative constructions of language that the universe allows through its own infinity. The generic is ultimately the superabundance of being such as it is withdrawn from the grasp of language, once an excess of determinations engenders an effect of indeterminacy.

In 1963, Paul Cohen furnished proof that even in very robust language situations, such as that of set theory, there exist universes in which generic multiplicities present themselves.[5] Since, as Lacan repeatedly asserted, mathematics is the science of the real, we can be assured that this singular subtraction from the mark of oneness that language stamps upon the pure multiple is genuinely real.

I have already said the undecidable is a subtraction from a norm of evaluation and the indiscernible a subtraction from the remarking of a difference. We can add that the generic is infinite subtraction from the subsumption of the multiple beneath the One of the concept.

Finally, consider a language situation and its principles of evaluation. Once again, consider single place expressions of the kind $F(x)$. Among the admissible values for statements in this language situation – for instance the true, the false, the possible, or any other – let's establish one value once and for all, which we shall call the nominating value. We shall then say that an expression $F(x)$ *names* a term a_1 belonging to that universe if that term is the *only one* which, when substituted for x, gives to the statement $F(a_1)$ the nominating value.

For example, take two terms – a_1 and a_2 – as our universe. Our language allows the expression 'x is bigger than a_2'. We will suppose that the nominating value is the true value. If a_1 is actually bigger than a_2, then the expression 'x is bigger than a_2' names the term a_1. And 'a_1 is bigger than a_2', which is the nominating value, is effectively true, while 'a_2 is bigger than a_1', which is *not* the nominating value, is false. But the universe comprises only a_1 and a_2. Therefore, a_1 is the only term in the universe which, when substituted for x, yields a statement with the nominating value.

The fact that an expression names a term means that it is provides a schema for its proper name. As always, the 'proper' presupposes the unique. The named term is unique because it gives to the expression that names it the fixed nominating value.

Accordingly, a term in the universe is 'unnameable' *if it is the only one in that universe that is not named by any expression.*

One should be attentive here to the doubling of the unique. A term is named only in so far as it is the unique term that confers upon an expression the nominating value. A term is unnameable only in so far as it is the unique term that subtracts itself from that uniqueness.

The unnameable is that which subtracts itself from the proper name and is alone in doing so. Thus the unnameable is the proper of the proper – so singular that it cannot even tolerate having a proper name; so singular in its singularity as to be the only one not to have a proper name.

We find ourselves here on the verge of paradox. For if the uniqueness of the unnameable consists in not having a proper name, then it seems the unnameable falls under the name of anonymity, which is proper to it alone. Isn't 'the one who has no name' the name of the unnameable? The answer would seem to be yes, since the unnameable is the only one to operate this subtraction.

The fact that uniqueness is doubled seems to imply that one form of uniqueness is the ruin of the other. It becomes impossible to subtract oneself from the proper name if this subtraction's uniqueness provides the basis for the propriety of a name.

As a result, there would seem to be no proper of the proper, which is to say, no singularity of that which subtracts itself from all self-doubling through the name of its singularity.

But this is only the case so long as the expression 'having no proper name' is possible in the language situation in which one is operating. Alternatively, this is only the case so long as the expression 'there is no expression $F(x)$ for which the unnameable term alone provides a nominating value' can itself be an expression in the language. For only this expression about expressions can serve to name the unnameable, thereby engendering the paradox.

Yet it is generally not the case that an expression can refer to all possible expressions in a language. In this instance, the not-all prevents the deployment of the putative paradox. For if you state 'there is no expression $F(x)$ such that this or that' you are in fact presupposing, albeit negatively, that all of the language can be inscribed in the unity of an expression. This in turn would require the language situation to be capable of a high degree of metalinguistic reflexivity, which could be sustained only at the price of a paradox even more damaging than the one under consideration.

Moreover, in 1968 the mathematician Furkhen proved that it is possible to suppose the existence of the unnameable without contradiction. Furkhen presents a fairly simple language situation – something like a fragment of the theory of the arithmetical successor, supplemented with a small part of set theory – such that it allows for a model in which one term and one term only remains nameless. Consequently, this is a model in which the unnameable –i.e., the subtractive reduplication of uniqueness, or the proper of the proper – well and truly exists.

Let us recapitulate. We have the undecidable as subtraction from the norms of evaluation, or subtraction from the Law; the indiscernible as subtraction from the marking of difference, or subtraction from sex; the generic as infinite and excessive subtraction from the concept, as pure multiple or subtraction from the One; and, finally, the unnameable as subtraction from the proper name, or as a singularity subtracted from singularisation. These are the analytical figures of being through which the latter is invoked whenever language loses its grip.

What we must now do is move from the analytic of subtraction to its dialectic, and establish the latter's topological linkage. The frame for this linkage is set out in the 'gamma' diagram below.

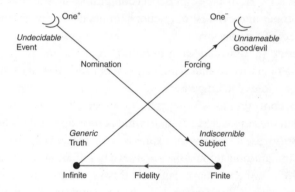

I should point out that only now do we enter fully into the realm of philosophy, since everything discussed so far is shared between philosophy and mathematics, and hence between philosophy and ontology.

Speaking of ontology, let it be said in passing that Lacan had no qualms about calling it a disgrace – a disgrace of sense, or of the senses. A culinary disgrace, I would add, a family disgrace for philosophy, not a form of good housekeeping but a disgrace for the philosophical household. But for me 'ontology' is just another name for mathematics – or, to be more precise, 'mathematics' is the name of ontology as a language situation. I thereby evade the place where disgrace dwells. What we have here is a subtraction of ontology as a whole from philosophy, which is now simply the language situation in which truths – in the plurality of their procedures – become pronounceable as Truth – in the singularity of its inscription.

But let's return to the gamma diagram.

It represents the trajectory of a truth, regardless of its type. I maintain that there are four types of truth: scientific, artistic, political, and amorous. My diagram is philosophical in that it renders the four types of truth compossible through a formal concept of Truth.

Notice how the four figures of subtraction are distributed according to the register of pure multiplicity. This also designates the latent being of these acts.

The undecidable and the unnameable are coupled by their common presupposition of the one: a single statement in the case of the undecidable; the uniqueness of what evades the proper name in the case of the unnameable. Yet the position of the one within the subtractive effect differs in each case.

Because it is subtracted from the effect of the norm of evaluation, the undecidable statement falls outside the compass of what can be inscribed, since what defines the possibilities of inscription is precisely to be governed by the norm. Thus Gödel's statement is absent from the domain of the provable because neither it nor its negation can be admitted into it. Consequently, we could say that the undecidable statement supplements the language situation governed by the norm. I indicate this in the diagram by the plus sign appended to the one.

The unnameable, on the contrary, is embedded in the intimate depths of presentation. It bears witness to the flesh of singularity and thus provides the point-like ground for the entire order in which terms are presented. This radical underside of naming, this folding of the proper back upon itself, designates that in being which undermines the principle of the one, such as it has been established by language in the naming of the proper. This weakening of the one of language by the point-like ground of being is indicated in the diagram by appending the minus sign to the one.

As for the indiscernible and the generic, they are coupled by their common presupposition of the multiple. Indiscernibility is said of at least two terms, since it is a difference without a concept. And the generic, as we have seen, requires an infinite dissemination of the terms in the universe, since it provides the schema for a subset that is subtracted from all predicative unity.

But here, once again, the type of multiple differs in each case. The criterion for the kind of multiple implied in the indiscernible is constituted by the places marked out in a discerning expression. Since every effective expression in a language situation is finite, the multiple of the indiscernible is necessarily finite. The generic, on the contrary, requires the infinite.

Thus the gamma diagram superimposes the logical figures of subtraction onto an ontological distribution. There is a quadripartite distribution of the one-more, the one-less, the finite, and the infinite. A truth circulates within this exhaustive quadripartite structure, which accounts for the ways in which being is given. Similarly, the trajectory of a truth is traced by the complete logic of subtraction.

Let us now follow this trajectory.

In order for the process of a truth to begin, something must happen. As Mallarmé would put it, it is necessary that we be not in a predicament where nothing takes place but the place. For the place as such (or structure) gives us only repetition, along with the knowledge which is known or unknown within it, a knowledge that always remains in the finitude of its being. I call the advent, the pure supplement, the unforeseeable and disconcerting addition: 'event'. It is, to quote the poet once more, that which is 'sprung from the croup and the flight'.[6] A truth arises in its novelty – and every truth is a novelty – because a hazardous supplement interrupts repetition. Indistinct, a truth begins by surging forth.

But from the outset, this surging forth provides the basis for the undecidable. For the norm of evaluation that governs the situation, or structure, cannot be applied to the statement 'this event belongs to the situation'. Were such a statement to be decidable, then clearly the event would already be subject to the norms of repetition, and consequently would not be evental. Every statement implying the naming of the event harbours an intrinsic undecidability. And no assessment, no exhibition, can compensate for the insufficiency of the norm. For hardly has the event surged forth than it has already disappeared. It is nothing but the flash of a supplementation. Its empirical character is that of an eclipse. That is why it will always be necessary to say that it took place, that it was given in the situation, and this unverifiable statement, subtracted from the norm of evaluation, constitutes a supplementation vis-à-vis the realm of what language decides: it is well and truly in this one-more that undecidability is played out.

A truth's first step is to wager on this supplement. One decides to hold to the statement 'the event has taken place', which comes down to deciding the undecidable. But of course, since the undecidable is subtracted from the norm of evaluation, this decision is an axiom. It has no basis other than the presupposed vanishing of the event. Thus every truth passes through the pure wager on what has being only in disappearing. The axiom of truth – which always takes the form 'this took place, which I can neither calculate nor demonstrate' – is simply the affirmative obverse of the subtraction of the undecidable.

It is in the wake of this subtraction that the infinite procedure of verifying the true begins. It consists in examining within the situation the consequences of the axiom. But this examination itself is not guided by any established law. Nothing governs its trajectory, because the axiom that supports it has decided independently of any appeal to the norms of evaluation. Thus it is a hazardous trajectory, one without a concept. The successive choices that make up the verification are devoid of any aim that would be representable in the object or supported by a principle of objectivity.

But what is a pure choice, a choice without a concept? Obviously, it is a choice faced with two indiscernible terms. If there is no expression to discern two terms in a situation, one may be certain that the choice whereby the verification proceeds through one term rather than the other has no basis in any objective difference between them. It is then a question of an absolutely pure choice, free from any presupposition other than that of having to choose, in the absence of any distinguishing mark in the presented terms, the one through which the verification of the consequences of the axiom will first proceed.

This situation has frequently been registered in philosophy, under the name 'freedom of indifference'. This is a freedom that is not governed by any noticeable difference, a freedom that faces up to the indiscernible. If there is no value by which to discriminate what you have to choose, it is your freedom as such which provides the norm, to the point where it effectively becomes indistinguishable from chance. The indiscernible is the subtraction that establishes a point of coincidence between chance and freedom. Descartes will make of this coincidence God's prerogative. He even goes so far as to claim that, given the axiom of divine freedom, the choice of 4 rather than 5 as the answer to the sum $2 + 2$ is the choice between two indiscernibles. In this instance, the norm of addition is that from which God is axiomatically subtracted. It is his pure choice that will retroactively constitute the norm, which is to say actively verify it or turn it into truth.

Putting God aside, I will maintain that it is the indiscernible that coordinates the subject as pure *punctum* in the process of verification. A subject is that which disappears between two indiscernibles, or that which is eclipsed through the subtraction of a difference without concept. This subject is that throw of the dice which does not abolish chance but effectuates it as verification of the axiom that grounds it. What was decided at the point of the undecidable event will proceed through *this* term, in which the local act of a truth is represented – without reason or marked difference, and indiscernible from its other. The subject, fragment of chance, crosses the distance-less gap that the subtraction of the indiscernible inscribes between two terms. In this regard the subject of a truth is in effect genuinely indifferent: the indifferent lover.[7]

Clearly, the act of the subject is essentially finite, as is the presentation of indiscernibles in its being. Nevertheless, the verifying trajectory goes on, investing the situation through successive indifferences. Little by little, what takes shape behind these acts begins to delineate the contour of a subset of the situation – or of the universe wherein the evental axiom verifies its effects. This subset is clearly infinite and remains beyond the reach of completion. Nevertheless, it is possible to state that if it is completed, it will ineluctably be a generic subset.

For how could a series of pure choices engender a subset that could be unified by means of a predicate? This could only be the case if the trajectory of a truth was secretly governed by a concept or if the indiscernibles wherein the subject is dissipated in its act were actually discerned by a superior intellect. This is what Leibniz thought, for whom the impossibility of indiscernibles was a consequence of God's computational intellect. But if there is no God to compute the situation, if the indiscernibles are genuinely indiscernible, the trajectory of truth cannot coincide in the infinite with any concept whatsoever. And as a result, the verified terms compose – or rather, if one supposes their infinite totalization, *will have* composed – a generic subset of the universe. Indiscernible in its act or as subject, a truth is generic in its result or being. It is subtracted from every recollection of the multiple in the one of a designation.

Thus there are two reasons, and not just one, for maintaining that a truth is scarcely-said.

The first is that, since it is infinite in its being, a truth can be represented only in the future perfect. It will have taken place as generic infinity. Its taking-place, which is also its localized relapse into knowledge, is given in the finite act of a subject. There is an incommensurability between the finitude of its act and the infinity of its being. This incommensurability is also what relates the verifying exposition of the evental axiom to the infinite hypothesis of its completion; or what relates the indiscernible subtraction, which founds the subject, to the generic subtraction, wherein is anticipated the truth that the subject is a subject *of*. This is the relation between the almost nothing, the finite, and the almost everything, the infinite. Whence the fact that every truth is scarcely-said, since what is said about it is always tied to the local order of verification.

The second reason is intrinsic. Since a truth is a generic subset of the universe, it does not let itself be summarized by any predicate, it is not constructed by any expression. This is the nub of the matter: there is no expression for truth. Whence the fact that it is scarcely-said, since ultimately the impossibility of constructing truth by means of an expression comes down to the fact that what we *know* of truth is only knowledge – that which, always finite, is arranged in the background of pure choices.

The fact that a truth is scarcely-said articulates the relation between the indiscernible and the generic, which is governed by an undecidable axiom.

Nevertheless, the generic or subtractive power of a truth can be anticipated as such. The generic being of a truth is never presented, but we can know, formally, that a truth will always have taken place as a generic infinity. Whence the possibility of a fictive disposition of the effects of its having-taken-place. From the vantage point of the subject, it is always possible to hypothesize a universe wherein the truth through which the subject is constituted will have completed its generic totalization. What would the consequences of such a hypothesis be for the universe in which truth proceeds infinitely? Thus the axiom, which decides the undecidable on the basis of the event, is followed by the hypothesis, which fictively maintains a Universe supplemented by this generic subset whose finite, local delineations are supported by the subject through the trial of the indiscernible.

What is it that obstructs such a hypothesis? What limits the generic power of a truth projected through the fiction of its completion, and hence of its being wholly-said? I maintain that this obstacle is none other than the unnameable.

The anticipating hypothesis as to the generic being of a truth is obviously a *forcing* of the scarcely-said. This forcing enacts the fiction of an all-saying from the vantage of an infinite and generic truth. But then there is a great temptation to exert this forcing on the most intimate, most subtracted point of the situation, and to try to force that which testifies to the situation's singularity, that which does not even have a proper name, the proper of the proper, which is anonymous but for which 'anonymous' is not even the adequate name.

Let us say that forcing, which represents the infinitely generic character of truth in the future perfect, encounters its radical limit in the possibility that its power of all-saying in truth will result in a truth ultimately giving its own name to the unnameable.

The constraint that the infinite, or the subtractive excess of the generic, exerts on the weakness of the one at the point of the unnameable, may give rise to the desire to name the unnameable, to appropriate the proper of the proper through naming.

But it is in this very desire, which every truth puts on the agenda, that I perceive the figure of evil as such. To force a naming of the unnameable is to deny singularity as such; it is the moment in which, in the name of a truth's infinitely generic character, the resistance of what is absolutely singular in singularity, of that share of being of the proper which is subtracted from naming, appears as an obstacle to the deployment of a truth seeking to ensure its dominion over the situation. The imperialism of a truth – its worst desire – consists in invoking generic subtraction in order to force the subtraction of the unnameable, so that it may vanish in the light of naming.

We will call this a disaster. Evil is the disaster of a truth when the desire to force the naming of the unnameable is unleashed in fiction.

It is commonly held that evil is the negation of what is present and the denial of what is affirmed, that it is murder and death, that it is opposed to life. I would say instead that it is the denial of a subtraction. It is not self-affirmation that evil affects, but rather always that which is withdrawn and anonymous in the weakness of the one. Evil is not disrespect for the name of the other, but rather the will to name *at any price*.

Moreover, it is also commonly held that evil is mendacity, ignorance, murderous stupidity. But, alas, evil has the process of a truth as its radical condition. There is evil only in so far as there is an axiom of truth at the point of the undecidable, a trajectory of truth at the point of the indiscernible, an anticipation of the being of truth at the point of the generic, and the forcing in truth of a naming at the point of the unnameable.

If the forcing of the unnameable subtraction is a disaster, it is because it affects the situation as a whole by pursuing within it singularity as such, for which the unnameable is the emblem. In this sense, the desire in fiction to suppress the fourth subtractive operation unleashes a capacity for destruction latent in every truth, in the precise sense in which Mallarmé could write that 'Destruction was my Beatrice'.[8]

Accordingly, the ethics of a truth consists entirely in exercising a sort of restraint with regard to its powers. It is important that the combined effect of the undecidable, the indiscernible, and the generic – or of the event, the subject, and truth – should acknowledge as the fundamental limit for its trajectory that unnameable which Samuel Beckett chose as the title for one of his books.

Samuel Beckett was certainly not unaware of the hidden ravages inflicted on the subtraction of the proper by the desire for truth. He even saw in it the ineluctable violence of thought, when he has his Unnamable say this: 'I only think . . . once a certain degree of terror has been exceeded.'[9] But he also knew that the ultimate guarantee for the possibility of a peace among truths is rooted in the reserve of non-saying; in the limit of the voice vis-à-vis that which shows itself; in that which is subtracted from the absolute imperative to speak the truth. This is also what he intended when in *Molloy* he reminded us that '[t]o restore silence is the role of objects'[10] and when in *How It Is* he congratulates himself on the fact that 'the voice being so ordered I quote that of our total life it states only three quarters'.[11]

Subtracting lies at the source of every truth. But subtraction is also what, in the guise of the unnameable, governs and sets a limit to the subtractive trajectory. There is only one maxim in the ethics of a truth: do not subtract the last subtraction.

Which is something that Mallarmé, with whom I wish to conclude, says with customary precision in his 'Prose (for des Esseintes)'.

There is always the danger that a truth – however errant and incomplete it may be – takes itself, in the words of the poet, for an 'age of authority'. It then wants everything to be triumphantly named in the Summer of revelation. But the heart of what is, the 'southland' (*midi*) of our unconsciousness of being, does not and must not have a name. The site of the true, which is subtractively constructed – or, as the poet puts it elsewhere, the flower that a contour of absence has separated from every garden – itself remains, in its intimate depth, subtracted from the proper name. The sky and the map testify that this land did not exist. But it does exist, and this is what wears thin the authoritarian truth, for which only what has been named through the power of the generic exists. This erosion must be sustained by safeguarding the proper and the nameless. Let us conclude then by reading Mallarmé's poem, wherein everything I have said is dazzlingly rendered:

L'ère d'autorité se trouble
Lorsque, sans nul motif, on dit
De ce midi que notre double
Inconscience approfondit

Que, sol de cent iris, son site
Ils savent s'il a bien été
Ne porte pas de nom que cite
L'or de la trompette d'été.

The age of authority wears thin
When, without reason, it is stated
Of this southland which our twin
Unconsciousness has penetrated

That, soil of a hundred irises, its site,
They know if it was really born:
It bears no name that one could cite,
Sounded by summer's golden horn.[12]

CHAPTER 10
TRUTH: FORCING AND THE
UNNAMEABLE[1]

When a philosopher makes a claim about truth, is it not natural – 'natural' in a sense which etymology upholds through thoroughgoing artifice – for him to do so from the bias of his love? Doubtless, the Platonic gesture – registered, acclaimed, then reviled through the centuries – persists in discerning a connotation of superior intensity in the wise friendship of *philosophia*; especially when it is in the shelter of wisdom that we discover truth's enigma and, as a result, at the heart of serene friendship that we encounter the tempest of love. As Lacan demonstrated in his strange appropriation of a real *Symposium*, it is through this transference (in every sense of the word) that philosophy is able to proclaim itself 'love of truth'.

Thus when Lacan insists that the position of the psychoanalyst surely does not consist in loving truth, there can be no doubt that he is maintaining the stance he ended up describing as that of an 'anti-philosophy'.

Yet in doing so, Lacan clearly appoints himself educator for every philosophy to come. In my view, only those who have had the courage to work through Lacan's anti-philosophy without faltering deserve to be called 'contemporary philosophers'. There are not many of them. But it is as a contemporary philosopher that I will here endeavour to elucidate what I declare to be a return of truth. Let's say that I'm speaking here as a philosopher-subject supposed to know anti-philosophy[2] – and hence as a lover of truth supposed to know what little faith can be afforded to the protestations made in the name of such a love.

Lacan delineates his concept of the love of truth in the seminar entitled *The Reverse of Psychoanalysis*, which has recently been published in an edition I shall simply take as it is, without entering into the controversies that invariably attend the inscription of the living word into the dead letter.[3]

In this seminar, Lacan makes the radical claim that since truth is primordially a kind of powerlessness or weakness; if there is such a thing as the love of truth, it can only be the love of this powerlessness, the love of this weakness. It's worth noting that in this claim Lacan for once echoes

Nietzsche, for whom truth is in a certain regard the impotent form of power, or the name that the powerless give to power in order to disguise it.

But Lacan immediately distances himself from the Dionysian preacher. For Lacan, the weakness wherein truth dwells is not rooted in revenge or resentment. That which affects truth with an insurmountable restriction is, obviously enough, castration. Truth is the veil thrown over the impossibility of saying it all, of saying all of truth. It is both what can only be half-said and what disguises this acute powerlessness that restricts the access to saying – in an act of pretence, whereby it transforms itself into a total image of itself. Truth is the mask of its own weakness. In which regard Lacan now echoes Heidegger, for whom truth is the very veiling of being in its withdrawal. Except that Lacan distances himself completely from the pathos with which Heidegger characterizes the becoming-distress of the veil and the forgetting. For castration is structural, it is structure itself, so that for Lacan there can be no place for the primordially uncastrated, which is what the pre-Socratic thinkers and poets ultimately are for Heidegger.

What then, for Lacan, is the love of truth, given this authoritative status of structure? We must not shy away from the consequences: it is purely and simply *the love of castration.*

We are so accustomed to thinking of castration in terms of horror that we are astonished to hear Lacan discussing it in terms of love. Nevertheless, Lacan does not hesitate. In the seminar dated 14 January 1970 we read:

The love of truth is the love of that weakness whose veil we have lifted; it is the love of that which is hidden by truth, and which is called castration.[4]

Thus, under the guise of the love we bear toward it, truth affects castration with a veiling. Castration thereby manifests itself stripped of the horror that it inspires as a pure structural effect.

The philosopher will reformulate the matter as follows: truth is bearable for thought, which is to say, philosophically lovable, only in so far as one attempts to grasp it in what drives its *subtractive* dimension, as opposed to seeking its plenitude or complete saying.

So let us try to weigh truth in the scales of its power and its powerlessness, its process and its limit, its affirmative infinity and its essential subtraction – even if this weighing, and the concomitant desire to attain a precise measure of truth's indispensable mathematical connection (not to mention the demands of brevity), entails approximation.

I shall construct the scales for this weighing of truth by means of a quadruple disjunction:

1. The disjunction between transcendence and immanence. Truth is not of the order of something which stands above the givenness of experience; it proceeds or insists within experience as a singular figure of immanence.

2. The disjunction between the predicable and the non-predicable. There exists no single predicative trait capable of subsuming and totalizing the components of a truth. This is why we will say that a truth is nondescript or generic.

3. The disjunction between the infinite and the finite. Conceived in its being, as something that cannot be completed, a truth is an infinite multiplicity.

4. The disjunction between the nameable and the unnameable. A truth's capacity for disseminating itself into judgements within the field of knowledge is blocked by an unnameable point, whose name is forced only at the cost of disaster.

Thus a truth finds itself quadruply subtracted from the exposition of its being. It is neither a *supremum*, visible in the glare of its self-sufficiency, nor that which is circumscribed by a predicate of knowledge, nor that which subsists in the familiarity of its finitude, nor that whose erudite fecundity is blessed with boundless power.

To love truth is not only to love castration, but to love the figures in which its horror is drawn and quartered: immanence, the generic, the infinite, and the unnameable.

Let us consider them one by one.

That truth, or at least *our* truth, is purely immanent was one of Freud's simplest yet most fundamental insights. Freud was uncompromising in his defence of this principle, especially against Jung. It would be no exaggeration to say that one of Lacan's primary motivations was to mobilize this Freudian insight against the scientistic and moralistic objectivism of the Chicago school.

I will use the word 'situation' – the most anodyne word imaginable – to designate the multiple made up of circumstances, language, and objects, wherein some truth can be said to operate. We will say that this operation is *in* the situation, and is neither its end, nor its norm, nor its destiny. Similarly, the experience of the analyst clearly shows that a truth works through the subject – especially through his suffering – in the situation of analysis itself. Truth comes into being within this situation through the successive operations that make up the analysis. Moreover, it is a mistake to think that the existence of this truth constitutes a pre-given norm for what is observed in the analysis, or that it is a matter of discovering or revealing the truth, as though it were some secret entity buried, so to speak, in the deep exteriority of the situation. The whole point is that there is no depth, and depth is just another name – treasured by the hermeneuts – for transcendence.

Where does a truth come from then, if its process is strictly immanent and if it is not given as the secret depth or intimate essence of the situation? How can it advance within the situation if it has not always already been given within it? Lacan's genius lay in seeing that, as with Columbus's egg, the answer is already contained in the question. If a truth cannot originate from its being given, it must be because it has its origin in a disappearance. I call 'event' this originary disappearance supplementing the situation for the 'duration of a lightning flash; situated within it only in so far as nothing of it subsists; and insisting *in truth* precisely in so far as it cannot be repeated as presence. Obviously, the event is the philosophical analogue of (for example) what Freud called the primal scene. But since the latter is endowed with the force of truth only through its abolition, and has no place other than the disappearance of the having-taken-place, it would be futile to ask, using the realist categories proper to the situation, whether it is accurate or merely represents a fiction. This question remains genuinely undecidable, in the logical sense. Except that the effect of truth consists in retroactively validating the fact that at the point of this undecidable there was the disappearance – acutely real and henceforth immanent to the situation – not only of the undecidable, but of the very question of the undecidable.

Such is the first subtractive dimension of truth, whose immanence depends upon the undecidability of what that immanence retraces.

What then is a truth the truth of? There can be truth only of the situation wherein truth insists, because nothing transcendent to the situation is given to us. Truth is not a guarantor for the apprehension of something transcendent to the situation. Since a situation, grasped in its pure being, is only ever a particular multiple, this means that a truth is only ever a sub-multiple of that multiple, a subset of the set named 'situation'. Such is the rigour of the ontological requirement of immanence. Because a truth proceeds within a situation, what it bears witness to does not in any way exceed the situation. We could say a truth is *included* in that which it is the truth of.

Let me open a cautionary parenthesis at this stage. Cautionary because I have to admit that I am not, nor have ever been, nor will probably ever be either an analyst or an analysand, or even a psychoanalytic patient. I am the unanalysed. Can the unanalysed say something about analysis? You will have be the judge of that. It seems to me from what I have said so far that, if truth is at stake in analysis, it is not so much a truth of the subject as a truth of the analytical situation as such; a truth which, no doubt, the analysand will henceforth have to cope with, but which it would be one-sided to describe as belonging to him or her alone. Analysis seems to me a situation wherein the analysand is provided with the painful opportunity for encountering a truth, for *crossing* a truth along his path. He emerges from this encounter either armed or disarmed. Perhaps this approach sheds some light on the mysteries of what Lacan, no doubt thinking of the real as impasse, called 'the pass'.

But we now find ourselves precisely in the domain of the impasse. I said that a truth comes into being at the end of its process only as a subset of the situation-set. Yet the situation registers any number of subsets. Indeed, this provides the broadest possible definition of knowledge: to name subsets of the situation. The function of the language of the situation consists in gathering together the elements of the situation according to one or other predicative trait, thereby constituting the extensional correlate for a concept. A subset – such as those of cats or dogs in a perceptual situation, or of hysterical or obsessive traits and symptoms in an analytical situation – is captured through concepts of the language on the basis of indices of recognition attributable to all the terms or elements that fall under this concept. I call this conceptual and nominal swarming of forms of knowledge, the encyclopedia of the situation. The encyclopedia is what classifies subsets. But it is also the polymorphous interweaving of forms of knowledge that language continually elicits.

Yet if a truth is merely a subset of the situation, how does it distinguish itself from a rubric of knowledge? This question is philosophically crucial. It is a matter of knowing whether the price of immanence may not be purely and simply the reduction of truth to knowledge; in other words, a decisive concession to all the variants of positivism. More profoundly, the question is whether immanence may not entail some sort of neoclassical regression that would forsake the impetus given by Kant, and later retrieved by Heidegger, to the crucial distinction between truth and knowledge, which is also the distinction between thought and cognition. Simplifying somewhat, this neoclassical version of immanence would basically end up claiming that once you have diagnosed an analysand's *case*, which is to say, recognized him as hysterical or obsessive or phobic; once you have established the predicative trait inscribing him in the encyclopedia of the analytical situation, the real work has been done. It is then only a matter of *drawing consequences*.

Because of the way in which he envisaged his fidelity to Freud, Lacan categorically rejected this nosological vision of the analytical situation. To that end, he took up the modern notion of a non-conceptual gap between truth and forms of knowledge and projected it onto the field of psychoanalysis. Not only did he distinguish between truth and knowledge, he also showed that a truth is essentially unknown; that it quite literally constitutes a *hole* in forms of knowledge.

In doing so – and this is in my opinion a point whose consequences have yet to be fully grasped – Lacan declared that psychoanalysis was not a form of knowledge but a way of thinking.

Yet despite the claims of those who would like to effect a theological recuperation of psychoanalysis – and they are indefatigable, rather like someone who has figured out how to turn pig-feed into a communion wafer – and who like to indulge in delectable speculations about the transcendence of the Big Other, Lacan himself, on the whole, refused any compromise about the immanence of truth.

He thereby had to force our impasse and establish that, although reducible to a depthless subset of the situation, a truth of the situation is nonetheless heterogeneous to all those subsets registered by forms of knowledge.

This is the fundamental meaning of the maxim concerning 'half-saying'. That a truth cannot be entirely said means that its all, the subset that it constitutes within the situation, cannot be captured by means of a predicative trait that would turn it into a subsection of the encyclopedia. The truth at stake in the analysis of such and such a woman cannot be assimilated to the fact that she is, as they say, a hysteric. There is no doubt that many of the components of the truth operating in this situation possess the distinctive traits of what, in the register of knowledge, is called hysteria. But to say so is not to do anything *in truth*. For the truth in question necessarily organizes other components, whose traits are not pertinent as far as the encyclopedic concept of hysteria is concerned, and it is only in so far as these components subtract the set from the predicate of hysteria that a truth, rather than a form of knowledge, proceeds in its singularity. Thus however confident the diagnosis of hysteria and the consequences drawn from it may be, not only do they not constitute a saying of truth, they do not even constitute its half-saying, since the fact that they are ascribable to knowledge entails that they *completely* miss the dimension of truth.

A truth is a subset of the situation but one whose components cannot be totalized by means of a predicate of the language, however sophisticated that predicate. Thus a truth is an indistinct subset; so nondescript in the way it gathers together its components that no trait shared by the latter would allow the subset to be identified by knowledge.

Obviously, it is because it is included within the situation in the form of a singular indeterminacy of its concept, and because it is subtracted from the classificatory grasp of the language of the encyclopedia, that such a subset is a truth of the situation as such, an immanent production of its pure multiple being, a truth of its being qua being – as opposed to a knowledge of this or that regional particularity of the situation.

As is so often the case, mathematics bolsters Lacan's insight. At the beginning of the 1960s, the mathematician Paul Cohen showed how, for a given set, it was possible to identify subsets of it possessing all the characteristics outlined above. Cohen calls a subset that has been subtracted from every determination in terms of a fixed expression of the language a *generic* subset. Moreover, he uses a demonstrative procedure to prove that the hypothesis that generic subsets exist is consistent.

Twenty years earlier, Gödel had provided a rigorous definition for the idea of a subset named in knowledge. These are subsets whose elements validate a fixed expression of the language. Gödel had called these *constructible* subsets. But Cohen's generic subsets are non-constructible. They are too indeterminate to correspond to, or be totalized by, a single predicative expression.

There can be no doubt that the opposition between constructible sets and generic sets provides a purely immanent ontological basis for the opposition between knowledge and truth. In this regard, Cohen's demonstration that the existence of generic subsets is consistent amounts to a genuinely modern proof that truths can exist and that they are irreducible to any encyclopedic datum whatsoever. Cohen's theorem mobilizes the ontological radicality of the matheme to consummate the modernity inaugurated by the Kantian distinction between thought and knowledge.

That a truth is generic rather than constructible, as Lacan brilliantly intuited in his maxim about truth's half-saying, also implies that a truth is infinite – our third disjunction.

This point seems to rebut every philosophy of finitude, in spite of the way Lacan inscribed finitude at the heart of desire through the thesis of the *objet petit a*. The being that sustains desire resides entirely in this object, which is also its cause. And since the defining characteristic of the *objet petit a* is that it is always a *partial* object, its finitude is constitutive.

But the dialectic of the finite and the infinite is extremely tortuous in Lacan, and I dare say the philosopher's eye here glimpses the limit, and hence the real, of what psychoanalysis is capable when conceived as a form of thinking, which is indeed how Lacan envisaged it.

That a truth is infinite constitutes an objection to the philosophical rumination on finitude only if that truth remains immanent, and hence only in so far as it touches on the real. If truth is transcendent, or supra-real, it can very well, under the name 'God' or some other name – such as 'the Other' – consign the entire destiny of the subject to finitude.

I said that Lacan sided with the immanence of truth. But I added: 'on the whole'. For, strictly speaking, he observes the constraint of immanence only within what could be called the primordial motivation of his thought. Elsewhere, we encounter significant oscillations, arising from Lacan's tendency to equivocate when it comes to severing every link with the hermeneutics of finitude to which, alas, the majority of contemporary philosophizing is ultimately reducible. Today, this hermeneutics of finitude seems to be in the process of reinstalling a pious discourse, a religiosity whose little God would seem to constitute the minimum of transcendence compatible with that democratic conviviality to which we are told there is no longer any conceivable alternative.

There is no doubt that we owe to Lacan, and specifically to his implacable insistence on the distinction between the logic of sense and the logic of truth, the conceptual apparatus required to expose the abjection of pious discourse. As for democratic conviviality, we know it was not Lacan's forte. Moreover, that it is not even a satisfactory ideal becomes more apparent every day when we consider those who lay claim to his legacy.

Nevertheless, the equivocation on Lacan's part persists. It is this equivocation that leads him to say in *Or Worse . . .*[5] – to choose just one example among many – that Cantor's non-denumerable transfinite cardinals represent 'an object which I would have to characterize as mythic'. I would counter that it is not possible to proceed very far in drawing the consequences of the infinity of the true without insisting that non-denumerable cardinals are real, not mythic.

To advance beyond Lacan perhaps we must above all put our trust in the matheme on this particular point – which is, of course, another way of remaining faithful to the master. This entails first and foremost that we hold fast to the affirmation, by way of mathematical proof, that every truth is infinite.

Let us suppose that a truth were finite. As a finite subset of the situation, it is made up of the terms a_1, a_2, and so on up to a_n, where n fixes the intrinsic dimension of this truth. In other words, it is a truth comprising n components. It immediately follows that there exists a predicate appropriate to this subset, which, since it is inscribed in the encyclopedia, falls under the purview of knowledge. This is to say that a finite subset could not be generic. It is necessarily constructible. Consider the predicate 'identical with a_1, or identical with a_2, . . . or identical with a_n', which is always available in the language of a situation. The set made up of the terms in question – i.e. the terms a_1, a_2, and so on up to a_n – is exactly circumscribed by this predicate. In other words, this predicate constructs this subset; it identifies it in the language, thereby excluding the possibility of its being generic. Consequently, it is not a truth. QED.

The infinity of a truth immediately implies that it cannot be completed. For the subset that it constitutes, and which is delineated on the basis of the eventuell disappearance, is composed through a succession that inaugurates a time – e.g. the highly particular time proper to analysis. Whatever the intrinsic norm governing its extension, such a time remains irremediably finite. And so the truth that unfolds within it does not attain the complete composition of its infinite being. Freud's genius was to grasp this point in the guise of the infinite dimension of analysis, which always leaves open, like a gaping chasm, the truth that slips into the time inaugurated by analysis.

We now seem to find ourselves driven back to castration, as to that which truth veils, thereby granting us permission to love it.

For if a truth remains open onto the infinity of its being, how are we to gauge its power? To say that truth is half-said is to say too little. The relation between the finitude proper to the time of its composition – a time founded by the event of a disappearance – and the infinity of its being is a relation without measure. It is better to say instead that a truth is little-said, or even that a truth is almost not spoken. Is it then legitimate to speak of a power of the true, a power required in order to found the concept of its eventual powerlessness? In the seminar I quoted at the outset, Lacan plainly states that 'it seems to be among the analysts, and among them in particular, that, invoking certain taboo words with which their discourse is festooned, one never notices what truth – which is to say, powerlessness – is'.[6] I concur. But in order to be neither like those festooned analysts, nor simply jealous of the festooned, we shall have to think the powerlessness of a truth, which presupposes that we first be able to conceive its power.

I conceive of this power – perhaps already recognized by Freud in the category of 'working through' – in terms of the concept *of forcing*, which I take directly from Cohen's mathematical work. Forcing is the point at which a truth, although incomplete, authorizes anticipations of knowledge concerning not what is but *what will have been if truth attains completion*.

This anticipatory dimension requires that truth judgements be formulated in the future perfect. Thus while almost nothing can be said about what a truth is, when it comes to what happens *on condition that that truth will have been*, there exists a forcing whereby almost everything can be stated.

As a result, a truth operates through the retroaction of an almost nothing and the anticipation of an almost everything.

The crucial point, which Paul Cohen settled in the realm of ontology, i.e. of mathematics, is the following: you certainly cannot straightforwardly name the elements of a generic subset, since the latter is at once incomplete in its infinite composition and subtracted from every predicate which would directly identify it in the language. But you can maintain that *if* such and such an element *will have been* in the supposedly complete generic subset, *then* such and such a statement, rationally connectable to the element in question, is, or rather will have been, correct. Cohen describes this method – a method constraining the correctness of statements *according to an anticipatory condition bearing on the composition of an infinite generic subset* – as that *of forcing*.

I say 'correct' or 'correctness' because Lacan superimposes the opposition between the correct and the true onto the opposition between knowledge and truth. But it is necessary to see why the statement caught up in forcing cannot, without serious confusion, be called true. For its value is determined only according to a condition of existence which pertains to a generic subset, and hence according to a condition of truth.

I use the term *veridical* to describe the value of a 'forced' statement. It simultaneously indicates the gap as well as the connection with truth. Thus, extrapolating from Cohen's matheme to what it prescribes for the philosopher, we will say that a truth proceeds in situation, devoid of the power either to say or to complete itself. In this sense truth is absolutely castrated, almost not being what it is. Nevertheless, with regard to any given statement, truth has the power to anticipate the following conditional judgement: if this or that component will have figured in a supposedly complete truth, then the statement in question will have been either veridical or erroneous. The power of a truth, deployed in the dimension of the future perfect, consists in legislating about what is veridically sayable, in anticipation of its own existence. Obviously, what is veridically sayable is a matter of knowledge, and the category of the veridical is a category of knowledge. Consequently, we will say that although a truth is castrated with regard to its own immediate power, it is all-powerful with regard to possible forms of knowledge. The bar of castration does not fall between truth and knowledge. It separates truth from itself, thereby releasing truth's power of hypothetical anticipation within the encyclopedic field of knowledge. This power is that of forcing.

I maintain that the analytical experience is built on such a basis. That which, little by little, comes to be articulated in the course of analysis is not only that which weaves the interminable infinity of the true into a finite, metered time, but also – and especially with regard to the rare interventions of the analyst – the anticipatory marking of what it will have been possible to say veridically, in so far as this or that sign, act, or signifier will have been supposed as a component of the truth. We know that this anticipatory marking depends upon the future perfect tense of the empirical completion of analysis, beyond which any supposition as to truth's completion becomes impossible, since the situation has been terminated and with it the forcing of a possible veridicality proper to the judgements about that situation. This testifies as to how an enunciated veridicality can be called knowledge, but knowledge *in truth*. As to what this knowledge truly is, this knowledge 'forced' by the treatment, the analysand is our sole witness, operating through a retroaction that balances the anticipation of forcing.

Once again, as the unanalysed, I need to sound a note of caution here and remark that I am not sure if it is appropriate to call the act of the analyst an interpretation. I would prefer to call it a forcing – despite the word's scandalously authoritarian ring. For it is always a matter of intervening according to the suspended hypothesis of a truth taking its course in the analytical situation.

I do not think it too forceful to register a hint of doubt as to the value of interpretation in many of the dead master's texts. This should not be too surprising when one recalls that all sorts of hermeneuts, stepping into the breach opened up by the faithful Paul Ricoeur, have tried to make the term 'interpretation' bear the burden of the putative link between psychoanalysis and the revamped forms of pious discourse. Let me be blunt: I do not believe analysis consists in interpretation. It is ruled by truth, not meaning. But it certainly does not consist in *discovering* truth, since, truth being generic, we know it is vain to hope that it could be uncovered. The sole remaining hope is that analysis would consist in forcing a knowledge into truth through the risky game of anticipation, by means of which a generic truth in the process of coming into being delivers in fragmentary fashion a constructible knowledge.

Having gauged the power of truth, must we say it extends to all those statements that circulate in the situation in which it operates, without exception – even if only on condition of the wager about its coming into being as a multiple? Does truth, in spite (and because) of its generic nature, possess the power of naming all imaginable veridicalities?

To respond affirmatively would be to disregard the return of castration, and of the love that binds us to it through truth, in the terminal form of an absolute obstacle – a term which, although given in the situation, is radically subtracted from the grip of veridical evaluation. There is a point that is unforceable, so to speak. I call this point the unnameable, while in the realm of psychoanalysis Lacan called it enjoyment.

Let us consider a situation in which a truth proceeds as the trace of a vanished event; a situation immanently supplemented by the becoming of its own truth. For a generic truth is the paradox of a purely internal anonymous supplement, an immanent addition. What is the real for such a configuration?

Let us rigorously distinguish between being and the real. This distinction is already operative in Lacan's very first seminar, since on 30 June 1954 he claims that the three fundamental passions – love, hate and ignorance – can be inscribed 'only in the realm of being, and not in that of the real'.[7] Thus, if the love of truth is a passion, this love is certainly directed toward the being of truth, but it falters upon encountering its real.

As far as the being of truth is concerned, we have already acquired its concept: it is that of a generic multiplicity subtracted from the constructions of knowledge. To love truth is to love the generic as such and this is why, as in all love, we have here something that goes astray, something that evades the order of language, something that is maintained in the errancy of an excess through the power of the forcings it permits.

Nevertheless, there remains the question of the real upon which this very errancy and the power that it founds come to falter.

In this regard, I would say that in the realm determined by a situation and the generic becoming of its truth, what testifies to a real is a single term or point – one and only one – where the power of truth is cut short. When it comes to this term, no anticipatory hypothesis about the generic subset can allow judgement to be forced. It is a genuinely unforceable term. No matter how advanced the process of truth, this term may never be prescribed in such a way that it would be conditioned by this truth. No matter how great the transformative resources proper to the immanent tracing of the true, no naming is appropriate for this term of the situation. That is why I call it unnameable. Unnameable should be understood not in terms of the available resources of knowledge and the encyclopedia, but in the precise sense in which it remains out of reach for the veridical anticipations founded on truth. It is not unnameable 'in itself', which would be meaningless, but unnameable with regard to the singular process of a truth. The unnameable emerges only in the domain of truth.

This sheds some light on why, in the situation of the psychoanalytic treatment, which is precisely one of the sites wherein one supposes a truth to be at work, enjoyment is at once what that truth deploys in terms of the real and what remains forever subtracted from the veridical expanse of the sayable. This is because, from the perspective of psychoanalytical truth, or the truth of the situation of treatment, enjoyment is precisely the point of the unnameable that constitutes a stumbling block for the forcings permitted by this truth.

It is imperative to insist that this term is *unique*. There cannot be two or more unnameables for a singular truth. The Lacanian maxim, 'there is oneness', is here fastened to the irreducible real, to what could be called the 'grain of the real' jamming the machinery of truth, whose power consists in being the machinery of forcings and hence the machinery for producing finite veridicalities from the vantage point of a truth that cannot be accomplished. Here, the jamming effected by the One-real is opposed to the path opened up by veridicality.

This effect of oneness in the real, elicited by the power of truth, constitutes truth's powerless obverse. This is signalled straight away by the peculiar difficulty that arises when it comes to *thinking* this effect. How can we think that which subtracts itself from every veridical naming? How can we think in truth that which is excluded from the powers of truth? Is to think it not also thereby to name it? And how could we ever name the unnameable?

Lacan's response to this paradoxical appeal is never explicitly spelled out. When it comes to trans-phallic or secondary *jouissance*, one sees Lacan resorting to the triangle of the feminine, the infinite and the unsayable, about which the least that can be said is that it seems to hark back to a pre-Freudian era. That feminine enjoyment ties the infinite to the unsayable, and that mystical ecstasy provides evidence for this, is a theme I would characterize as cultural. One feels that, even in Lacan, it has not yet been submitted to a radical test by the ideal of the matheme.

Perhaps one of the sources of Lacan's difficulties resides in the paradox of the unnameable, a paradox which I will formulate as follows: if the unnameable is unique within the domain of a truth, is it not then nameable precisely on account of this property? For if what is not named is unique, not being named functions *as its proper name*. Ultimately, wouldn't 'the unnameable' be the proper name for the real of a situation traversed by its truth? Wouldn't unsayable enjoyment be the name for the real of the subject, once he or she comes to grips with his or her truth, or with *a* truth within the therapeutic situation?

But then the unnameable is named in truth; it is forced, and truth possesses a genuinely boundless reservoir of power.

Here once again, mathematics comes to our aid. In 1968, the logician Furkhen proved that the uniqueness of the unnameable is no objection to its existence. Furkhen created a mathematical situation in which the resources of the language, along with its capacities for naming, are clearly defined, and in which there exists one term, and one term only, which cannot receive a name, which means that it cannot be identified by means of an expression of the language.

Consequently, in the register of the matheme, it is perfectly consistent to maintain that one term and one term only in a given situation remains unforceable for a generic truth. It is thus that, in the situation supplemented by its truth, the real of that supplementation is attested to. No matter how powerful a truth is, no matter how capable of veridicality it proves to be, this power comes to falter upon a single term, which at a stroke effects the swing from all-powerfulness to powerlessness and displaces our love of truth from its appearance, the love of the generic, to its essence, the love of the unnameable.

Not that the love of the generic is nothing. By itself, it is radically distinct from the love of opinions, which is the passion of ignorance; or from the disastrous desire for complete constructibility. But the love of the unnameable lies beyond even the generic, and it alone allows the love of truth to be maintained without disaster or dissolution coming to affect the veridical in its entirety. For where truth is concerned, only by undergoing the ordeal of its powerlessness do we discover the ethic required for assuming its power.

The circumstances in which we find ourselves in this autumn of 1991 enjoin me to conclude, in an apparently incongruous manner, with Vladimir Ilyich Ulyanov, also known as Lenin, whose statues it is fashionable nowadays to tear down.

Let us note in passing that, were a Lacanian tempted to join in the zeal of those now toppling statues, he or she would do well to reflect on the following paragraph from the seminar dated 20 March 1973, which begins thus:

> Marx and Lenin, Freud and Lacan are not coupled in being. It is via the letter they found in the Other that, as beings of knowledge, they proceed two by two, in a supposed Other.[8]

Thus the would-be Lacanian toppler of Lenin's statues has to explain why Lacan identified himself as Freud's Lenin.

Let's add that, at a time when many analysts are worried about their relation to the state, even if only in the monumental guise of the Inland Revenue and the European Union, they would surely do better to consider Lenin's writings than those of the statue-topplers – supposing such writings exist.

Lenin felt obliged to write: 'Theory is all-powerful because it is true.' This is not incorrect, since forcing subordinates to itself in anticipatory fashion the expanse of the situation through a potentially infinite network of veridical judgements. But, once again, this is only to say the half of it. It is necessary to add: 'Theory is powerless, because it is true.' This second half of the statement's correctness is supported by the fact that forcing finds itself in the impasse of the unnameable. But on its own, this second half of correctness is no more capable of staving off disaster than the first.

Thus Lenin seems to have adopted a relation of love vis-à-vis castration that veils the latter in that half of power which it founds. By way of contrast, it is only too apparent that the statue-topplers seem to have adopted the direct love of powerlessness which does nothing but pave the way for situations devoid of truth.

Is this oscillation inevitable? I don't think so. Under the stern guarantee of the matheme, we can advance into that open expanse wherein the love of truth is related to castration from the twofold perspective of power and powerlessness, of forcing and the unnameable. All that is required of us is to hold both to the veridical and to what cannot be completed; to analysis terminable *and* interminable. Or, as Samuel Beckett puts it in the final words of a book which is not called *The Unnamable* for nothing: 'you must go on, I can't go on, I will go on.'[9]

CHAPTER 11
KANT'S SUBTRACTIVE ONTOLOGY

If at first sight it appears that Kant has no ontology, since he seems to declare the very idea inconsistent, this is because he is above all the philosopher of relation, of the linkages between phenomena, and this constitutive primacy of relation forbids all access to the being of the thing as such. Are not Kant's famous categories of experience a veritable conceptual catalogue of every conceivable kind of relation (inherence, causality, community, limitation, totality, etc.)? Is it not for Kant a question of showing that the ultimate basis for the *bound* character of representations cannot be sought in the being of the represented and must be superimposed upon it through the constituting synthetic power of the transcendental subject? It might seem as if the Kantian solution to the problem of structured representation amounted to identifying the pure inconsistent multiple (or being qua being, in my conception of ontology) with the phenomenality of the phenomenon, and the counting-as-one (in my vocabulary, being qua given or being 'in situation') with relation, which is itself set out on the basis of the structuring activity of the subject. The experience of the phenomenal manifold would be rendered consistent through the power of counting-as-one (i.e. the universal linkages) that the subject imposes upon experience.

But that is not the case. For in one of his most radical insights, Kant firmly distinguishes between *binding* (*Verbindung*), which is synthesis of the manifold of phenomena, and *unity* (*Einheit*), which provides the originary basis for binding as such: 'Binding is representation of the synthetic unity of the manifold. The representation of this unity cannot therefore arise out of the binding. On the contrary, it is what, by adding itself to the representation of the manifold, first makes possible the concept of the binding.'[1]

Here then it seems that, far from being resolved through the categories of relation, the problem of how the inconsistent manifold comes to be counted-as-one must have been decided in advance in order for relational synthesis to be possible. Kant sees very clearly that the consistency of multiple-presentation is originary, and that the relations whereby phenomena arise out of that multiple-presentation are merely derivative realities of experience.

The question of the qualitative unity of experience puts relation in its place, which is secondary. It is first necessary to ground the fact that experience presents unified multiplicities; only then is it possible to think the origin of phenomenal relations.

In other words, it is necessary to understand that the source of the *order* in experience (the synthetic unity of the manifold) cannot be the same as that of the *one*. The place of the former is in the transcendental system of categories. The latter is necessarily a special function, one which Kant certainly ascribes to the understanding, but which is already presupposed in categorial 'functioning'. Kant calls this supreme function of the understanding – the guarantor of the general unity of experience, and hence of 'the law of the one' – 'originary apperception'. If we set aside the subjective connotation in the notion of originary apperception, which is conceived of by Kant as the '*transcendental* unity of self-consciousness',[2] and focus strictly on its functioning, we should have no difficulty recognizing in it what I call the counting-as-one, which Kant applies to representation in general, conceived as a universal abstract situation. Originary apperception is the name for the fact that nothing can enter into presentation without having been submitted a priori to the determination of its unity: 'Synthetic unity of the manifold of intuitions, as generated *a priori*, is thus the ground of the identity of apperception itself, which precedes *a priori* all *my* determinate thought.'[3] What makes boundedness possible is not the bind as such, which, from this point of view, in-exists, but the pure faculty of binding, which is not reducible to effective relations since only the one can account for it; it is the originary law for the consistency of the multiple, the capacity for 'bringing the manifold of given representations under the unity of apperception'.[4]

Thus Kant clearly conceives of the distinction between the counting-as-one as guarantor of consistency and originary structure for all presentation, and binding, which characterizes all *representable* structures, in terms of the gap between pure originary apperception (the function of unity) and the system of categories (the function of synthetic binding) within the transcendental activity of the understanding.

But Kant introduces originary apperception only as a precondition for a complete solution to the problem of relation. It is the attempt to elucidate order, which is for him the correlate of knowledge, that enjoins him to think the one. What I mean is this (which has been compellingly indicated by Heidegger): what is always problematic in Kant is not so much the critical radicality of his conclusions, in which regard he excels in audacity, but rather the singular narrowness of the means of access to this radicality. In truth, his problematic does not have its origin in the question of the possibility of presentation in general. The primary question for him is that of knowing how a priori synthetic judgements are possible, by which he means those universally acknowledged bindings which he believes to be operative in Euclidian mathematics or Newtonian physics. Although it has its point of departure in what is probably an erroneous analysis of the form of scientific statements, the rigour of his procedure leads him to radical conditions and conclusions – such as those of unity and binding. But the limiting effect of the point of departure extends into the consequences, which do not always clearly deliver the full extent of their significance.

To approach the 'there is oneness' in terms of the 'there is binding' entails certain consequences for the doctrine of the one. There is in Kant a distinct trace of the fact that the supreme function of the counting-as-one is invoked only because an originary consistency is ultimately required in order to support the binding activity of the categories. As a result, this 'one' will be conceived only for the needs of binding, the concept of consistency will be limited to what is required by the intrinsically relational nature of the phenomenal manifold, and the fundamental structure of presentation will be subordinated to the illusory structure of representation. This trace, which reduces the originary presentation of the multiple-as-one to the status of necessary condition for the conception of representable bindings, resides in the fact that, in Kant, the one-multiple is limited to the form of the object. Ultimately, if Kant is only able to think the one-multiple in terms of the narrow representability of the object, it is because the movement of his discourse subordinates the question of presentative consistency to the resolution of the critical problem, which is conceived of as an epistemological problem. Kantian ontology, which Heidegger characterizes so aptly, labours beneath the shade of its inception in the pure logic of cognition.

But the category of the object is not pertinent when it comes to designating what exists in so far as the latter manifests itself in situation as the counted-one of the pure multiple. Only from the perspective of binding does the object designate the one. The object is the aspect of the existent that is representable according to the illusion of the bind. The word 'object' is no more than an equivocal compromise between two entirely separate problematics: that of the counting-as-one of the inconsistent multiple (the appearance of being), and that of the connected, empirical character of existents. The notion of object is an equivocation, one that corresponds to that other typically Kantian equivocation, which ascribes both the supreme function of unity – originary apperception – and the categorial function of binding to the single term 'understanding'.

When Kant writes that 'the transcendental unity of apperception is that unity through which all the manifold given in an intuition is united in the concept of an object',[5] he reduces the one-multiple to the object in such a way as to allow the same term to also designate what is bound in representation by these bindings. Correlated with originary apperception as the unity available to it in the manifold of presentations, the object will also be correlated with the categories conceived as 'concepts of an object in general, by means of which the intuition of an object is regarded as *determined* in respect of one of the *logical functions* of judgment'.[6] That what exists in experience is also an object within it is evidence of the 'double register' in which Kant's argument operates: at once ontological, in accordance with the one (which is not) of being (which is multiple); and epistemological, in accordance with the logical form of judgement. But aside from the fact that it is supposed to provide a basis for the bind or relation – which Hume was finally right to consider a pure fiction, devoid of being – the trouble with this equivocation concerning the object is that it weakens the radical distinction, boldly proposed by Kant, between the origin of the one and the origin of relation.

For Kant holds to his conviction that the a priori conditions for the binding of phenomena must include, under the name of object, the supreme condition of the one as that which provides stability for what is manifested in the field of representations. What other meaning can we give to the famous formulation: 'the conditions of the *possibility of experience* in general are likewise conditions of the *possibility of the objects of experience*',[7] given that the word 'object' here explicitly serves as a pivot between the condition for the consistency of presentation (referring back to the multiple as such, or the originary structure), and the derivative condition of the link between representable 'objects' (referring back to empirical multiplicity, or illusory situations)?

Granted, Kant is well aware that what is left undetermined by the object is 'the being of the object', its objectivity, the pure 'something in general = x' that provides a basis for the being of binding without that x itself ever being presented or bound. And we also know that x is the pure or inconsistent multiple, and hence that the object, in so far as it is the correlate of the apparent binding, is devoid of being. Kant has an acute sense of the subtractive nature of ontology, of the void through which the presentative situation is conjoined to its being. By the same token, the existent-correlate of originary apperception conceived as non-existent operation of the counting-as-one is not, strictly speaking, the object, but rather the form of the object in general – which is to say, that absolutely indeterminate being from which the very fact that there is an object originates. At the most intense point in his ontological meditation, Kant comes to conceive of the operation of the count as *the correlation of two voids*.

Kant splits both terms in the subject/object pairing. The empirical subject, which exists 'according to the determinations of our state in inner sense' and which is changeable, without fixity or permanence, has as its correlate represented phenomena, which 'as representations, [have] their object, and can themselves in turn become objects of other representations'.[8] The transcendental subject, as given in originary apperception – the supreme guarantor of objective unity (and hence of the unity of the representation of objects), relative to which 'representations of objects is alone possible',[9] 'pure, originary, unchangeable consciousness'[10] – has as its correlate an object 'which cannot itself be intuited by us'[11] because it is the form of objectivity in general, the 'transcendental object = x',[12] which is distinct from empirical objects. This object is not one among 'several' objects because it is *the general concept of consistency for all possible bound objectivity*, the principle that provides that oneness on the basis of which there are objects available *for* binding. The transcendental object is 'throughout all our knowledge one and the same = x'.[13]

So on the one hand we have the subject of experience (immediate self-consciousness) with its multiple correlates, the objects bound in representation; and on the other we have originary apperception (pure, singular consciousness) with its correlate, the object of objectivity, the postulated x from which bound *objects* derive their unitary form.

But the feature common both to originary apperception as transcendental proto-subject and this x as transcendental proto-object is that, as the primitive, invariant forms required for the possibility of representation, this subject and this object remain absolutely un-presented: they are referred to, over and above all possible experience, only as the void withdrawn from being, for which all we have are names.

The subject of originary apperception is merely a necessary 'numerical unity', an immutable power of oneness, and is unknowable as such. Kant's entire critique of the Cartesian *cogito* is based on the impossibility of maintaining the transcendental subject's absolute power of oneness as an instance of knowledge, as the determination of a point of the real. Originary apperception is an exclusively logical form, an empty necessity: 'beyond this logical meaning of the "I", we have no knowledge of the subject in itself, which as substratum underlies this "I", as it does all thoughts'.[14]

As for the transcendental object = x, Kant explicitly declares that it 'is nothing to us – being as it is something that has to be distinct from all our representations'.[15]

The subtractive radicality of Kantian ontology culminates in grounding representation in the relation between an empty logical subject and an object that is nothing.

Moreover, I cannot accept Heidegger's account of the differences between the first and second editions of the *Critique of Pure Reason*. For Heidegger, Kant retreated 'from the doctrine of the transcendental imagination'. According to Heidegger's exegesis, the 'spontaneous impetus' of the first version posited the imagination as that 'third faculty' (beside those of sensibility and understanding) providing a basis for the regime of the one and thereby guaranteeing the possibility of ontological knowledge. Heidegger reproaches Kant for failing to go further in exploring this 'unknown root' of the essence of man and for reducing the imagination to a mere operation of the understanding. Kant, he says, 'perceived the unknown and was forced to retreat. It was not just that the transcendental power of imagination frightened him, but rather that in between [the two editions] pure reason as reason drew him increasingly under its spell'.[16]

In my opinion, Kant's decision not to resort to the positivity of a third faculty (the imagination), his reduction of the problem of the one to that of a mere operation of the understanding, testify to his critical intransigence and his refusal to concede anything to the aesthetic prestige of the ontologies of presence. The 'prestige of pure reason' may well be another name for this intransigence when faced with the great temptation. For Kant, this is also where the genuine danger lies: that of having to acknowledge, from the perspective of the transcendental subject as well as from that of the object = x, the crucial significance of the void, thereby illuminating – for the first time independently of all negative theology – the paths of a subtractive ontology.

Is this to say that Kant's enterprise is entirely successful? No, because it continues to bear the trace of the fact that the origin of the deduction lies in the theory of binding. Kant effectively ascribes the foundational function to the *relation* between two voids. He does so, in the final analysis, because he is attempting to ground the 'there is' of objects, the objectivity of the object, which is the sole support for the deployment of the categorial binding of the manifold of representations. For Kant, the object remains the sole name for the one in representation. The synthetic unity of consciousness is required not only for knowledge of the object, but because it 'is a condition under which every intuition must stand *in order to become an object for me*. For otherwise, in the absence of this synthesis, the manifold would *not* be united in one consciousness'.[17] The subordination of theory to the knowledge of universal relations (its epistemological intent) forces the power of the counting-as-one to admit representable objects as its consequence and splits the void in conformity with the general idea of the subject/object relation, which remains the unquestioned framework for ontology as such.

Kantian Critique hesitates on the threshold of the ultimate step, which consists in positing that relation is not, and that this non-being of relation *differs in kind* from the non-being of the one, so that it is impossible to arrange an identitarian symmetry between the void of the counting-as-one (the transcendental subject) and the void as name of being (the object = x). Naturally, this gesture would also posit that the object is not the category through which thought gains access to the being of representations. It would also accept the dissolution of both object and relation in pure multiple presentation, without thereby relapsing into Humean scepticism.

Nevertheless, Kant is an extremely scrupulous and rigorous philosopher. There is no doubt he saw how, in wanting to ground the universality of relations, he was in fact opening up an unthinkable abyss between the withdrawal of the transcendental object and the absolute unity of originary apperception; between the ontological site of binding and the function of the one. The hesitations and retractions attested to by the major differences between the two editions of the *Critique of Pure Reason*, which have a particular bearing on the status of the transcendental subject, do not, in my opinion, stem from hesitations over the role of imagination. They are the price to be paid for the problematic relation between the narrowness of the premises (examination of the form of judgments) and the extent of the consequences (the void as point of being). It is clear that the root of this difficulty lies in the notion of object – a topic to which Heidegger devotes a decisive exegesis. Kant burdens himself with a notion that, pertinent though it may be for a critical doctrine of binding, should be dissolved by the operations of ontology.

By the same token, faced with the abyss opened up in being by the double naming of the void (according to the subject and according to the object), Kant will take up the problem again but from another angle, by asking himself where and how these two voids can in turn be counted as one. To answer these questions, an entirely different framework will be necessary, which is to say, a situation other than the epistemological one. What is essentially at stake in the *Critique of Pure Reason* is the demonstration that both the void of the subject and the void of the object belong to a single realm of being, which Kant will call the supra-sensible. From this point of view, far from being the instance of 'metaphysical' regression it is sometimes regarded as, the second Critique constitutes a *necessary* dialectical reworking of the ontological impasses of the first. Its aim, in a different situation (that of voluntary action), is to count as one that which, in the cognitive situation, remained the enigmatic correlate of two absences.

Nevertheless, in the register of knowledge, Kant's powerful ontological intuitions remain tethered to a starting point restricted to the form of judgement (which, it must be said, is the lowest degree of thinking), while in the order of localization, they remain tied to a conception of the subject which makes of the latter a protocol of constitution, whereas it can, at best, only be a result.

In spite of this, we can hold on to the notion that the question of the subject is that of identity, and hence of the one, with the proviso that the subject be understood, not as the empty centre of a transcendental realm but rather as the operational unity of a multiplicity of effectuations of identity. Or as the *multiple ways of being self-identical.*

CHAPTER 12
EIGHT THESES ON THE UNIVERSAL

1. Thought is the proper medium of the universal

By 'thought', I mean the subject in so far as it is constituted through a process that is transversal relative to the totality of available forms of knowledge. Or, as Lacan puts it, the subject in so far as it constitutes a hole in knowledge.

Remarks:

a. That thought is the proper medium of the universal means that nothing exists as universal if it takes the form of the object or of objective legality. The universal is essentially 'anobjective'. It can be experienced only through the production (or reproduction) of a trajectory of thought, and this trajectory constitutes (or reconstitutes) a subjective disposition.

   Here are two typical examples: the universality of a mathematical proposition can only be experienced by inventing or effectively reproducing its proof; the situated universality of a political statement can only be experienced through the militant practice that effectuates it.

b. That thought, as subject-thought, is constituted through a process means that the universal is in no way the result of a transcendental constitution, which would presuppose a constituting subject. On the contrary, the opening up of the possibility of a universal is the precondition for there being a subject-thought at the local level. The subject is invariably summoned as thought at a specific point of that procedure through which the universal is constituted. The universal is at once what determines its own points as subject-thoughts and the virtual recollection of those points. Thus the central dialectic at work in the universal is that of the local, as subject, and the global, as infinite procedure. This dialectic is constitutive of thought as such.

Consequently, the universality of the proposition 'the series of prime numbers goes on forever' resides both in the way it summons us to repeat (or rediscover) in thought a unique proof for it, but also in the global procedure that, from the Greeks to the present day, mobilizes number theory along with its underlying axiomatic. To put it another way, the universality of the practical statement 'a country's illegal immigrant workers must have their rights recognized by that country' resides in all sorts of militant effectuations through which political subjectivity is actively constituted, but also in the global process of a politics, in terms of what it prescribes concerning the State and its decisions, rules and laws.

c. That the process of the universal or truth – they are one and the same – is transversal relative to all available instances of knowledge means that the universal is always an incalculable emergence, rather than a describable structure. By the same token, I will say that a truth is intransitive to knowledge, and even that it is essentially unknown. This is another way of explaining what I mean when I characterize truth as unconscious.

I will call *particular* whatever can be discerned in knowledge by means of descriptive predicates. But I will call *singular* that which, although identifiable as a procedure at work in a situation, is nevertheless subtracted from every predicative description. Thus the cultural traits of this or that population are particular. But that which, traversing these traits and deactivating every registered description, universally summons a thought-subject, is singular. Whence thesis 2:

2. Every universal is singular, or is a singularity

Remarks:

There is no possible universal sublation of particularity as such. It is commonly claimed nowadays that the only genuinely universal prescription consists in respecting particularities. In my opinion, this thesis is inconsistent. This is demonstrated by the fact that any attempt to put it into practice invariably runs up against particularities which the advocates of formal universality find intolerable. The truth is that in order to maintain that respect for particularity is a universal value, it is necessary to have first distinguished between good particularities and bad ones. In other words, it is necessary to have established a hierarchy in the list of descriptive predicates. It will be claimed, for example, that a cultural or religious particularity is bad if it does not include within itself respect for other particularities. But this is obviously to stipulate that the formal universal already be included in the particularity. Ultimately, the universality of respect for particularities is only the universality of universality. This definition is fatally tautological. It is the necessary counterpart of a protocol – usually a violent one – that wants to eradicate genuinely particular particularities (i.e. immanent particularities) because it freezes the predicates of the latter into self-sufficient identitarian combinations.

Thus it is necessary to maintain that every universal presents itself not as a regularization of the particular or of differences, but as a singularity that is subtracted from identitarian predicates; although obviously it proceeds via those predicates. The subtraction of particularities must be opposed to their supposition. But if a singularity can lay claim to the universal by subtraction, it is because the play of identitarian predicates, or the logic of those forms of knowledge that describe particularity, precludes any possibility of foreseeing or conceiving it.

Consequently, a universal singularity is not of the order of being, but of the order of a sudden emergence. Whence thesis 3:

3. Every universal originates in an event, and the event is intransitive to the particularity of the situation

The correlation between universal and event is fundamental. Basically, it is clear that the question of political universalism depends entirely on the regime of fidelity or infidelity maintained, not to this or that doctrine, but to the French Revolution, or the Paris commune, or October 1917, or the struggles for national liberation, or May 1968. *A contrario*, the negation of political universalism, the negation of the very theme of emancipation, requires more than mere reactionary propaganda. It requires what could be called an *evental revisionism*. Thus, for example, Furet's attempt to show that the French Revolution was entirely futile; or the innumerable attempts to reduce May 1968 to a student stampede toward sexual liberation. Evental revisionism targets the connection between universality and singularity. Nothing took place but the place, predicative descriptions are sufficient, and whatever is universally valuable is strictly objective. *In fine*, this amounts to the claim that whatever is universally valuable resides in the mechanisms and power of capital, along with its statist guarantees.

In that case, the fate of the human animal is sealed by the relation between predicative particularities and legislative generalities.

For an event to initiate a singular procedure of universalization, and to constitute its subject through that procedure, is contrary to the positivist coupling of particularity and generality.

In this regard, the case of sexual difference is significant. The predicative particularities identifying the positions 'man' and 'woman' within a given society can be conceived in an abstract fashion. A general principle can be posited whereby the rights, status, characteristics and hierarchies associated with these positions should be subject to egalitarian regulation by the law. This is all well and good, but it does not provide a ground for any sort of universality as far as the predicative distribution of gender roles is concerned. For this to be the case, there has to be the suddenly emerging singularity of an encounter or declaration; one that crystallizes a subject whose manifestation is precisely its subtractive experience of sexual difference. Such a subject comes about through an amorous encounter in which there occurs a disjunctive synthesis of sexuated positions. Thus the amorous scene is the only genuine scene in which a universal singularity pertaining to the Two of the sexes – and ultimately pertaining to difference as such – is proclaimed. This is where an undivided subjective experience of absolute difference takes place. We all know that, where the interplay between the sexes is concerned, people are invariably fascinated by love stories; and this fascination is directly proportional to the various specific obstacles through which social formations try to thwart love. In this instance, it is perfectly clear that the attraction exerted by the universal lies precisely in the fact that it subtracts itself (or tries to subtract itself) as an asocial singularity from the predicates of knowledge.

Thus it is necessary to maintain that the universal emerges as a singularity and that all we have to begin with is a precarious supplement whose sole strength resides in there being no available predicate capable of subjecting it to knowledge.

The question then is: what material instance, what unclassifiable effect of presence, provides the basis for the subjectivating procedure whose global motif is a universal?

4. A universal initially presents itself as a decision about an undecidable

This point requires careful elucidation.

I call 'encyclopedia' the general system of predicative knowledge internal to a situation: i.e. what everyone knows about politics, sexual difference, culture, art, technology, etc. There are certain things, statements, configurations or discursive fragments whose valence is not decidable in terms of the encyclopedia. Their valence is uncertain, floating, anonymous: they exist at the margins of the encyclopedia. They comprise everything whose status remains constitutively uncertain; everything that elicits a 'maybe, maybe not'; everything whose status can be endlessly debated according to the rule of non-decision, which is itself encyclopedic; everything about which knowledge enjoins us not to decide. Nowadays, for instance, knowledge enjoins us not to decide about God: it is quite acceptable to maintain that perhaps 'something' exists, or perhaps it does not. We live in a society in which no valence can be ascribed to God's existence; a society that lays claim to a vague spirituality. Similarly, knowledge enjoins us not to decide about the possible existence of 'another politics': it is talked about, but nothing comes of it. Another example: are those workers who do not have proper papers but who are working here, in France (or the United Kingdom, or the United States . . .) part of this country? Do they belong here? Yes, probably, since they live and work here. No, since they don't have the necessary papers to show that they are French (or British, or American . . .), or living here legally. The expression 'illegal immigrant' designates the uncertainty of valence, or the non-valence of valence: it designates people who are living here, but don't really belong here, and hence people who can be thrown out of the country, people who can be exposed to the non-valence of the valence of their presence here as workers.

Basically, an event is what decides about a zone of encyclopedic indiscernibility. More precisely, there is an implicative form of the type: $E \rightarrow d(\varepsilon)$, which reads as: every real subjectivation brought about by an event, which disappears in its appearance, implies that ε, which is undecidable within the situation, has been decided. This was the case, for example, when illegal immigrant workers occupied the church of St. Bernard in Paris: they publicly declared the existence and valence of what had been without valence, thereby deciding that those who are here belong here and enjoining people to drop the expression 'illegal immigrant'.

I will call ε the evental statement. By virtue of the logical rule of *detachment*, we see that the abolition of the event, whose entire being consists in disappearing, leaves behind the evental statement ε, which is implied by the event, as something that is at once:

- a real of the situation (since it was already there);

- but something whose valence undergoes radical change, since it was undecidable but has been decided. It is something that had no valence but now does.

Consequently, I will say that the inaugural materiality for any universal singularity is the evental statement. It fixes the present for the subject-thought out of which the universal is woven.

Such is the case in an amorous encounter, whose subjective present is fixed in one form or another by the statement 'I love you', even as the circumstance of the encounter is erased. Thus an undecidable disjunctive synthesis is decided and the inauguration of its subject is tied to the consequences of the evental statement.

Note that every evental statement has a declarative structure, regardless of whether the statement takes the form of a proposition, a work, a configuration or an axiom. The evental statement is implied by the event's appearing–disappearing and declares that an undecidable has been decided or that what was without valence now has a valence. The constituted subject follows in the wake of this declaration, which opens up a possible space for the universal.

Accordingly, all that is required in order for the universal to unfold is to draw all the consequences, within the situation, of the evental statement.

5. The universal has an implicative structure

One common objection to the idea of universality is that everything that exists or is represented relates back to particular conditions and interpretations governed by disparate forces or interests. Thus, for instance, some maintain it is impossible to attain a universal grasp of difference because of the abyss between the way the latter is grasped, depending on whether one occupies the position of 'man' or the position of 'woman'. Still others insist that there is no common denominator underlying what various cultural groups choose to call 'artistic activity'; or that not even a mathematical proposition is intrinsically universal, since its validity is entirely dependent upon the axioms that support it.

What this hermeneutic perspectivalism overlooks is that every universal singularity is presented as the network of consequences entailed by an eventual decision. What is universal always takes the form $\varepsilon \rightarrow \pi$, where ε is the eventual statement and π is a consequence, or a fidelity. It goes without saying that if someone refuses the decision about ε, or insists, in reactive fashion, on reducing ε to its undecidable status, or maintains that what has taken on a valence should remain without valence, then the implicative form in no way enjoins them to accept the validity of the consequence, $\pi\pi$. Nevertheless, even they will have to admit the universality of the form of implication as such. In other words, even they will have to admit that if the event is subjectivated on the basis of its statement, whatever consequences come to be invented as a result will be necessary.

On this point, Plato's apologia in the *Meno* remains irrefutable. If a slave knows nothing about the eventual foundation of geometry, he remains incapable of validating the construction of the square of the surface that doubles a given square. But if one provides him with the basic data and he agrees to subjectivate it he will also subjectivate the construction under consideration. Thus the implication that inscribes this construction in the present inaugurated by geometry's Greek emergence is universally valid.

Someone might object: 'You're making things too easy for yourself by invoking the authority of mathematical inference.' But they would be wrong. Every universalizing procedure is implicative. It verifies the consequences that follow from the eventual statement to which the vanished event is indexed. If the protocol of subjectivation is initiated under the aegis of this statement, it becomes capable of inventing and establishing a set of universally recognizable consequences.

The reactive denial that the event took place, as expressed in the maxim 'nothing took place but the place', is probably the only way of undermining a universal singularity. It refuses to recognize its consequences and cancels whatever present is proper to the eventual procedure.

Yet even this refusal cannot cancel the universality of implication as such. Take the French Revolution: if, from 1792 on, this constitutes a radical event, as indicated by the immanent declaration which states that revolution as such is now a political category, then it is true that the citizen can only be constituted in accordance with the dialectic of Virtue and Terror. This implication is both undeniable and universally transmissible – in the writings of Saint-Just, for instance. But obviously, if one thinks there was no Revolution, then Virtue as a subjective disposition does not exist either and all that remains is the Terror as an outburst of insanity inviting moral condemnation. Yet even if politics disappears, the universality of the implication that puts it into effect remains.

There is no need to invoke a conflict of interpretations here. This is the nub of my sixth thesis:

6. The universal is univocal

In so far as subjectivation occurs through the consequences of the event, there is a univocal logic proper to the fidelity that constitutes a universal singularity.

Here we have to go back to the evental statement. Recall that the statement circulates within a situation as something undecidable. There is agreement both about its existence and its undecidability. From an ontological point of view, it is one of the multiplicities of which the situation is composed. From a logical point of view, its valence is intermediary or undecided. What occurs through the event does not have to do with the being that is at stake in the event, nor with the meaning of the evental statement. It pertains exclusively to the fact that, whereas previously the evental statement had been undecidable, henceforth it will have been decided, or decided as true. Whereas previously the evental statement had been devoid of significance, it now possesses an exceptional valence. This is what happened with the illegal immigrant workers, who demonstrated their existence at the St. Bernard church.

In other words, what affects the statement, in so far as the latter is bound up in an implicative manner with the evental disappearance, is of the order of the *act*, rather than of being or meaning. It is precisely the register of the act that is univocal. It just so happened that the statement was decided, and this decision remains subtracted from all interpretation. It relates to the yes or the no, not to the equivocal plurality of meaning.

What we are talking about here is a logical act, or even, as one might say echoing Rimbaud, a logical revolt. The event decides in favour of the truth or eminent valence of that which the previous logic had confined to the realm of the undecidable or of non-valence. But for this to be possible, the univocal act that modifies the valence of one of the components of the situation must gradually begin to transform the logic of the situation in its entirety. Although the being-multiple of the situation remains unaltered, the logic of its appearance – the system that evaluates and connects all the multiplicities belonging to the situation – can undergo a profound transformation. It is the trajectory of this mutation that composes the encyclopedia's universalizing diagonal.

The thesis of the equivocity of the universal refers the universal singularity back to those generalities whose law holds sway over particularities. It fails to grasp the logical act that universally and univocally inaugurates a transformation in the entire structure of appearance.

For every universal singularity can be defined as follows: it is the act to which a subject-thought becomes bound in such a way as to render that act capable of initiating a procedure which effects a radical modification of the logic of the situation, and hence of what appears in so far as it appears.

Obviously, this modification can never be fully accomplished. For the initial univocal act, which is always localized, inaugurates a fidelity, i.e. an invention of consequences, that will prove to be as infinite as the situation itself. Whence thesis 7:

7. Every universal singularity remains incompletable or open

All this thesis requires by way of commentary concerns the manner in which the subject, the localization of a universal singularity, is bound up with the infinite, the ontological law of being-multiple. On this particular issue, it is possible to show that there is an essential complicity between the philosophies of finitude, on the one hand, and relativism, or the negation of the universal and the discrediting of the notion of truth, on the other. Let me put it in terms of a single maxim: The latent violence, the presumptuous arrogance inherent in the currently prevalent conception of human rights derives from the fact that these are actually the rights of finitude and ultimately – as the insistent theme of democratic euthanasia indicates – the rights of death. By way of contrast, the evental conception of universal singularities, as Jean-François Lyotard remarked in *The Differend*, requires that human rights be thought of as the rights of the infinite.

8. Universality is nothing other than the faithful construction of an infinite generic multiple

What do I mean by generic multiplicity? Quite simply, a subset of the situation that is not determined by any of the predicates of encyclopedic knowledge; that is to say, a multiple such that to belong to it, to be one of its elements, cannot be the result of having an identity, of possessing any particular property. If the universal is for everyone, this is in the precise sense that to be inscribed within it is not a matter of possessing any particular determination. This is the case with political gatherings, whose universality follows from their indifference to social, national, sexual or generational origin; with the amorous couple, which is universal because it produces an undivided truth about the difference between sexuated positions; with scientific theory, which is universal to the extent that it removes every trace of its provenance in its elaboration; or with artistic configurations whose subjects are works, and in which, as Mallarmé remarked, the particularity of the author has been abolished, so much so that in exemplary inaugural configurations, such as the *Iliad* and the *Odyssey*, the proper name that underlies them – Homer – ultimately refers back to nothing but the void of any and every subject.

Thus the universal arises according to the chance of an aleatory supplement. It leaves behind it a simple detached statement as a trace of the disappearance of the event that founds it. It initiates its procedure in the univocal act through which the valence of what was devoid of valence comes to be decided. It binds to this act a subject-thought that will invent consequences for it. It faithfully constructs an infinite generic multiplicity, which, by its very opening, is what Thucydides declared his written history of the Peloponnesian war – unlike the latter's historical particularity – would be: xατιμα εs αει, 'something for all time'.

CHAPTER 13
POLITICS AS A TRUTH PROCEDURE

When, and under what conditions, can an event be said to be political? What is the 'what happens' in so far as it happens politically?

We will maintain that an event is political, and that the procedure it engages exhibits a political truth, only under certain conditions. These conditions pertain to the material of the event, to the infinite, to its relation to the state of the situation, and to the numericality of the procedure.

1. An event is political if its material is collective, or if the event can only be attributed to a collective multiplicity. 'Collective' is not a numerical concept here. We say that the event is ontologically collective to the extent that it provides the vehicle for a virtual summoning of all. 'Collective' means immediately universalizing. The effectiveness of politics relates to the affirmation according to which 'for every x, there is thought'.

    By 'thought', I mean any truth procedure *considered subjectively*. 'Thought' is the name of the subject of a truth procedure. The use of the term 'collective' is an acknowledgement that if this thought is political, it belongs to all. It is not simply a question of address, as it is in the case of other types of truth. Of course, every truth is addressed to all. But in the case of politics, the universality is intrinsic, and not simply a function of the address. In politics, the possibility of the thought that identifies a subject is at every moment available to all. Those that are constituted as subject of a politics are called the *militants* of the procedure. But 'militant' is a category without borders, a subjective determination without identity, or without concept. That the political event is collective prescribes that all are the virtual militants of the thought that proceeds on the basis of the event. In this sense, politics is the single truth procedure that is not only generic in its result, but also in the local composition of its subject.

    Only politics is intrinsically required to declare that the thought that it is is the thought of all. This declaration is its constitutive prerequisite. All that the mathematician requires, for instance, is at least one other mathematician to recognize the validity of his proof. In order to assure itself of the thought that it is, love need only assume the two. The artist ultimately needs no one. Science, art and love are aristocratic truth procedures. Of course, they are addressed to all and universalize their own singularity. But their regime is not that of the collective. Politics is impossible without the statement that people, taken indistinctly, are capable of the thought that constitutes the post-evental political subject. This statement claims that a political thought is topologically collective, meaning that it cannot exist otherwise than as the thought of all.

That the central activity of politics is the *gathering* is a local metonymy of its intrinsically collective, and therefore principally universal, being.

2. The effect of the collective character of the political event is that politics presents as such the infinite character of situations. Politics summons or exhibits the infinity of the situation. Every politics of emancipation rejects finitude, rejects 'being towards death'. Since a politics includes in the situation the thought of all, it is engaged in rendering explicit the subjective infinity of situations.

Of course, every situation is ontologically infinite. But only politics summons this infinity immediately, as subjective universality.

Science, for example, is the capture of the void and the infinite by the letter. It has no concern for the subjective infinity of situations. Art presents the sensible in the finitude of a work, and the infinite only intervenes in it to the extent that the artist destines the infinite to the finite. But politics treats the infinite as such according to the principle of the same, the egalitarian principle. This is its starting-point: the situation is open, never closed, and the possible affects its immanent subjective infinity. We will say that the numericality of the political procedure has the infinite as its first term; whereas for love this first term is the one; for science the void; and for art a finite number. The infinite comes into play in every truth procedure, but only in politics does it take the first place. This is because only in politics is the deliberation about the possible (and hence about the infinity of the situation) constitutive of the process itself.

3. Lastly, what is the relation between politics and the state of the situation, and more particularly between politics and the State, in both the ontological and historical senses of the term?

The state of the situation is the operation which, within the situation, codifies its parts or sub-sets. The state is a sort of metastructure that exercises the power of the count over all the sub-sets of the situation. Every situation has a state. Every situation is the presentation of itself, of what composes it, of what belongs to it. But it is also given as state of the situation, that is, as the internal configuration of its parts or sub-sets, and therefore as re-presentation. More specifically, the state of the situation re-presents collective situations, whilst in the collective situations themselves, singularities are not re-presented but presented. On this point, I refer the reader to my *Being and Event*, Meditation 8.[1]

A fundamental datum of ontology is that the state of the situation always exceeds the situation itself. There are always more parts than elements; i.e. the representative multiplicity is always of a higher power than the presentative multiplicity. This question is really that of power. The power of the State is always superior to that of the situation. The State, and hence also the economy, which is today the norm of the State, are characterised by a structural effect of separation and superpower with regard to what is simply presented in the situation.

It has been mathematically demonstrated that this excess is not measurable. There is no answer to the question about *how much* the power of the State exceeds the individual, or how much the power of representation exceeds that of simple presentation. The excess is errant. The simplest experience of the relation to the State shows that one relates to it without ever being able to assign a measure to its power. The representation of the State by power, say public power, points on the one hand to its excess, and on the other to the indeterminacy or errancy of this excess.

We know that when politics exists, it immediately gives rise to a show of power by the State. This is obviously due to the fact that politics is collective, and hence universally concerns the parts of the situation, thereby encroaching upon the domain from which the state of the situation draws its existence. Politics summons the power of the State. Moreover, it is the only truth procedure to do so directly. The usual symptom of this summoning is the fact that politics invariably encounters repression. But repression, which is the empirical form of the errant superpower of the State, is not the essential point.

The real characteristic of the political event and the truth procedure that it sets off is that a political event fixes the errancy and assigns a measure to the superpower of the State. It fixes the power of the State. Consequently, the political event interrupts the subjective errancy of the power of the State. It configures the state of the situation. It gives it a figure; it configures its power; it measures it.

Empirically, this means that whenever there is a genuinely political event, the State reveals itself. It reveals its excess of power, its repressive dimension. But it also reveals a measure for this usually invisible excess. For it is essential to the normal functioning of the State that its power remain measureless, errant, unassignable. The political event puts an end to all this by assigning a visible measure to the excessive power of the State.

Politics puts the State at a distance, in the distance of its measure. The resignation that characterizes a time without politics feeds on the fact that the State is not at a distance, because the measure of its power is errant. People are held hostage by its unassignable errancy. Politics is the interruption of this errancy. It exhibits a measure for state power. This is the sense in which politics is 'freedom'. The State is in fact the measureless enslavement of the parts of the situation, an enslavement whose secret is precisely the errancy of superpower, its measurelessness. Freedom here consists in putting the State at a distance through the collective establishment of a measure for its excess. And if the excess measured, it is because the collective can measure up to it.

We will call *political prescription* the post-eventual establishment of a fixed measure for the power of the State.

We can now proceed to elaborate the numericality of the political procedure.

Why does every truth procedure possess a numericality? Because there is a determination of each truth's relation to the different types of multiple that singularize it: the situation, the state of the situation, the event, and the subjective operation. This relation is expressed by a number (including Cantorian or infinite numbers). Thus the procedure has an abstract schema, fixed in some typical numbers which encode the 'traversal' of the multiples that are ontologically constitutive of this procedure.

Let us give Lacan his due: he was the first to make a systematic use of numericality, whether it be a question of assigning the subject to zero as the gap between 1 and 2 (the subject is what falls between the primordial signifiers S1 and S2), of the synthetic bearing of 3 (the Borromean knotting of the real, the symbolic and the imaginary), or of the function of the infinite in feminine *jouissance*.

In the case of politics, we said that its first term, which is linked to the collective character of the political event, is the infinite of the situation. It is the simple infinite, the infinite of presentation. This infinite is determined; the value of its power is fixed.

We also said that politics necessarily summons the state of the situation, and therefore a second infinite. This second infinite is in excess of the first, its power is superior, but in general we cannot know by how much. The excess is measureless. We can therefore say that the second term of political numericality is a second infinite, the one of State power, and that all we can know about this infinite is that it is superior to the first, and that this difference remains undetermined. If we call σ the fixed infinite cardinality of the situation, and ε the cardinality that measures the power of the State, then apart from politics, we have no means of knowing anything other than: ε is superior to σ. This indeterminate superiority masks the alienating and repressive nature of the state of the situation.

The political event prescribes a measure for the measurelessness of the State through the suddenly emergent materiality of a universalizable collective. It substitutes a fixed measure for the errant ε; one that almost invariably remains superior to the power σ of simple presentation, of course, but which is no longer endowed with the alienating and repressive powers of indeterminacy. We will use the expression π(ε) to symbolize the result of the political prescription directed at the State.

The mark π designates the political function. It is exercised in several spaces (though we shall not go into the details here) correlated with the places of a singular politics ('places' in the sense defined by Sylvain Lazarus).[2] This function is the trace left in the situation by the vanished political event. What concerns us here is its principal efficacy, which consists in interrupting the indeterminacy of state power.

The first three terms of the numericality of the political procedure, all of which are infinite, are ultimately the following:

1. The infinity of the situation, which is summoned as such through the collective dimension of the political event, which is to say, through the supposition of thought's 'for all'. We will refer to it as σ.

2. The infinity of the state of the situation, which is summoned for the purposes of repression and alienation because it supposedly controls all the collectives or sub-sets of the situation. It is an infinite cardinal

number that remains indeterminate, though it is always superior to the infinite power of the situation of which it is the state. We will therefore write: $\varepsilon > \sigma$.

3. The fixing by political prescription, under an evental and collective condition, of a measure for state power. Through this prescription, the errancy of state power is interrupted and it becomes possible to use militant watchwords to practise and calculate the free distance of political thinking from the State. We write this as $\pi(\varepsilon)$, designating a determinate infinite cardinal number.

Let us try to clarify the fundamental operation of prescription by giving some examples. The Bolshevik insurrection of 1917 reveals a weak State, undermined by war, whereas tsarism was a paradigmatic instance of the quasi-sacred indeterminacy of the State's superpower. Generally speaking, insurrectionary forms of political thought are tied to a post-evental determination of the power of the State as being very weak or even inferior to the power of simple collective representation.

By way of contrast, the Maoist choice of prolonged war and the encirclement of the cities by the countryside prescribes to the State what is still an elevated measure of its power and carefully calculates the free distance from this power. This is the real reason why Mao's question remains the following: how can red power exist in China? Or, how can the weakest prevail over the strongest in the long run? Which is to say that, for Mao, $\pi(\varepsilon)$ – the prescription concerning the power of State – remains largely superior to σ the infinity of the situation such as it is summoned by the political procedure.

This is to say that the first three components of numericality – the three infinites σ, ε, $\pi(\varepsilon)$ – are affected by each singular political sequence and do not have any sort of fixed determination, save for that of their mutual relations. More specifically, every politics proceeds to its own post-evental prescription vis-à-vis the power of the State, so that it essentially consists in creating the political function π in the wake of the evental upsurge.

When the political procedure exists, such that it manages a prescription vis-à-vis the State, then and only then can the logic of the same, that is, the egalitarian maxim proper to every politics of emancipation, be set out.

For the egalitarian maxim is effectively incompatible with the errancy of state excess. The matrix of inequality consists precisely in the impossibility of measuring the superpower of the state. Today, for example, it is in the name of the necessity of the liberal economy – a necessity without measure or concept – that all egalitarian politics are deemed to be impossible and denounced as absurd. But what characterizes this blind power of unfettered Capital is precisely the fact that it cannot be either measured or fixed at any point. All we know is that it prevails absolutely over the subjective fate of collectives, whatever they may be. Thus in order for a politics to be able to practise an egalitarian maxim in the sequence opened by an event, it is absolutely necessary that the state of the situation be put at a distance through a strict determination of its power.

Non-egalitarian consciousness is a mute consciousness, the captive of an errancy, of a power which it cannot measure. This is what explains the arrogant and peremptory character of non-egalitarian statements, even when they are obviously inconsistent and abject. For the statements of contemporary reaction are shored up entirely by the errancy of state excess, i.e. by the untrammelled violence of capitalist anarchy. This is why liberal statements combine certainty about power with total indecision about its consequences for people's lives and the universal affirmation of collectives.

Egalitarian logic can only begin when the State is configured, put at a distance, measured. It is the errancy of the excess that impedes egalitarian logic, not the excess itself. It is not the simple power of the state of the situation that prohibits egalitarian politics. It is the obscurity and measurelessness in which this power is enveloped. If the political event allows for a clarification, a fixation, an exhibition of this power, then the egalitarian maxim is at least locally practicable.

But what is the figure for this equality, the figure for the prescription whereby each and every singularity is to be treated collectively and identically in political thought? This figure is obviously the 1. To finally count as one what is not even counted is what is at stake in every genuinely political thought, every prescription that summons the collective as such. The 1 is the numericality of the same, and to produce the same is that which an emancipatory political procedure is capable of. The 1 disfigures every non-egalitarian claim.

To produce the same, to count each one universally as one, it is necessary to work *locally*, in the gap opened between politics and the State, a gap whose principle resides in the measure $\pi(\varepsilon)$. This is how a Maoist politics was able to experiment with an agrarian revolution in the liberated zones (those beyond the reach of the reactionary armies), or a Bolshevik politics was able to effect a partial transfer of certain state operations into the hands of the soviets, at least in those instances where the latter were capable of assuming them. What is at work in such situations is once again the political function π, applied under the conditions of the prescriptive distance it has itself created, but this time with the aim of producing the same, or producing the real in accordance with an egalitarian maxim. One will therefore write: $\pi(\pi(\varepsilon)) \Rightarrow 1$ in order to designate this doubling of the political function which works to produce equality under the conditions of freedom of thought/ practice opened up by the fixation of state power.

We can now complete the numericality of the political procedure. It is composed of three infinites: that of the situation; that of the state of the situation, which is indeterminate; and that of the prescription, which interrupts the indeterminacy and allows for a distance to be taken vis-à-vis the State. This numericality is completed by the 1, which is partially engendered by the political function under the conditions of the distance from the State, which themselves derive from this function. Here, the 1 is the figure of equality and sameness.

The numericality is written as follows: σ, ε, $\pi(\varepsilon)$, $\pi(\pi(\varepsilon)) \Rightarrow 1$.

What singularizes the political procedure is the fact that it proceeds from the infinite to the 1. It makes the 1 of equality arise as the universal truth of the collective by carrying out a prescriptive operation upon the infinity of the State; an operation whereby it constructs its own autonomy, or distance, and is able to effectuate its maxim within that distance.

Conversely, let us note in passing that, as I established in *Conditions*,[3] the amorous procedure, which deploys the truth of difference or sexuation (rather than of the collective), proceeds from the 1 to the infinite through the mediation of the two. In this sense – and I leave the reader to meditate upon this – politics is love's numerical inverse. In other words, love begins where politics ends.

And since the term 'democracy' is today decisive, let me conclude by providing my own definition of it, one in which its identity with politics will be rendered legible.

Democracy consists in the always singular adjustment of freedom and equality. But what is the moment of freedom in politics? It is the one wherein the State is put at a distance, and hence the one wherein the political function π operates as the assignation of a measure to the errant superpower of the state of the situation. And what is equality, if not the operation whereby, in the distance thus created, the political function is applied once again, this time so as to produce the 1? Thus, for a determinate political procedure, the political adjustment of freedom and equality is nothing but the adjustment of the last two terms of its numericality. It is written: $[\pi(\varepsilon)—\pi(\pi(\varepsilon))\Rightarrow 1]$. It should go without saying that what we have here is the notation of democracy. Our two examples show that this notation has had singular names: 'soviets' during the Bolshevik revolution, 'liberated zones' during the Maoist process. But democracy has had many other names in the past. It has some in the present (for example: 'gathering of the Political Organization and of the collective of illegal immigrant workers from the hostels'[4]); and it will have others in the future.

Despite its rarity, politics – and hence democracy – has existed, exists, and will exist. And alongside it, under its demanding condition, metapolitics, which is what a philosophy declares, with its own effects in mind, to be worthy of the name 'politics'. Or alternately, what a thought declares to be a thought, and under whose condition it thinks what a thought is.

SECTION III
LOGICS OF APPEARANCE

CHAPTER 14
BEING AND APPEARANCE

Let's consider the following remark, in its almost matchless banality: today logic is a mathematical discipline, which in less than a century has attained a degree of complexity equal to that of any other living region of this science. There are logical theorems, especially in the theory of models, whose arduous demonstration synthesizes methods drawn from apparently distant domains of the discipline (from topology or transcendental algebra) and whose power and novelty are astonishing.

But the most astonishing thing for philosophy is the lack of astonishment elicited by this state of affairs. As recently as Hegel, it was perfectly natural to call *Logic* what is obviously a vast philosophical treatise. The first category of this treatise is being, being qua being. Moreover, this treatise includes a long discussion that seeks to establish that, as far as the concept of the infinite is concerned, mathematics represents only the immediate stage of its presentation and must be sublated by the movement of speculative dialectics. As recently as Hegel, only this dialectics fully deserved the name of 'logic'.

That mathematization finally won the dispute over the identity of logic is a veritable gauntlet thrown down at the feet of philosophy, the discipline that historically established the concept of logic and set out its forms.

The question is therefore the following: what is the status of logic, and what is the status of mathematics, such that the destiny of the one is to be inscribed in the other? But this inscription itself determines a sort of torsion that puts the very question we've just posed into question. For if there is a discipline that requires the conduct of its discourse to be strictly logical, this discipline is indeed mathematics. Logic seems to be one of the a priori conditions for mathematics. How is it possible then that this condition finds itself as though injected into what it conditions, to the point that it no longer constitutes anything but a regional disposition?

There can be little doubt that the mediation between logic as a philosophical prescription and logic as a mathematical discipline has its basis in what it has become customary to call the *formal* character of logic. We know that, in the preface to the second edition of the *Critique of Pure Reason*, Kant attributes to this character the fact that logic, 'from the earliest times',[1] has entered the secure path of a science. It is because logic gives an 'exhaustive exposition and strict proof of the formal rules of all thought'[2] that, as Kant argues, it has not needed to take either one step forward or backwards ever since the time of Aristotle. Its success is entirely bound up with the fact that it abstracts from every object, and consequently ignores the great partition between the transcendental and the empirical.

One can therefore state the following, which I think is the most widespread conviction today: since formal logic is not tied to any figure of the empirical givenness of objects, it follows that its destiny is mathematical, for the precise reason that mathematics is itself a formal theoretical activity – in the sense that Carnap, for example, distinguishes the formal sciences (i.e. logic and mathematics) from the empirical sciences, the paradigm of which is physics.

Nevertheless, it will be noted immediately that this solution could not belong to Kant, who is consistently faithful to the ontological intuitions that I've already outlined in 'Kant's Subtractive Ontology'. For Kant, mathematics, which requires the form of temporal intuition in the genesis of arithmetical objects and the form of spatial intuition in the genesis of geometrical objects, can in no way be regarded as a formal discipline. This is why all mathematical judgements, even the simplest, are synthetic – unlike logical judgements, which remain analytic. It will also be noted that the attribution of immutability, supposedly characteristic of logic since its Aristotelian inception, and which, is linked by Kant to its formal character, is doubly erroneous, both in terms of history and foresight. It is historically inaccurate, because Kant takes no account of the complexity of the history of logic, which from the Greeks onward precludes any assumption of the unity and fixity Kant attributes to logic. Specifically, Kant entirely effaces the fundamental difference in orientation between the predicative logic of Aristotle and the propositional logic of the Stoics, a difference from which Claude Imbert has very recently drawn important consequences.[3] And it amounts to a failure of foresight, because it is clear that, ever since its successful mathematization, logic has never ceased to take giant steps forward – which is why it is one of the great cognitive endeavours of the twentieth century.

It is altogether peculiar, nonetheless, that Kant's thesis, which was intended to emphasize both the merits of logic and its restriction to the general forms of thinking, is exactly the same as Heidegger's, the aim of which is entirely different, i.e. to indicate the forgetting of being, one of whose principal effects is the formal autonomy of logic. We know that for Heidegger logic – the product of a scission between *phusis* and *logos* – is the potentially nihilistic sovereignty of a *logos* from which being has withdrawn. But in order to reach this historial determination of logic, what does Heidegger tell us about its obvious characteristics? Very simply, that logic is 'the science of thinking, the doctrine of the rules of thinking and the forms of what is thought',[4] from which he infers, exactly like Kant, that 'it has taught the same thing since antiquity'.[5] Formalism and immutability seem to be linked to one another and to confirm a vision of logic that confines it either to what lies on this side of the partition between the empirical and the transcendental (Kant), or to the technical process of a nihilistic enframing of the totality of beings (Heidegger).

When all's said and done, it is difficult to accept as indisputable the claim that the mathematization of logic is a consequence of its formal character. Either this thesis comes up against the fact that mathematization has given a formidable impetus to logic, which contradicts the immutability supposedly imposed on it by its formal character; or it assumes that mathematics itself is purely formal, which in turn demands that we ask what distinguishes it from logic. Now, in the course of the 20th century, this 'logicist' project, which effectively sought to reduce mathematics to logic, ran aground, beset by the paradoxes and impasses that had dogged it ever since Frege's fundamental work. Thus, although entirely mathematized, logic itself seems to prescribe that mathematics as a whole cannot be reduced to it.

We are thus led back to our question as a question. What does it mean, for thinking, that logic can be identified today as mathematical logic? We should be astonished by this established syntagm. We must ask: what is logic, and what is mathematics, such that it is possible and even necessary to speak of a mathematical logic? My abiding conviction is that it is impossible to respond to this question without first passing through a third term, one which is present from the outset, but whose absence is signalled by the very syntagm 'mathematical logic'. This third term is 'ontology', the science of being qua being.

In any case, it is this third term that allows Aristotle – the founder of what Kant and Heidegger understand by the word 'logic' – to interrogate the formal necessity of the first principles of every discourse that lays claim to consistency. That thinking being, being qua being, demands the determination of the axioms of thinking in general is Aristotle's thesis in book Γ of the *Metaphysics*. As he states: 'to him who studies being qua being belongs the inquiry into [the axioms] as well'.[6] This is why the initial declaration according to which there exists a science of the entity qua entity finds itself as though traversed, rather than realized, by a long process legitimating first the principle of non-contradiction ('we have now posited that it is impossible for anything at the same time to be and not to be'[7]); and then the principle of the excluded middle ('of one subject we must either affirm or deny one predicate'[8]). There can be no doubt that these principles today have the status of logical laws, to the extent that the acceptance or rejection of the second (the excluded middle) distinguishes two fundamental orientations in contemporary logic: the classical one, which validates reasoning by *reductio ad absurdum*, and the intuitionist one, which only admits constructive proofs. Thus it is indisputable that, for us, Aristotle establishes logic as that through which ontology must be mediated. Anyone who declares the existence of a science of being qua being will be required to ground the formal axioms for all transmissible discourse. So let us agree that, for Aristotle, ontology prescribes logic.

But why is this the case? In order to understand this point, it is necessary to investigate the second of Aristotle's key statements – after the recognition of the existence of ontology – the one that sums up the difficulty he discerns in the science of the entity qua entity. This is the statement that the entity is said to be in many senses, but also πρos εν, in the direction of (or toward) the one, or in the possible grasp of the one. Aristotle's thesis is that ontology is not in a position to constitute itself through an immediate and univocal grasp of its putative object. The entity as such is only exposed to thought in the form of the one, but it remains caught up in the equivocity of sense. It is therefore necessary to conceive ontology not as the science of an object given or experienced in its apparent unity, but as a construction of unity for which we have only the direction – πρos εν, toward the one. This direction is in turn all the more uncertain in that it starts out from an irreducible equivocity. It follows that to hold to this direction, to engage oneself in the construction of a unified aim for the science of being, presumes the determination of the minimal conditions for the univocity of the discourse, rather than of the object. What universal and univocal principles does a consistent discourse rest upon? Consensus regarding this point is necessary, if only in order to take up the direction of the one, and to try to reduce the initial equivocity of being. Logic deploys itself precisely in the interval between the equivocity of being and the constructible univocity toward which this equivocity signals. This is what the formal character of logic must be reduced to. Let's say, metaphorically, that logic stands in the void that, for thought, separates the equivocal from the univocal, in so far as it is a question of the entity qua entity. This void is connected by Aristotle to the preposition *pros*, which indicates, for ontological discourse, the direction in which this discourse might constructively breach the void between the equivocal and the univocal.

In the end, it is to the precise extent that ontology assumes the equivocity of sense as its starting-point that it in turn prescribes logic as the exhibition, or making explicit, of the formal laws of consistent discourse, or as the examination of the axioms of thinking in general.

We should immediately note that, for Aristotle, the choice of the equivocal as the immediate determination of the entity grasped in its being precludes any ontological pretension on the part of mathematics. This is because mathematics possesses two traits, both of which were fully recognized by Aristotle, in particular in books B and M of the *Metaphysics*. On the one hand, it is devoted to the univocal, meaning that for Aristotle mathematical things (the μαθηματικα) are eternal, incorruptible, immobile. But this univocity comes at the price of the admission that the being of mathematical things is, as I have shown elsewhere,[9] only a pseudo-being, a fiction. Mathematics is not capable of offering any access whatsoever to the determination of the entity qua entity. Mathematics is linked to pure logic in that it is a fictional construction of eternity; one whose destiny is ultimately, like that of every fiction, not ontological but aesthetic. Therefore, it immediately follows from the notion that ontology is rooted in equivocity that logic is prescribed as the formal science of the principles of consistent discourse, and that mathematical univocity is merely a rigorous aesthetics. This is the Aristotelian knot that ties together ontology, logic and mathematics.

There are several ways of untying this knot, but they are all Platonic in one way or another. For since they stipulate that it must be possible to say being in one sense alone, they all re-establish mathematical univocity as the (at least provisional) paradigm for ontology. More specifically, they all restore to mathematics the pertinence of the category of truth, which is necessarily the mediating instance between the act of thought and the act of being. This restoration of the theme of mathematical truth stands opposed to Aristotle's relativistic and aesthetic stance, in which the de-ontologization of mathematics puts the beautiful in place of the true.

We could say that whoever thinks that mathematics is of the order of rigorous fiction – a linguistic fiction, for example – transforms it into an aesthetic of pure thought, which is essentially Aristotelian. And this is indeed why the opposition Plato/Aristotle has been one of the great motifs in my recent work.

Note that the place of logic differs essentially in each of the two options that we're faced with. What, for an Aristotelian, accounts for the force of logic, including its force with regard to mathematics? It's the fact that logic – which is purely formal and absolutely universal, does not presuppose any ontological determination, and is linked to the consistency of discourse in general – is the compulsory norm for the passage from the equivocity of being to the unity that this equivocity signals toward. But for a Platonist these characteristics are tantamount to weaknesses. This is because for a Platonist mathematics thinks idealities whose ontological status is undeniable, whereas pure logic remains empty. To sublate logic, it would be necessary for it to reach a level of mathematization that would allow it to share with mathematics the ontological dignity that the Platonist accords to the μαθηματικα. Whereas, for the Aristotelian, it is precisely the purely formal aspect of logic that keeps it from falling prey to the aesthetic mirage of the μαθηματικα, those non-existent quasi-objects. It is the principled, linguistic and non-objective character of logic that accounts for the discursive interest it holds for ontology.

We could say that the Platonic configuration is an ontological promotion of mathematics that deposes logic, whilst the Aristotelian configuration is an ontological prescription of logic that deposes mathematics.

In this sense, the position I am about to argue for is – to speak like Robespierre berating the factions – simultaneously ultra-Platonist and citra-Platonist.[10]

It is ultra-Platonist in so far as, by pushing the recognition of the ontological dignity of mathematics to its extreme, I reaffirm that ontology is nothing other than mathematics itself. What can rationally be said of being qua being, of being devoid of any quality or predicate other than the sole fact of being exposed to thought as entity, is said – or rather *written* – as pure mathematics. What's more, the actual history of ontology coincides exactly with the history of mathematics.

But our position will also be citra-Platonist, in so far as we will not presuppose the deposition of logic. Indeed, we shall see that by asserting the radical identity of ontology and mathematics we can identify logic otherwise than as a formal discipline regulating the use of consistent discourse. We can wrest logic away from its grammatical status, separate it from what is currently referred to as the 'linguistic turn' in contemporary philosophy.

It is undeniable that this turn is essentially anti-Platonist. For the Socrates of the *Cratylus*, the maxim is that we philosophers begin from things, not from words. This could also be stated as follows: we begin from mathematics, and not from formal logic: Let no one enter here who is not a geometer. To reverse the linguistic turn, which ultimately serves only to secure the tyranny of the Anglo-American philosophy of ordinary language, is tantamount to accepting that, in mathematical thought or in mathematics as a thought, it is the real, and not mere words, which is at stake.

For a long time, I was convinced that this sublation of Platonism implied the deposition of formal logic, understood as the privileged point of entry into rational languages. In doing so, I shared the characteristically French suspicion with which Poincaré and Brunschvicg regarded what they called logistics. It was only at the cost of a long, arduous study of the most recent formulations of logic, and by grasping their mathematical correlations – a study which I have only recently completed, and of which I present here only the outline or programme – that I came to understand the following: by allowing the insight that mathematics is the science of being qua being to illuminate logic, so that logic becomes deployed as an immanent characteristic of possible universes rather than as a syntactical norm, logic is finally placed once more under an ontological, rather than linguistic, prescription. And although this prescription involves taking up the Aristotelian gesture again, it does so in terms of an entirely different orientation.

Thus it is possible to do justice – a justice meted out by being itself, so to speak – to the enigmatic syntagm 'mathematical logic'. Once fully unpacked, this syntagm will now mean the following: the plurality of logics instituted by an ontological decision.

That ontology realizes itself historically as mathematics is the opening thesis of my book *Being and Event*, and I have neither the intention nor the possibility of reiterating the arguments behind this claim here, since I have already established its principal points in the first part of this volume.[11]

What is relevant for us here with regard to the question of logic is a thesis derived from the one mentioned above, or rather, a theorem that can be deduced from the fundamental axioms of set-theory, and therefore from the principles of the ontology of the multiple. This theorem ordinarily takes the following form: there is no set of all sets. This non-existence means that thought is not capable of sustaining, without collapsing, the hypothesis that a multiple (i.e. a being) comprises all thinkable beings. Once it is related to the category of totality, this fundamental theorem indicates the non-existence of being as a whole. In certain regards, and in accordance with a transposition of the physical into the metaphysical, it decides Kant's first Antinomy of pure reason in favour of the Antithesis: 'The world has no beginning, and no limits in space; it is infinite as regards both time and space.'[12] Of course, it is not a matter here either of time or space, nor even of the infinite, which, as we've said again and again, is nothing but a simple actual determination of being in general, and is not as such problematic. Instead, let us posit the following: it is impossible for thought to grasp as a being a multiple that would supposedly comprise all beings. Thought falters at the very point of what Heidegger calls 'being in its totality'. The fact that this claim is a theorem once we have assumed that ontology *is* mathematics, and hence that the properties of being qua being can be demonstrated, means that it must be understood in the strong sense: *it is an essential property of being qua being that there cannot exist a whole of beings, once beings are thought solely on the basis of their beingness.*

A crucial consequence of this property is that every ontological investigation is irredeemably *local*. In effect, there can exist no demonstration or intuition bearing upon being qua totality of beings, or even qua general place wherein beings are set out. This incapacity is not only a de facto inaccessibility, or a limit that would transcend the capacities of reason. On the contrary, it is reason itself which determines that the impossibility of the whole is an intrinsic property of the being-multiple of the entity.

To put it succinctly: a determination in thought of what can be rationally said about the entity qua entity, and therefore about the pure multiple, always assumes as the place for this determination, not the whole of being, but a particular being, even though the scale of this being may be that of an infinity of infinites.

Being is exposed to thought only as a local site of its own untotalizable deployment.

But this localization of the site of an ontological cognition, which in *Being and Event* I call a situation, affects being, since qua pure multiple being does not contain in its being something that could ground the limits of the site in which it exposes itself. The entity, qua entity, is multiple, pure multiple, multiple without-one, or multiple of multiples. It shares this determination with *all other entities*. But what is designated by 'all other entities' doesn't exist; it has no being. Consequently, in so far as the aforementioned determination is given, it is given in a site, or in a situation, which in turn, thought in its being qua being, is a multiple-being. This situation is not that of the ontological generality of being, which would be the non-existent whole of entities that share the determination of their being as pure multiplicity. A being can only assert its beingness in a site whose local character cannot be inferred from this beingness as such.

We will call that aspect of a being which is linked to the constraint of a local or situated exposition of its being-multiple, the 'appearance' of this being. Clearly, it is intrinsic to the being of entities to appear, in so far as being as a whole does not exist. All being is being-there: this is the essence of appearance. Appearance is the site, the 'there' of being-multiple when the latter is thought in its being. Within this framework, appearance in no way presupposes depend on space, time, or, more generally, any transcendental field. Appearance does not depend on the presupposition of a constituting subject. Being-multiple does not appear *for* a subject. Rather, it is of the essence of being to appear, once it is admitted that, since a being cannot be situated according to the whole, it must assert its being-multiple with regard to a non-whole, that is, with regard *to another particular being*, which determines the being of the 'there' in being-there.

Appearance is an intrinsic determination of being. But it is immediately evident that since the localization of being, which constitutes its appearance, implies another particular being – its site or situation – appearance as such is what binds or re-binds a being to its site. The essence of appearance is relation.

Now, being qua being is, for its part, absolutely unbound. This is a fundamental characteristic of the pure multiple, such as it is thought within the framework of a theory of sets. There are only multiplicities, nothing else. None of them, taken on its own, is linked to any other. In a theory of sets, even functions must be thought of as pure multiplicities, which means that they are equated with their graph. The beingness of beings presupposes nothing save for its immanent composition, that is, its status as a multiple of multiples. This excludes that there may be, strictly speaking, a being of relation. Being, thought as such, in a purely generic manner, is subtracted from any bond.

However, to the extent that it is intrinsic to being to appear, and thus to be *a* singular entity, it can only do so by affecting itself with a primordial bond relating it to the entity that situates it. It is appearance, and not being as such, that superimposes the world of relation upon ontological unbinding.

This clarifies something that seems empirically obvious and that gives rise to a kind of reversal of Platonism *tout court* in the wake of the combination of ultra-Platonism and citra-Platonism. Platonism seems to say that appearance is equivocal, mobile, fleeting, unthinkable, and that it is ideality, including mathematical ideality, that is stable, univocal, and exposed to thought. But we moderns can maintain the opposite. It is the immediate world, the world of appearances, that is always given as solid, linked, consistent. This is a world of relation and cohesion, one in which we have our habits and reference points; a world in which being is ultimately held prisoner by being-there. And it is being in itself, conceived as mathematicity of the pure multiple, or even as the physics of quanta, which is anarchic, neutral, inconsistent, unbound, indifferent to signification, having no ties with anything other than itself.

Of course, Kant already adopted as his starting-point the notion that the phenomenal world is always related and consistent. For him, the question that this world poses to us is indeed already the reversal of Plato. For it is not the inconsistency of representation that constitutes a problem, but rather its cohesion. What needs to be explained is the fact that appearance composes a world that is always bound and re-bound. There can be no doubt that the *Critique of Pure Reason* is preoccupied with interrogating the logic of appearance.

But Kant infers from the conditions of this logic of appearance that being in itself remains unknowable for us, and consequently postulates the impossibility of any rational ontology. For Kant – and this conceptual link is neither Aristotelian nor Platonist – the logic of appearance deposes ontology.

For me, on the contrary, ontology exists as a science, and being in itself attains to the transparency of the thinkable in mathematics. Except that this transparency only accords to being the senseless rationality of the pure multiple. Being qua being is caught up in the infinite task of its knowledge, which constitutes the historicity of mathematics. Consequently, it becomes possible to say that it is appearance as such that requires that there be a logic, because it is logic that establishes the 'there' of being-there as relation. The ontological base is nothing but the tendency toward inconsistency that characterizes pure multiplicity such as it is thought in mathematics.

This sheds light on our initial problem. Let's say that logic is what makes appearance *as an intrinsic dimension of being* into the object of a science. Whereas mathematics is the science of being qua being. In so far as appearance, i.e. relation, is a constraint that affects being, the science of appearance must itself be a component of the science of being, and therefore of mathematics. It is required that logic be mathematical logic. But in so far as mathematics apprehends being qua being on this side of its appearance and hence in its fundamental unbinding, it is also necessary that mathematics not be confused with logic in any way.

Consequently, we will posit that within mathematics logic is the movement of thought whereby the being of appearance – that is, what affects being in so far as it is being-there – is grounded.

Appearance is nothing but the logic of a situation, which is always, in its being, *this* situation. Logic as a science restores the logic of appearance as the theory of situational cohesion in general. This is why logic is not the formal science of discourse, but the science of possible universes, thought according to the cohesion of appearance, which is itself the intrinsic determination of the unbinding of beings qua beings.

On this point, we are very close to Leibniz. Logic is that which is valid for every possible universe; it is the principle of coherence, which can be demanded for every existent once it has appeared. But we're also far from Leibniz. For what, when thought in its being, is not governed by any harmony or principle of reason, but on the contrary is disseminated into an inconsistent, groundless multiple.

We must then ask ourselves how and where, from within the domain of mathematics, we can illuminate the mathematical status of logic as the mathematical theory of possible universes, or the general theory of the cohesion of being-there, or the theory of the relational consistency of appearance.

In this regard, we cannot remain content with the formalization of logic such as has been realized from Boole and Frege, all the way up to the sophisticated developments of Gödel, Tarski or Kleene. Admirable as it may be, this formalization remains a simple aftereffect of the initial constructions of both Aristotle, originator of the predicate calculus and the theory of proof, and the Stoics, precursors of propositional calculus and modal logic. This logical formalism assumes, as did the Greeks, that logic consists in constructing formal languages; it consolidates the idea that logic is nothing but the hard core of a generalized rational grammar. In this sense, this version of formalism is inscribed in philosophy's linguistic turn. It believes it can do without ontological prescription and overlooks the intrinsic identity of logic and appearance, or being-there. Its mathematical appearance is derivative and extrinsic, since it is nothing but a calculating literalization, an accidental univocity. All told, in this figure of logic, mathematization is nothing but formalization. Now the essence of mathematics is in no way formalization. Mathematics is a thought, a thought of being qua being. Its formal transparency is a direct consequence of the absolutely univocal character of being. Mathematical writing is the transcription or inscription of this univocity.

In order that logic may call itself mathematical in the full sense of the term, two conditions must be satisfied, which the theory of formal languages is very far from bringing together.

First condition: Logic must emerge from within the movement of mathematics itself, and not as the will to establish an extrinsic linguistic framework for mathematical activity. In giving birth to the ontological theory of sets, Cantor was not preoccupied with general and extrinsic aims, but with problems that were intrinsic to the topology and classification of real numbers. The mathematical character of logic will only be elucidated if the gesture that establishes and demarcates it effectively reproduces the fundamental theme that concerns us here: that appearance is an intrinsic dimension of being, and therefore that logic, which is the science of appearance, is itself called, summoned, from within the science of being, which is to say from within mathematics.

Second condition: Logic must not be pegged to grammatical and linguistic analysis; its primary question must not be that of propositions, judgements or predicates. Logic must primarily provide a mathematical conception of the being of a universe of relations; or tell us what a possible situation of being is, when it is thought in its relational cohesion; or again, what being-there is, as the bound essence of the ineluctable localization of being.

Consequently, a contemporary theory of logic, whose singularity we've already caught more than a glimpse of, must obey these two conditions and break with the linguistic, formalistic, and axiomatic protocol to which all of modern logic seems to have been confined. This theory, we repeat, is the theory of categories, whose product is the theory of *topoi* – an appropriate name, since it is in effect the place of being that is at stake.

This theory was outlined by Eilenberg and MacLane in the 1940s,[13] on the basis of the immanent requirements of modern algebraic geometry. Our first condition is thereby satisfied. This theory sets out, under the concept of *topos*, a conception of what constitutes an acceptable, or possible, universe such that a given mathematical situation may be localized within it. The logical dimension of this presentation of a universe is entirely immanent to the given universe. It presents itself as a mathematically assignable characteristic of the universe, and not as a formal and linguistic exteriority. Our second condition is thereby satisfied.

This is certainly not the place to enter into the technical details of what is currently called the categorial presentation of logic, or theory of elementary *topoi.* I will only retain three traits of this theory here, traits that are appropriate to the philosophical questions that concern us.

1. The theory of *topoi* is descriptive and not really axiomatic. The classical axioms of set-theory fix the untotalizable universe of the thinking of the pure multiple. We could say that set-theory constitutes an ontological decision. The theory of *topoi* defines, on the basis of an absolutely minimal concept of relation, the conditions under which it is acceptable to speak of a universe for thinking, and consequently to speak of the localization of a situation of being. To borrow a Leibnizian metaphor: set-theory is the fulminating presentation of a singular universe, in which what there is is thought, according to its pure 'there is'. The theory of *topoi* describes possible universes and their rules of possibility. It is akin to the inspection of the possible universes which for Leibniz are contained in God's understanding. This is why it is not a mathematics of being, but a mathematical logic.

2. In a *topos*, the purely logical operators are not presented as linguistic forms. They are constituents of the universe, and in no way formally distinct from the other constituents. A category, i.e. a *topos*, is defined on the basis of an altogether general and elementary notion: a relation oriented from an object *a* toward an object *b*, a relation which is called an arrow, or morphism. In a *topos*, negation, conjunction, disjunction, implication, quantifiers (universal and existential), are nothing but arrows, whose definitions can be provided. Truth is nothing but an arrow of the *topos*, the truth-arrow. And logic is nothing but a particular power of localization immanent to such and such a possible universe.

3. The theory of *topoi* provides a foundation for the plurality of possible logics. This point is of crucial importance. If, in effect, the local appearance of being is intransitive to its being, there is no reason why logic – which is the thinking of appearance – should be one. The relational form of appearance, which is the manifestation of the 'there' of being-there, is itself multiple. The theory of *topoi* permits us to fully comprehend, on the basis of the mathematicity of possible universes, where and how logical variability – which is also the contingent variability of appearance – is marked with respect to the strict and necessary univocity of multiple-being. For example,

there can be classical *topoi* which intrinsically validate the law of the excluded middle, or the equivalence between double negation and affirmation; but there can also be non-classical ones, which do not validate these two principles.

For these reasons, as well as for many others which can only be illuminated by the laborious mathematical construction of the concept of *topos*, we can assert that this theory really is mathematical logic as such. Which is to say that within ontology the theory of *topoi* is the science of appearance; the science of what it means for every truth of being to be irremediably local.

For all that, the theory of *topoi* culminates in magnificent theorems on the local and the global. It develops a sort of geometry of truth, giving a fully rational sense to the concept of local truth. In it we can read – in the transparency of the theorem, so to speak – that the science of appearance is also the science of being qua being, in this inflection inflicted by the place that destines a truth to being.

Aristotle's desire, that logic be prescribed by ontology, is thereby fulfilled. Not, however, on the basis of the equivocity of being, but, on the contrary, on the basis of its univocity. This is what leads philosophy, conditioned by mathematics, to rethink being according to what I regard as its contemporary programme: to understand how it is possible for a situation of being to be at once a pure multiplicity on the edge of inconsistency, and the solid and intrinsic binding of its appearance.

It is only then that we know why, when a truth shows itself, when being seems to displace its configuration under our very eyes, it is always despite appearance, in a local collapse of the consistency of appearance, and therefore in a temporary cancellation of all logic. For what comes to the surface at that point, displacing or revoking the logic of the place, is being itself, in its redoubtable and creative inconsistency, that is, in its void, which is the placelessness of every place.

This is what I call an event. For thought, the event is to be located at the internal joint that binds mathematics and mathematical logic. The event arises when the logic of appearance is no longer capable of localizing the multiple-being it harbours within itself. We are then, as Mallarmé would say, in the environs of the vagueness wherein all reality comes to be dissolved. But we also find ourselves where there's a chance that – as far as possible from the fusion of a place with the beyond, that is, from the advent of another logical place – a constellation, cold and brilliant, will arise.

CHAPTER 15
NOTES TOWARD A THINKING OF APPEARANCE

I. The philosophical starting point we've chosen involves showing the logical inconsistency of any concept of an absolute totality or reference, perhaps in the sense that Heidegger spoke of 'being in its totality'. The demonstrable thesis is that this concept is inconsistent, that is to say, it gives rise to a formal contradiction. I wish to argue that this concept of totality cannot be appropriated by thought.

It could be objected that the inconsistent character of a concept does not preclude its existence. This is an identifiable philosophical thesis, the 'chaotic' thesis. Here we shall try to engage thought in a different path. Clearly, this implies an element of decision.

When one makes this choice – a 'rationalist' choice in the broadest sense of the term – one assumes the philosophical axiom according to which the 'there is' is intrinsically thinkable. One thereby assumes a variant of the dictum from Plato's *Parmenides*: 'It is the same to think and to be'. It is impossible to ascribe to being traits of inconsistency which would render a thinking of being untenable. One implicitly maintains a co-belonging of being and thought.

Ultimately, that there is no Whole is a consequence of the idea that everything is intrinsically thinkable. Now the absolute totality cannot be thought. This is the Platonist orientation in its absolute generality. The exposure to the thinkable is what Plato calls an Idea. The statement 'For everything that is, there is an idea' could serve as the axiom for our enterprise. This does not mean that the idea is actual.

Let me open a historical parenthesis: for Plato, is there an idea of all that there is? This question is broached in the preliminary discussion of the *Parmenides*, when it is argued that besides the idea of the good or the beautiful there is the idea of hair or mud. This is why Plato will declare himself a Parmenidean, whence the 'parricide' of the *Sophist*. As he declares in Book VI of the *Republic*: 'What is absolutely, is absolutely knowable.' This is a decision of thought beyond which it is difficult to ascend. Chaos is set aside, not as an objective composition, in the sense in which all meaning is denied to the universe, but rather in the sense that one would acknowledge that it is possible for something to be, whilst remaining totally inappropriate to thought.

This could be expressed in the following terms: if the universe is conceived as the totality of beings, there is no universe. One can also understand by universe a situation considered as a local referent, since there is no total referent. It seems this is what Lucretius believed. This position follows from the intuition that there is no whole.

When one possesses a thinking of the multiple and the void of the sort that we find in atomism, one assumes that there is no totality. This is what separates the Epicureans from the Stoics, for whom the totality as such essentially exists. On this basis, I maintain that the history of philosophy has no unity, being originally split into two orientations. Consequently, the usage of the notion of metaphysics is inconsistent.

II. The mainspring of the logical demonstration of the inconsistency of the absolute totality is Russell's paradox. It is necessary to recall the logical context of this paradox. Our starting-point is to be located in the conceptual confidence of Frege, for whom once a concept is given it makes sense to speak of all the objects that fall under this concept. This is what is referred to as the *extension* of the concept. Extension is not an empirical given.

Frege demands that the consideration of totality be a consistent intellectual operation. Here we must distinguish between the consistent and the representable. The totality of blue objects is consistent in the register of pure thought, but it is not representable. In a certain sense, there is something Platonic in all this. The concept becomes the correlate of the totality of the objects it covers. This is what Plato calls 'participation' (in the idea).

This position constitutes an *extensional Platonism*. Extension takes place in the medium of total recollection. Contradiction is introduced via the empty set. It is this extensional Platonism that is undermined by Russell's paradox, which constructs a concept that does not have extension in the aforementioned sense. A certain kind of confidence in the concept is thereby undermined. This development is related to the Kantian tradition of critique, which introduces a limit in the use of the concept. One cannot put one's trust in the concept when it comes to the existence of its extension. This issue is intimately connected to the relationship between language and reality. In Frege, who distinguishes sense from reference, every concept has a reference. This means that language refers either to reality per se or to a particular reality. One can then legitimately speak of the reality designated by language. What we have then is a referential concept of language. Russell's paradox tells us that it is not true that one can argue that language always refers to a reality. In other words, it is not true that language prescribes an existence for thought. This last point is crucial.

At this point we find ourselves subject to two requirements: (a) there is no totality; (b) there is no extensional Platonism.

A parenthesis: we are confronted here by the notorious problem of what it means to speak of fictitious entities. By and large, for the empiricist it comes down to the empty set, while for the rest it is not necessary for the unicorn to exist in order for us to be able to speak of it. In Anglo-American philosophy this question has given rise to numerous speculative subtleties. In our view, one cannot maintain that every well-defined concept has a consistent extension. It is possible to maintain that a well-defined predicate can 'inconsist' for thought.

III. How were all of these matters actually dealt with? What direction was followed? We can identify three paths:

1. The first argues that Russell's paradox proves one must pay attention to existence. This position is shared by the ensemble of constructivist and intuitionist orientations. It precludes demonstrations of existence by *reductio ad absurdum*. One must always be able to exhibit at least one case. This is a drastic orientation, since, among other things, it refuses the principle of the excluded middle. Its great representative is Brouwer, working at the beginning of the 20th century. It can also be encountered in the development of computer science. Arguably, it draws the ultimate consequences of the various critiques of the ontological argument for the existence of God. Incidentally, it should be noted that God has proved an extraordinary field for the exercise of rational thought, much like speculations concerning angels. In effect, both God and angels are existences that cannot be experiences – outside of mysticism. The essence of rational theology is the same as that of mathematics, which works with idealities. In logic, this translates into the problem of the relation that a concept bears to its reference. In other words, theology prepares the ground for logic.

2. The hierarchical path, whose great representative is Russell. This is the path that Russell adopts in the *Principia Mathematica*. The underlying principle is that whenever one attributes a property to a given object, the property must always be considered as pertaining to a different

level than that of the object to which it is applied. Predication is only possible from top to bottom; this is what is referred to as the 'theory of types'. One thereby eschews any circularity. This is also a Platonic universe, but one that has been rendered completely hierarchical. Within it, every concept is originarily associated with a number. The result is extraordinarily difficult to manipulate. Consequently, it will be necessary to introduce simplifying axioms (axioms of reducibility). This theory has recently re-emerged, on account of its appropriateness to the theory of categories.

3. The most operational orientation: to limit every exercise of predication to a presupposed existence. Here one begins by availing oneself of some existent. One will speak of all the x's having property P, provided they are already placed within a set. A separation has been effected. The great name that graces this operation is that of Zermelo. This is an extensional Platonism, but a situated one. All the same, it means that existence always precedes the separating activity of the concept. One will have to avail oneself of an existence, since it no longer suffices merely to avail oneself of a concept. Thus there will be initial declarations of existence, and hence existential axioms. The difficulty will concern these axioms. Zermelo's path pulls the question of existence onto the side of decision. It will be necessary to declare at least one existence, for example that of the empty set, or that of the infinite set. This is a complex point, since one moves from 'affirming the whole' to 'affirming something'. Characteristically, this entails 'affirming the nothing'. Existence will therefore be 'punctuated', as the object of a local division rather than as a placement within the Whole. Once this is done, predicative separation enters the frame.

In order to argue that everything which exists possesses an idea, it is necessary to maintain that something exists. This existence is not empirical, it is a decision of thought. Therefore, an initial non-empirical existence is required. This requirement is more Cartesian than Platonist. For Descartes there is an absolutely initial point of existence. In my view, Zermelo's axiom is a Cartesian rectification of Platonism. The cogito is a pure point of existence, the first figure of an existence without qualities. For Descartes, 'I am' each time I think in or about this point. This point of existence is beset by a constitutive instability; it is a vanishing 'I am'. We encounter here the staging of modern rationality, for which the point of existence bears the name of 'subject'.

The conclusion to be drawn is that the only being we shall admit is a situated one. Every assertion of existence must be referred to a situation – x belongs to S. No existence is allowed which does not presuppose another, except for the one decided axiomatically. This is the consequence of the fact that there is no Whole.

There will be two ways of saying x: (1) in itself, as a pure, mathematically assignable multiplicity, and (2) in so far as it exists, in terms of its belonging to a situation. Ontologically, x is said as a pure multiplicity that leaves the question of its existence undecided. When x is said mathematically, the possible and the real become indiscernible. It is from this standpoint that mathematics is an ontology. But otherwise, in so far as it exists, x is situated, it exists in a situation (or in several). This status is not prescribed by x itself. This is why the belonging of x to the situation is called its *appearance*.

Appearance is what is thinkable about x in so far as it belongs to S. The appearance of x is distinct from its being: x is also thinkable as a pure multiple. Appearance is x situated in S; x in situation; x in the place where it happens to be.

This is a distinctly non-Aristotelian thesis. For Aristotle, every physical being has a natural place. There are situations which are particularly adequate for a being x to belong to. For example, the place of heavy things will be down below. This means that the place is involved in the being of x. There is an affinity between being and the situation; this is the problem of 'elective affinities'. We will posit that there is no natural place. Consequently, the site of a being is not inferred from its constitutive properties, even if every being is situated.

Appearance is really distinct from being. Being in situation is not transitive to its multiple composition. We bid farewell to the idea of nature: appearance is not natural. For Aristotle, what is not natural is violent. Consider, for instance, the difference he outlines between the falling stone and the thrown stone. In our view, on the contrary, there is something violent about appearance.

We are thereby introduced to an elementary set-up for thought:

1. There are only multiples.
2. Every element is a being.
3. Every being is situated.
4. Appearance is distinct from being.

How does the difference between being and appearance offer itself to thought? What is it to think a being in its appearance? Let us say we have x in situation, and we propose to interrogate ourselves about the difference between x and y. This question forces itself upon us because there needs to be a principle of differentiation within the situation. Thinking in situation must therefore be a thinking of relation in the broadest sense of the term. We know the ontological difference between the two, because x and y are multiples which are the same if and only if they possess the same elements (axiom of extensionality). This does not in any way bring the situation into play. It is an ontological criterion of differentiation, which is independent of the question of knowing how x and y appear. It says nothing about differentiation within a situation, i.e. about appearance. If we consider appearance to be thinkable (because everything is thinkable, as the *Parmenides* instructs us), we are obliged to suppose that there exists a different relation which is thinkable within appearance.

We need a theory of difference according to appearance, over and above the fact that this difference may be phenomenologically obvious. This is what we will call the *transcendental*: the entire apparatus which must be presupposed in order to be able to think difference within appearance. Obviously, these differences within appearance will differ from the differences within being. What is at stake in the transcendental is the difference between the differences in being and the differences in appearance. As in Kant, there will also be a connection between the two, except that for us the thing in itself is perfectly thinkable. There are indeed a noumenon and a phenomenon, but the noumenon is knowable.

Our concern will be the exposition of the transcendental. This exposition will be carried out by moving back and forth between the condition and the conditioned. At first, we will proceed in an abstract fashion. The fact that appearance differs from being does not mean that there is no being of appearance. What thought thinks in appearance is obviously the being of appearance, and includes the difference between being and appearance. This difficulty can also be encountered in Kant's exposition of the transcendental. The thinking of the being of appearance will therefore need to be distinguished from the thinking of a particular apparent. The aim is to enable a thinking of difference, and more generally of relation. This thinking will obviously be a thinking in situation.

Let's formally suppose that we are in a situation S. The question before us is that of the difference between x and y in so far as they appear in this situation. What do we require in order to ask this question?

As a general rule, there is no reason to suppose that the same laws of differentiation apply both to being and appearance. Our working hypothesis is that these laws are not the same, since we wish to give the greatest scope to the notion of situation.

In being there are no degrees of identity (again, according to the axiom of extensionality): it is either the same or not the same; thus, the difference is classical and conforms to the law of excluded middle. Appearance is not obliged to respect this law. Phenomenologically speaking, we know that it is not. What can be predicated about appearance? Degrees, surely. If there is no Whole, being in situation is a singular allocation. The situation introduces difference within difference. The ontological regulation is bivalent. This is not the case in appearance. The identity/difference logic can vary from one situation to another. Different transcendental configurations, i.e. effectively different regimes of difference, will be permitted. All this cannot be reduced to the One.

This multiplicity of transcendentals presupposes a multiplicity of measures. An operator of plus or minus will be necessary. The formal concept will be that of a *structure of order*. This concept gives rise to the idea of the plus or the minus, of an availability of the plus or minus for formalization. Basically, the transcendental of a situation S will be an ordered set, a figure of order.

The essence of alterity is anti-symmetry, which indicates that the two places of the relation are not equivalent. The axiom of anti-symmetry is a placement of differences. The places are not interchangeable. The relation of order organizes conditions of non-exchangeability. Saying that the transcendental is a relation of order means that it is a multiple endowed with a structure of order. Order is not a structure of the situation. Within the situation, there is an ordered set; the situation is not itself ordered.

The situation is not the transcendental. The situation does not appear in the situation, since no set is an element of itself (the axiom of foundation). The situation is not given, it does not appear, but the transcendental is an element of the situation and it appears. The inapparent structuring of S would entail that S is ordered. If the transcendental appears, it is because it falls under the law of the transcendental; the identity and difference of the transcendental are themselves regulated by the transcendental. In other words, the transcendental regulates itself. This is the classical objection to any appearance of the transcendental: how can something both appear and legislate over itself? The transcendental can appear, 'more or less'. There is an experience of the transcendental itself. The transcendental is not the situation itself, it is an element of the situation, and it appears. The structure of order is an operator of plus or minus. There is also a principle of minimality that comes down to not appearing. Something that is can not appear. Thus there is the existence of a minimum, which corresponds to non-appearance. This determines what two beings have in common from the standpoint of appearance (we encounter here the operator of conjunction of appearance).

We also need an operator of synthesis, which can respond to the question: what is a global appearance? This is what we will call the *envelope*.

To undertake the exposition of the transcendental is to forward the hypothesis that every situation of appearance obeys a structure which in turn obeys this imperative.

Everything we are about to say can be placed under the heading 'exposition of the transcendental', that is, under the aegis of what reveals the legislative character of appearance.

In the Kantian tradition, this involves the exposition of a number of categories.[1] In our own case these categories will be logico-ontological. In the Kantian tradition, transcendental is understood in terms of the subjective constitution of experience. We will instead expose the laws of appearance, respecting the principle that it is beings as such that appear (against the Kantian distinction between noumena and phenomena). In this regard, our conception is more Hegelian than Kantian. For Hegel, it is of the essence of being to manifest itself. This comes down to saying that it is of the being of appearance to manifest itself, that appearance is a dimension of being itself, a consequence of its localization, of the fact that there is no Whole. We must distinguish being-in-itself from being-there. Thinking the transcendental means thinking being as being-there, together with the operations that make it possible. The most important general objective is that of trying to think what happens to beings as such once they have had to appear. Beings are marked by appearance. In saying this, we still remain within an ontological discourse. It is indeed being which is at stake, including what happens to it in so far as it has to appear. This can also be formulated as follows: What happens to beings when there is no All? This is the question of the femininity of being in Lacan's sense, the question of the being that is not-all. Where in beings is their own appearance registered? If we abstract from totality, this is a Hegelian question. What happens to being is indeed something like a synthesis; it is true to say that some kind of unification is at work.

Consequently, this is a logical project in the strong sense of the term. There is an essential connection between appearance and logic: logic is the principle of order of appearance, its legislation (linguistic legality is only one of its aspects). In any case, this goes back to Kant.

In the *Critique of Pure Reason*, Kant calls the exposition of the transcendental the 'transcendental logic'. This is actually the title of the entirety of the second part, the first consisting in an 'aesthetic'. The second part of the *Critique* covers the analytic and the dialectic. Duality is here more important than triplicity. This means that the exposition of the categories and antinomies is carried out under the 'umbrella' of transcendental logic. The latter is already introduced by Kant in the Introduction to the second part. The essential point is that Kant introduces transcendental logic by opposing it to general logic. He speaks of the 'idea of a transcendental logic'.[2]

What does the opposition between general logic and transcendental logic mean? General logic is indifferent to the question of the origin – whether empirical or a priori – of knowledge. It comprises the principle of identity, the principle of non-contradiction and formal syllogism. But it does not register the trajectory of knowing. It relates to the formal result, independently of the process.

Transcendental logic interrogates the source of knowledge. It is concerned with the possibility of instances of a priori knowledge, of that knowledge which is capable of relating to any object whatsoever. It is a question of concepts the origin of which are neither empirical nor aesthetic (and therefore not a question of space and time). It is really a question of the thinking of objects, or, as Kant puts it, of the 'science of the pure understanding and of the rational knowledge of a priori objects'.[3] Only the laws of reason and the understanding are at stake.

We must retain two things from Kant's procedure. First, transcendental logic does indeed deal with the 'there is' as such, and is effectively concerned with the relation to objects. It is not a pure linguistic syntax; it is preoccupied with the relation that reason and the understanding have to objects. Second, there is no cognitive origin of any sort here, nor any empirical origin. This is why the object becomes any object whatsoever. Transcendental logic is a theory of concepts that relate a priori to any objects whatsoever; therefore, it is not indifferent to the source of knowledge, but to the particularity of the object. This is precisely the object = x. What is sought is the objectivity of the object.

For us, the transcendental is indeed what concerns the 'there is' in general. We will treat the object as a pure mark of objectivity. We too are dealing with the object = x. We will provide a protocol of identification for the object, but there will be no identity of the object, since this would belong to the register of effective or empirical givenness. The fundamental difference with regard to the Kantian orientation is that we do not accept the distinction between general and transcendental logic. It is the logic of objectivity as such that authorizes any logic whatsoever. For me, every logic is a logic of appearance; there is no other logic. Since every logic is real, there is no logic besides that of the appearance of beings as such, the logic of the real. This logic does not differ in any respect from a formal logic. We will fuse together what Kant holds apart. First, the distinction between phenomenon and noumenon (the in-itself, i.e. mathematics itself, is easier to know than appearance). Then the distinction between general and transcendental logic (as in Husserl's title: *Formal and transcendental logic*). Formal logic is a diagrammatic approach to transcendental logic: a particular section of transcendental logic.

Kant's guiding clue is the following: at the beginning of the 'transcendental analytic', in the first section, we find the 'analytic of concepts'. In the first chapter we encounter the argument under the heading 'On the clue to the discovery of all the pure concepts of the understanding.'[4] This is where we find the exposition of the transcendental.

A parenthesis: Kant's fundamental conviction is that this exposition of the transcendental can be completed. The transcendental can be exhaustively expounded as a list comprising the pure concepts of the understanding. This conviction is sometimes stated as follows: the new metaphysics – the non-dogmatic, critical metaphysics – can be successfully realized. Kant is the Aristotle of the transcendental. He begins and ends, like Aristotle, with general logic. It is a closed project.

We can therefore ask ourselves what the leading clue may be. It is almost immediately apparent that this leading clue is general logic. The truth is that it is the completion of the Aristotelian project that allows for the completion of the Kantian one (the table of judgements inherited from general logic). The leading clue which allows for the completion of the new critical metaphysics is Aristotle's logic. For Kant, the latter has not accomplished any progress ever since its creation.

We cannot endorse such an approach. First of all, general logic is subsumed by transcendental logic. Consequently, it cannot be used as a guide in the examination of the latter. Furthermore, even if this could be done, we would not be able to accept Kant's thesis about the static nature of logic, since for us logic has its own historicity. This means that our leading clue will not be provided by a theory of judgement. We must find another path.

A second remark is in order. We no longer possess the certainty regarding the closed or complete character of this exposition, which in Kant is linked to the idea that logic is complete. We are obliged to admit that our exposition is necessarily incomplete, but without being able to define this incompleteness. This proposition belongs to the exposition of the transcendental. It relates back to the essential incompleteness of mathematics. We cannot exclude possible mathematical reversals or transformations. Kant traces his exposition of the transcendental from a logic which he believes to be complete, and can therefore hope to complete his own endeavour. This is not the case for us, because we labour within the framework of an open mathematics.

What then will be our leading clue? We will agree to call it 'phenomenological'. It will consist of a minimal phenomenology of appearance, an abstract phenomenology of localization. Since there is no logical source, there is a phenomenological one. This means that we will need to introduce some descriptive principles valid for every situation.

1. The existence of a formalism of the plus and the minus.

2. A principle of minimality (this gives meaning to the not-all, and consequently to negation itself).

3. A principle of elementary connection (how it can be said that two things are there at the same time).

4. A synthetic principle (how a 'bundle' of appearance, a being-together-there, can be thought globally).

This is a minimal phenomenological matrix from which we will draw all of the possible variants of logic. Ontology (mathematics) will be our indispensable resource. In other words, we will propose an 'ontologization' of the phenomenological. The exposition of the transcendental means a thinking of the transcendental in the ambit of the ontologization of phenomenological access. These are the guidelines in accordance with which we will realize the general programme of a thinking of appearance.

CHAPTER 16
THE TRANSCENDENTAL

A. The inexistence of the Whole

If one posits the existence of a being of the Whole, it follows, from the fact that any being thought in its being is pure multiplicity, that the Whole is a multiple. A multiple of what? A multiple of all that there is. Or since 'what there is' is as such multiple, a *multiple of all multiples*.

If this multiple of all multiples does not count itself in its composition, it is not the Whole. For one would then possess the 'true' Whole only by adding to the given multiple-composition this identifiable supplementary multiple which is the recollection of all the 'other' multiples.

The Whole therefore enters into its own multiple composition. Or: the Whole presents itself, as *one* of the elements that constitute it as multiple.

We will agree to call *reflexive* a multiple (a being) which has the property of presenting itself in its own multiple composition. Engaging in an altogether classical consideration, we have just said that if the being of the Whole is presupposed, it must be presupposed as reflexive. Or that the concept of Universe entails, with regard to its being, the predicate of reflexivity.

If there *is* a being of the Whole, or if (it amounts to the same) the concept of Universe is consistent, one must admit that it is consistent to attribute to certain beings the property of reflexivity, since at least one of them possesses it, namely the Whole (which is). Moreover, we know that it is consistent *not* to attribute it to certain beings. Thus, since the set of the five pears in the fruit-bowl before me is not itself a pear, it cannot count itself in its composition. Thus there certainly are non-reflexive multiples.

If we now return to the Whole (to the multiple of all multiples), we see that it is logically possible, once we suppose that it is (or that the concept of Universe consists), to divide it into two parts: on the one hand, all the reflexive beings (there is at least one amongst them – the Whole itself – which, as we have seen, enters into the composition of the Whole), and on the other, all the non-reflexive beings (of which there are undoubtedly a great number). It is therefore consistent to take into consideration the multiple defined by the phrase 'all the non-reflexive multiples'. Or the phrase: 'all the beings that are absent from their own multiple-composition'.

It is clear that this multiple is not itself in doubt, since it is a part of the Whole, whose being has already been presupposed. Therefore it is presented by the Whole, which is the multiple of all beings.

Thus we know that within the Whole there is the multiple of *all* the non-reflexive multiples. Let us name this multiple *the Chimera*. Is the Chimera reflexive or non-reflexive? The question is pertinent, since 'reflexive' or 'non-reflexive' is, as we have already said, a partition of the Whole into two. This is a partition without remainder. Given a being, either it presents itself (it figures within its own multiple-composition), or it does not.

Now, if the Chimera is reflexive, it is because it presents itself. It is within its own multiple composition. But what is the Chimera? It is the multiple of all non-reflexive beings. If the Chimera is amongst these multiples, it is because it is not reflexive. But we have just presumed that it is: inconsistency.

Therefore, the Chimera is not reflexive. However, it is by definition the multiple of all non-reflexive multiples. If it is not reflexive, it is within this 'all', this whole, and therefore, it presents itself. It is reflexive. Inconsistency, once again.

Since the Chimera can be neither reflexive nor non-reflexive, and since this partition admits of no remainder, we must conclude that the Chimera is not. But the being of the Chimera followed necessarily from the being which was ascribed to the Whole. Therefore, the Whole has no being – which proves statement 1.

We have just reached a conclusion by means of proof. Is this really necessary? Would it not be simpler to consider the inexistence of the Whole as a matter of evidence? It seems that the supposition of the existence of the Whole relates back to those outdated ancient conceptions of the cosmos that envisaged it as the beautiful and finite totality of the world. This is indeed how Koyré understood it, when he entitled his studies on the Galilean 'epistemological break': *From the Closed World to the Infinite Universe*.[1] The argument concerning the 'disclosure' of the Whole is then rooted in the Euclidean infinity of space and in the isotropic neutrality of what inhabits it.

However, there are serious objections to this purely axiomatic treatment of detotalization.

First of all, it is being as such that we are here declaring cannot constitute a whole, not the world, or nature, or the physical universe. It is indeed a question of establishing that every consideration of being-in-totality is inconsistent. The question of the limits of the visible universe is but a secondary aspect of the ontological question of the Whole.

Moreover, even if one only considers the world, it quickly becomes obvious that contemporary cosmology falls on the side of its finitude (or its closure) rather than of its radical detotalization. This cosmology even re-establishes, with the theory of the Big Bang, the well-known metaphysical path going from the initial One (in this case, the infinitely dense 'point' of matter and its explosion) to the multiple-Whole (in this case, the galactic clusters and their composition).

The infinite discussed by Koyré is still too undifferentiated to acquire, with respect to the question of the Whole, the value of an irreversible break. Today we know, especially after Cantor, that the infinite can indeed be local, that it can characterize a singular being, and that it is not only – as is Newton's space – the property that marks the global place of every thing.

In the end, the question of the Whole, since it is essentially logical or ontological, cannot be decided in terms of physical or phenomenological evidence. It calls for an argument, the very one that mathematicians discovered at the beginning of the twentieth century, and which we have reformulated here.

B. Derivation of the thinking of a being on the basis of that of another being

A multiple-being can only be thought to the extent that its composition – i.e. the elements belonging to it – is determined. The multiple that has no elements thus finds itself immediately determined. It is the Void. All other multiple-beings are only 'mediately' determined, by considering the beings from which their elements derive. Therefore, the fact that multiple-beings can be thought implies that at least one being is determined in thought 'prior to them'.

As a general rule, the being of a multiple-being is thought on the basis of an operation that indicates how its elements derive from another being, whose determination is already effective. The axioms of the theory of multiples (or rational ontology) aim in great part at regulating these operations. Let us mention here at least two classical operations. We will say that given a being-multiple, it is consistent to think the being of another being, the elements of which are the elements of the elements of the first (this is the operation of immanent dissemination). And we will say that given a being, the possibility of thinking the other being whose elements are the parts of the first is guaranteed (this is the operation of 'extraction of parts', or of representation).

Ultimately, it is clear that every thinkable being is drawn from operations first applied to the void alone. A being will be the more complex the longer the operational chain that, on the basis of the void, leads to its determination. The degree of complexity is technically measurable: this is the theory of 'ontological rank'.

If there was a being of the Whole, doubtless we could separate within it any multiple by taking into account the properties that singularize this or that multiple. Moreover, there would be a universal 'place' of beings, on the basis of which both the existence of what is and the relations between beings would be arranged. In particular, the predicative separation would uniformly determine multiplicities by identification and differentiation within the Whole.

But, as we have just seen, there is no Whole. Therefore, there is no uniform procedure of identification and differentiation of beings. Thinking about any being is always a local question, in as much as it is derived from singular beings and is not inscribed in any multiple whose referential value would be absolutely general.

Let us consider this from a slightly different angle. From the inexistence of the Whole it follows that every multiple-being enters into the composition of other beings, without this plural (the others) ever being able to fold back upon a singular (the Other). For if all beings were elements of a single Other, the Whole would be. But since the concept of Universe 'inconsists', as vast as the multiple in which a singular being is inscribed may be, there exist others, not enveloped in the first multiple, in which this being is also inscribed.

In the end, there is no possible uniformity covering the derivations of the intelligibility of beings, nor a place of the Other in which all of them could be situated.

The identifications and relations of beings are always local. The site of these identifications and relations is what we call a world.

In the context of the operations of thought whereby the being of a being is guaranteed in terms of that of another being, one calls 'world' (for these operations) a multiple-being such that, if a being belongs to it, every being whose being is assured on the basis of the first – in accordance with the aforementioned operations – belongs to it equally.

Thus, a world is a multiple-being closed for certain derivations of being.

C. A being is thinkable only in as much as it belongs to a world

The possibility of thinking the being of a being follows from two things: one other being (at least), the being of which is guaranteed; and one operation (at least) which legitimates thought passing from this other being to the one whose being of which needs to be guaranteed. But the operation presumes that the space in which it is exercised, that is, the (implicit) being-multiple within which the operational passage takes place, is itself presentable. In other words, one can indeed say that the being of a being is always guaranteed in a local manner, in terms of the being of another being. Ultimately, this is the case because there is no Whole. But what precisely is the place of the local, if there is no Whole? This place is surely the site where operation operates. We are guaranteed one point in this place: the other being (or beings) on the basis of which the operation (or operations) give access to the being of the 'new' being. And the being thus guaranteed in its being names another point within the place. 'Between' these two points there is the operational passage, on the basis of the place as such.

Ultimately, what indicates the place is the operation. But what localizes an operation? Obviously, it is a world (for this operation). There where 'it' operates without existing, 'there' is the place where the being attains its thinkable being – its consistency. Thus, a being is exposed to the thinkable only in so far as – invisibly, in the guise of an operation that localizes it – it names, within a world, a new point. It is thus that a being appears in a world.

We can now think what the situation of a being is:

We call 'situation of being', for a singular being, the world in which it inscribes a local procedure of access to its being on the basis of other beings.

It is clear that, as long as it is, a being is situated by or appears in a world.

If we speak of a *situation of being* for a being, it is because it would be ambiguous, and ultimately mistaken, to speak too quickly about the *world of a being*, or about its being-in-the-world. In effect it goes without saying that a being, abstractly determined as pure multiplicity, can appear in different worlds. It would be absurd to think that there is an intrinsic link between such and such a being and such and such a world. The 'worldlification' of a (formal) being, which is its being-there or its appearance, is ultimately a logical operation: the access to a guarantee of its being. This operation is capable of appearing in numerous ways, and to carry along with it, as the bases for the derivations of being that it effects, entirely distinct worlds. Not only is there a plurality of worlds, but the 'same' being – ontologically the 'same' – generally co-belongs to different worlds.

In particular, man is the animal that appears in a great number of worlds. Empirically speaking, this animal is simply the being which, amongst all those whose being we acknowledge, appears most multiply. The human animal is the being of the thousand logics. We shall see, much later in our exposition, that, since it is capable of entering into the composition of a subject of truth, the human animal can even contribute to the appearance of a (generic) being for such and such a world. That is, it is capable of including itself in the ascent of appearance (the plurality of worlds, logical construction) towards being (the pure multiple, universality), and it can do this vis-à-vis a virtually unlimited number of worlds.

This capacity notwithstanding, the human animal cannot hope for a worldly proliferation as exhaustive as that of its principal competitor: the void. Since the void is the only immediate being, it follows that it figures in every world. In its absence, in effect, no operation has a starting point in being; no operation can operate without the void. Without the void there is no world, if by 'world' we understand the closed place of an operation. Conversely, where there is operation – that is, where there is world – the void can be registered.

Ultimately, man is the animal that desires the worldly ubiquity of the void. It is – as a logical power – the *voided* animal. This is the fugitive One of its infinite appearances.

The difficulty of this theme (the worldly multiplicity of a unity of being) derives from the following point: when a being is thought in its pure form of being, unsituated outside of intrinsic ontology (mathematics), one takes no consideration of the possibility that it has of belonging to different situations (to different worlds). The identity of a multiple is considered only from the narrow vantage point of its multiple composition. Of course, and as we've already remarked, this composition is itself only 'mediately' thought – save in the case of the pure multiple. It is validated, in the consistency of its being, only by being derived from multiple-beings whose being is guaranteed. And the derivations are in turn regulated by axioms. But the possibility for a being to be situated in heterogeneous worlds is not reducible to the mediate or derived character of every assertion regarding its being.

Let us consider, for example, some singular human animals – let's say Ariadne and Bluebeard. The world-fable in which they are given, in Perrault's tale, is well known: a lord kidnaps and murders a number of women. The last of them, doubtless because her relationship to the situation is different, discovers the truth and (depending on the variant) flees or gets Bluebeard killed. In short, she interrupts the series of feminine destinies. This woman, who is also the Other-woman of the series, is anonymous in Perrault's tale (only her sister is accorded the grace of a proper name, 'Anna, my sister Anna . . .'). In Bartok's brief and dense opera, *Bluebeard's Castle*, her name is Judith, while it is Ariadne in Maeterlinck's piece, *Ariadne and Bluebeard*, adapted by Paul Dukas into a magnificent yet almost unknown opera.

It would be a mistake to be surprised by our adopting as an example the logic of appearance of the opera by Maeterlinck-Dukas. The opera is essentially about the visibility of deliverance, about the fact that it is not enough for freedom to be (in this case under the name and acts of Ariadne), but that freedom must also appear, in particular to those who are deprived of it. Such is the case for the five wives of Bluebeard, who do not want to be freed. It is the case even though Ariadne frees them de facto (but not subjectively) and, from the beginning of the fable, sings this astonishing maxim: 'First, one must disobey: it's the first duty when the order is menacing and refuses to explain itself.'

In a brilliant and sympathetic commentary on *Ariadne and Bluebeard*, Olivier Messiaen, who was the respectful student of Paul Dukas, highlights one of the heroine's replies: 'My poor, poor sisters! Why then do you want to be freed, if you so adore your darkness?' Messiaen then compares this call directed at the submitted women to St John's famous declaration: 'The light shines in the darkness and the darkness has not understood.'[2] What is at stake, from one end to the other of this musical fable, is the relation between true-being (Ariadne) and its appearance (Bluebeard's castle, the other women). How does the light make itself present, in a world transcendentally regulated by the powers of darkness? We can follow the intellectualized sensorial component of this problem throughout the second act, which, in the orchestral score and the soaring vocals of Ariadne, is a terrible ascent toward light, and is something like the manifestation of a becoming-manifest of being, an effervescent localization of being-free in the palace of servitude.

But let us begin with some simple remarks. First of all, the proper names 'Ariadne' and 'Bluebeard' convey the capacity for appearing in narrative, musical or scenic situations that are altogether discontinuous: Ariadne before knowing Bluebeard, the encounter, Ariadne leaving the castle, Bluebeard the murderer, Bluebeard as child, Ariadne freeing the captives, Bluebeard and Ariadne in the sexual arena, etc. This capacity is in no way regulated by the set of genealogical constructions required in order to fix the referent of these proper names within the real. Of course, the vicissitudes that affect the two characters from one world to another presuppose that, under the proper names, a genealogical invariance authorizes the thought of the same. But this 'same' does not appear; it is strictly reduced to the names. Appearance is always the transit of a world; and the world in turn logically regulates what shows itself within it as being-there. Similarly, the set of whole natural numbers N, once the procedure of succession that authorizes its concept is given, does not by itself indicate that it can be either the transcendent infinite place of finite calculations, or a discrete sub-set of the continuum, or the reservoir of signs for the numbering of this book's pages, or what allows one to know which candidate holds the majority in an election, or something else altogether. Ontologically, these are indeed the 'same' whole numbers, which simply means that, if I reconstruct their concept on the basis of rational ontology, I will obtain the same ontological assertions in every case. But this constructive invariance no longer obtains in the potative univocity of signs, when the numbers appear in properly incomparable situations.

It is therefore guaranteed that the possibility of thinking a being grasped in the efficacy of its appearance includes something other than the ontological or mathematical construction of its multiple-identity. But what?

The answer is: a logic, whereby every being finds itself arranged and constrained as soon as it appears locally, and its being is thus affirmed as being-there.

In effect, what does it mean for a singular being to be there, once its being – which is a pure mathematical multiplicity – does not prescribe anything about this 'there' to which it is consigned? It necessarily means the following:

(a) That it differs from itself. Being-there is not the same as being qua being. It is not the same, because the thought of the being qua being does not envelop the thought of the being-there.

(b) That it differs from other beings from the same world. Being-there is indeed this being that (ontologically) is not an other, and its inscription with others in this world cannot abolish this differentiation. On the one hand, the differentiated identity of a being cannot account on its own for the appearance of this being in a world. But on the other hand, the identity of a world can no more account on its own for the differentiated being of what appears.

The key to the think of appearance is to be able to determine at one and the same time, where singular beings are concerned, the self-difference which imposes that being-there should not equal being qua being, and the difference to others which imposes that being-there, or the law of the world that is shared by these others, should not abolish being qua being.

If appearance is a logic, it is because it is nothing but the coding, world by world, of these differences.

The logic of the tale thus comes down to explicating in which sense, in situation after situation – love, sex, death, the vain preaching of freedom – Ariadne is something other than 'Ariadne', Bluebeard something other than 'Bluebeard'; but also how Ariadne is something other than Bluebeard's other wives, even though she is also one of them, and Bluebeard something other than a maniac, even though he is traversed by his repetitive choice, etc. The tale can only attain consistency to the extent that this logic is effective, so that we know that Ariadne is 'herself', and differs from Sélysette, Ygraine, Mélisande, Bellangère and Alladine (in the opera, these are the other women in the series, who are not dead and who refuse to be freed by Ariadne) – but also that she differs from herself once she has been affected by the world of the tale. The same can be said of 197, to the extent that when it is numbering a page or a certain quantity of voters it is indeed *this* mathematically constructible number, but also isn't, no more than it is 198, which nevertheless, standing right next to it, shares its fate, which is to appear on the pages of this book.

Since a being, having been rendered worldly, both is and is not what it is, and since it differs from those beings that, in an identical manner, are of its world, it follows that differences (and identities) in appearance are a question of more or less. The logic of appearance necessarily regulates degrees of difference, of a being with respect to itself and of the same with respect to others. These degrees bear witness to the way in which a multiple-being is marked by its coming-into-situation in a world. The consistency of this coming is guaranteed by the fact that the connections of identities and differences are logically regulated. Appearance, for any given world, is never chaotic.

For its part, ontological identity does not entail any difference with itself, nor any degree of difference with regard to another. A pure multiple is entirely identified by its immanent composition, so that it is senseless to say that it is 'more or less' identical to itself. And if it differs from an other, even if only by a single element among an infinity of others, it differs absolutely.

This is to say that the ontological determination of beings and the logic of being-there (of being in situation, or of appearing-in-a-world) are profoundly distinct. This is what we shall have to establish in the remainder of our argument.

D. Appearance and the transcendental

We shall call 'appearance' that which, of a being as such (a mathematical multiple), is caught in a situated relational network (a world), such that one can say that this being is more or less different from another being belonging to the same situation (to the same world). We shall call 'transcendental' the operational set which allows us to give meaning to the 'more or less' of identities and differences in a determinate world.

We posit that the logic of appearance is a transcendental algebra for the evaluation of the identities and differences that constitute the worldly 'place' of the being-there of a being.

The necessity of this algebra follows from everything that we have discussed up to now. Unless we suppose that appearance is chaotic, a supposition immediately disqualified by the incontestable existence of a thinking of beings, there must be a logic for appearance, capable of linking in the world evaluations of identity no longer supported by the rigid extensional identity of pure multiples (that is, by the being-in-itself of beings). We know immediately that every world pronounces upon degrees of identity and difference, without there being any reason to believe that these degrees, in so far as they are intelligible, depend on any 'subject' whatsoever, or even on the existence of the human animal. We know, from a sure source, that such and such a world preceded the existence of our species, and that, as in 'our' worlds, it stipulated identities and differences and had the power to deploy the appearance of innumerable beings. This is what Quentin Meillasoux calls 'the fossil argument': the irrefutable materialist argument that interrupts the idealist (and empiricist) apparatus of 'consciousness' and the 'object'. The world of the dinosaurs existed, it deployed the infinite multiplicity of the being-there of beings millions of years before there could be any question of a consciousness or a subject, whether empirical or transcendental. To deny this point is to indulge in a recklessly idealist axiomatic. We can be certain that there is no need of a consciousness in order to testify that beings are obliged to appear – to be there – under the logic of a world. Although appearance is irreducible to pure being (which is accessible to thought through mathematics alone), it is nonetheless what is imposed upon beings to guarantee their being once it is acknowledged that the Whole is impossible: beings must always manifest themselves locally, and there can be no possibility of subsuming the innumerable worlds of this manifestation. The logic of a world is what regulates this necessity, by affecting a being with a variable degree of identity (and therefore of difference) relative to the other beings of the same world.

This necessitates that there be a scale of these degrees in the situation – the transcendental of the situation – and that a being can only exist in a world in so far as it is indexed to this transcendental.

From the outset, this indexing concerns the double difference to which we have already referred. First of all, in a given world, what is the degree of identity between a being and this or that other being in the same world? Furthermore, what happens, in this world, to the identity between a being (*étant*) and its own being (*être*)? The transcendental organization of a world provides the protocol of response to these questions. Thus, the transcendental organization fixes the moving singularity of the being-there of a being in a determinate world.

If, for example, I ask in what sense Ariadne is similar to Bluebeard's other victims, I must be able to respond by an evaluative nuance – she is reflexively what the others are blindly – which is available in the organization of the story, or in its language, or (in the Maeterlinck-Dukas version) in the music, considered as the transcendental of the (aesthetic) situation in question. Inversely, the other women (Sélysette, Ygraine, Mélisande, Bellangère and Alladine) form a series; they can be substituted, the one for the other, in their relationship to Bluebeard: they are transcendentally identical, which is what marks their 'choral' treatment in the opera, their very weak musical identification. By the same token, I immediately know how to evaluate Bluebeard in love with Ariadne in terms of his lag with respect to himself (he finds it impossible to treat Ariadne like the other women, and thus stands outside what is implied by the referential being of the name 'Bluebeard'). Within the opera, there is something of a cipher for this lag, an extravagant element: for the duration of the last act, Bluebeard remains on the stage, but does not sing a single note or speak a single word. This is truly the limit value (exactly minimal, in fact) of an operatic transcendental: Bluebeard is absent from himself.

Similarly, I know that between the number 199 and the number 200, if indexed as pages of a book, there is of course a difference which is in a sense absolute; but I also know that, seen 'as pages', they are very close, that they are perhaps numbering variants of the same theme – say a dull repetition – so that it makes sense, in the world instituted by the reading of the book, to say (this being the transcendental evaluation proper to this book) that the numbers 199 and 200 are almost identical. This time we are dealing with the maximal value of what a transcendental can impose, in terms of identity, upon the appearance of numbers.

Thus the value of the identities and differences of a being to itself and of a being to others, varies transcendentally between an almost nil identity and a total identity, between absolute difference and in-difference.

It is therefore clear in what sense we call *transcendental* that which allows a local (or intra-worldly) evaluation of identities and differences.

To grasp the singularity of this use of the word 'transcendental', it is probably necessary to remark that, as in Kant, it concerns a question of possibility; but we also need to note that we are dealing with local dispositions and not with a universal theory of differences. To put it very simply: there are many transcendentals; the intra-worldly regulation of difference is itself differentiated. This is one of the main reasons why it is impossible here to argue for a unified 'centre' of transcendental organization such as the Kantian Subject.

Historically, the first great example of what one could call a transcendental inquiry ('How is difference possible?') was proposed by Plato in the *Sophist*. Let us take, he suggests, two crucial Ideas (supreme genera or kinds) – movement and rest, for example. What does it mean to say that these two Ideas are not identical? Since what makes the intelligibility of movement and rest possible is precisely their Idea, it is entirely impossible to respond to the question about their ideal difference by way of the supposed acknowledgement of an empirical difference (the evidence that a body in movement is not at rest). One possible solution consists in relying upon a third great Idea, inherited from Parmenides, one that seems to touch upon the problem of difference. This is the Idea of the Same, which bolsters the operation of the identification of beings, ideas included (any being is the same as itself). Couldn't we say that movement and rest are different because the Same does not subsume them simultaneously? It is at this point that Plato makes a remarkable decision – a truly transcendental decision. He decides that difference cannot be thought as the simple absence of identity. It is from this decision onwards, and in the face of its ineluctable consequences (the existence of non-being), that Plato breaks with Parmenides: contrary to what is argued by the Eleatic philosopher, the law of being makes it impossible for Plato to think difference solely with the aid of Idea of the Same. There must be a proper Idea of difference, an Idea that is not reducible to the negation of the Idea of the Same. Plato names this Idea 'the Other'. On the basis of this Idea, saying that movement is other than rest brings into play an underlying *affirmation* within thought (that of the existence of the Other, and ultimately that of the existence of non-being) instead of merely signifying that movement is not identical to rest.

The Platonic transcendental configuration is constituted by the triplet of being, the Same, and the Other, supreme genera or kinds that allow access to the thought of identity and difference in any configuration of thought. It is clear that the transcendental, whether the word itself is used or not, always comes down to the registering of a positivity of difference, to the refusal to posit difference as nothing but the negation of identity. This is what Plato declares by 'doubling' the Same with the existence of the Other.

What Plato, Kant and my own proposal have in common is the acknowledgement that the rational comprehension of differences in being-there (i.e., of intra-worldly differences) is not deducible from the ontological identity of the beings in question. This is because ontological identity says nothing about the localization of beings. Plato says: simply in order to think the difference between movement and rest, I cannot be satisfied with a Parmenidean interpretation that refers every entity to its identity with itself. I cannot limit myself to the path of the Same, the truth of which is nevertheless beyond dispute. I will therefore introduce a diagonal operator: the Other. Kant says: the thing-in-itself cannot account either for the diversity of phenomena or for the unity of the phenomenal world. I will therefore introduce a singular operator, the transcendental subject, which binds experience in its objects. And Badiou says: the mathematical theory of the pure multiple doubtlessly exhausts the question of the being of a being, save for the fact that its appearance – logically localized by its relations to other beings – is not ontologically deducible. It is therefore necessary to construct special logical machinery to account for the intra-worldly cohesion of appearance.

I have decided to put my trust in this lineage by retrieving the old word 'transcendental' in such a way as to purge it of its constituting and subjective tenor.

E. It must be possible to think in a world what does not appear within it

There are a number of ways that this point could be argued. The most immediate would be to assume that it is impossible to think the non-appearance of a being in a given world and to conclude that it is necessary that every being be thinkable as appearing within it. But this would entail said world localising every being. Consequently, this would reinstate the Universe or the Whole, the impossibility of which we have already stated.

We can also argue on the basis of the thought of being-there as necessarily including the possibility of a 'not-being-there', without which it would be identical to the thought of being qua being. For this possibility to be transcendentally effective, it must be possible for a zero degree of appearance to be exposed. In other words, the consistency of appearance requires there to be a transcendental marking, or a logical mark, of non-appearance. The possibility of thinking non-appearance rests on this marking, which is the intra-worldly index of the not-there of a being.

Finally, we can say that the evaluation of the degree of identity or difference between two beings would be ineffective if these degrees were themselves not situated on the basis of their minimum. That two beings are strongly identical in a determinate world makes sense to the extent that the transcendental measure of this identity is 'large'. But 'large' in turn has no meaning unless referred to 'less large' and finally to 'nil', which by designating zero-identity also allows a thinking of absolute difference. Ultimately, then, the necessity of a minimal degree of identity derives from the fact that worlds are never Parmenidean (unlike being as such, or the ontological situation, i.e., mathematics): they admit of absolute differences, which are thinkable within appearance only in so far as non-appearance is also thinkable.

These three arguments permit the conclusion that there exists, for every world, a transcendental measure of the not-appearing-in-this-world, which is evidently a minimum (a sort of zero) in the order of the evaluations of appearance.

Let us not forget, however, that, strictly speaking, a transcendental measure always pertains to the identity or difference of two beings in a determinate world. When we speak of an 'evaluation of appearance', as we have been doing from the start, this is only for the sake of expediency. For *what is measured or evaluated for the transcendental organization of a world is in fact the degree of intensity of the difference of appearance between two beings in this world, and not an intensity of appearance considered 'in itself'*.

In so far as it regards the transcendental, the thinking of the non-apparent comes down to saying that the identity between an ontologically determinate being and every being that really appears in a world is minimal (in other words, nil for what is internal to this world). Since it is identical to nothing that appears within a world, or (which amounts to the same) absolutely different from everything that appears within it, it can be said of this being that it does not appear within a given world. It is not there. This means that to the extent that its being is attested, and therefore localized, it is somewhere else, not there (it is in another world).

If this book has 256 pages – an uncertain thing at the moment of my writing – 321 does not appear within it, because none of the numbers that collect this paginated substance – 1 to 256, for example – can be said to be, even in a weak sense, identical to 321, with regard to this book as world.

This consideration is not an arithmetical (ontological) one. We have already noted that, after all, two arithmetically differentiated pages – 164 and 165, for example – can, on account of their sterile and repetitive aspect, be considered as transcendentally 'very identical' in terms of the world of the book. So that this argument, here on page 211, is 'almost' identical to the one proposed on page 208. This means that under certain relations, and in terms of the book-world in progress, the truth of the statement '211 equals 208' has some strong arguments in its favour. This is because the transcendental causes the emergence of intra-worldly traits, whereas prior to its functioning there are absolute ontological differences. This is all the more so in that it plays – whence the intelligibility of the localization of beings – upon degrees of identity: my two arguments are 'close', pages 164 and 165 'repeat', etc.

But as concerns page 321, it is not of the book in the following sense: no page is capable of being, whether in a strong or weak manner, identical to page 321. In other words, supposing that one wants to force page 321 to be co-thinkable in and for the world that is this book, one can at most say that the transcendental measure of the identity of '321' and of every page of this book-world is nil (minimal). One will conclude that the number 321 does not appear in this world.

The subtle point I am trying to make is that it is always through an evaluation of minimal identity that I make pronouncements about the non-apparent. It makes no sense to transform the judgement 'such and such a being is not there' into an ontological judgement. There is no being of not-being-there. What I can say of such a being, with respect to its localization – with respect to its ontological situation – is that its identity with such and such a being of this situation or this world is minimal, that is, nil according to the transcendental of this world. Appearance, which is the local or worldly attestation of a being, is logical through and through, and therefore relational. It follows that the non-apparent is a case of a nil degree of relation, and never a non-being pure and simple.

If I force the supposition of a very beautiful woman – Ava Gardner, let's say – to participate in the world of the cloistered (or dead?) wives of Bluebeard, it is on the basis of the eventual nullity of her identity to the series of spouses (her identity to Sélysette, Ygraine, Mélisande, Bellangère and Alladine has the minimum as its measure), but also of the zero degree of her identity to the other-woman of the series (Ariadne), that I will conclude that she does not appear within it – not on the grounds of some putative ontological absurdity affecting her marriage to Bluebeard. An absurdity, moreover, that would have been contravened had she come to play the role of Ariadne in Maeterlinck's opera, in which case it would have indeed been necessary – in accordance with the transcendental of the theatre-world – to pronounce oneself, via her acting, upon the degree of identity between 'her' and Ariadne, and therefore upon her apparent-interiority to the scenic version of the tale. This problem was already posed by Maeterlinck's mistress, Georgette Leblanc, of whom we can legitimately ask if (and to what extent) she is identical to Ariadne, since she claimed to be her model and even her genuine creator; this is particularly the case when Ariadne acknowledges (in an admirable aria penned by Dukas) that most women do not want to be freed. This identity is all the more strongly affirmed in that Georgette Leblanc, a singer, created the role of Ariadne after having been refused that of Mélisande in Debussy's opera, something that wounded her greatly. Yes, it makes sense to say that the degree of identity between (the fictional) Ariadne and (the real) Georgette Leblanc is very high.

This is how the question of a non-nil degree of identity between Georgette Leblanc and Ava Gardner could have arisen, or been there in a worldly connection logically instituted between writing, love, music, theatre and cinema. If this is not the case, it is because, in every attested world, the transcendental identity of Ava Gardner and Bluebeard's women takes the minimal value that it is possible to prescribe.

It also follows from this that there is an absolute difference between the matador Miguel Dominguin (Ava Gardner's notorious lover) and Bluebeard. At least this is the case in every attested world, including *The Barefoot Contessa*, Mankiewicz's very beautiful film, where the entire question is that of knowing whether Ava Gardner's beauty can pass unscathed from the matador to the prince. The film's transcendental response is 'no'. She dies.

As we will see, to die simply means to cease appearing, in a determinate world.[3]

F. The conjunction of two apparents in a world

One of the crucial aspects of the consistency of a world is that what sustains the co-appearance of two beings within it should be immediately legible. What does this legibility mean? Basically, that the intensity of the appearance of the part 'common' to the two beings – common in terms of appearance – allows itself to be evaluated. What is implied, in other words, is the evaluation of what these two beings have in common in so far as they are here, in this world.

Broadly speaking, the phenomenological or allegorical inquiry – taken here as a subjective guide and not as truth – immediately discerns three cases.

Case 1. Two beings are there, in the world, according to a necessary connection of their appearance. Thus, for example, a being which is the identifying part of another. Beholding the red leafage of virgin ivy upon a wall in autumn, I could say that it is arguably constitutive, in this autumnal world, of the being-there of the 'virgin ivy'. This virgin ivy in itself nonetheless coordinates many other things, including non-apparent ones, such as its deep and tortuous roots. In this case, the transcendental measure of what there is in common between the being-there of the 'virgin ivy' and the being-there 'red-leafage-unfurled' is identical to the logical value of the appearance of the 'red-leafage-unfurled', because it is the latter that identifies the former within appearance. The operation of the 'common' is in fact a sort of inclusive acknowledgement. A being, in so far as it is there, carries within it the apparent identity of another, which deploys it in the world as its part, but whose identifying intensity it in turn realizes.

Case 2. Two beings, in the logically structured movement of their appearance, entertain a relation to a third, which is the most evident (the 'largest') of that to which they have a common reference, from the moment that they co-appear in this world. Thus this country house in the autumn evening and the blood-red leafage of the virgin ivy have 'in common' the gravel band, visible near the roof as the ponderous matter of architecture, but also as the hollow base for the plant that creeps upon it. One will then say that the wall of the façade is what maximally conjoins the general appearance of the virgin ivy to the appearance – tiles and stones – of the house.

In case 1, one of the two apparents in the autumn world (the red leafage) was the common part of its co-appearance with the virgin ivy. In the present case, neither of the two apparents, the house or the ivy, have this function. A third term, which represents the stability of the world, maximally underlies the other two, and it is the stony wall of the façade.

Case 3. Two beings are situated in a single world without, however, the 'common' of their appearance itself being identifiable within appearance. Or again: the intensity of appearance of what the being-there of the two beings have in common is nil ('nil' obviously meaning that it is indexed to the minimal value – the zero – of the transcendental). Such is the case with the red leafage there before me, in the setting light of day, and – behind me, suddenly, on the path – the furious racket of a motorcycle skidding on the gravel. It is not that the autumnal world is dislocated, or split in two. It is simply the case that in this world, and in accordance with the logic that assures its consistency, what the apparent 'red leafage' and the apparent 'rumbling of the motorcycle' have in common does not itself appear. This means that the common here takes the value of minimal appearance, and that since its worldly value is that of 'unappearing', the transcendental measure of the intensity of appearance of the common part is in this case zero.

The three cases, allegorically grasped according to the perspective of a consciousness, can be objectified, independently of any idealist symbolism, in the following way: either the conjunction of two beings-there (or the common maximal part of their appearance) is measured by the intensity of appearance of one of them; or it is measured by the intensity of appearance of a third being-there; or, finally, its measure is nil. In the first case, we will say that the worldly conjunction of two beings is inclusive (because the appearance of the one carries with it that of the other). In the second case, that the two beings have an intercalary worldly conjunction. In the third case, that the two beings are disjoined.

Inclusion, intercalation and disjunction are the three modes of conjunction, understood as the logical operation of appearance. The link that we have just established with the transcendental measure of the intensities of appearance is now clear. The wall of the façade appears as borne – in its appearance – both by the visible totality of the house and by the virgin ivy, which masks, sections and reveals it. The measure of the wall's intensity of appearance is therefore certainly comparable to that of the house and the ivy. Comparable in the sense that the differential relation between intensities is itself measured in the transcendental. In fact, we can say that the intensity of appearance of the stone wall in the autumnal world is 'less than or equal to' that of the house, and to that of the virgin ivy. And it is the 'greatest' visible surface to be in this common relation to the two other beings.

Thus, in abstract terms, we have the following situation. Take two beings that are there in a world. Each of them has a value of appearance indexed by the transcendental of the same world; this transcendental is an ordering structure. The conjunction of these two beings – or the maximal common part of their being-there – is itself measured in the transcendental by the greatest value that is inferior, or equal, to both measurements of initial intensity.

Of course, it can be the case that this 'greatest value' is in fact nil (case 3). This means that no part common to the being-there of the two beings is itself there. The conjunction 'unappears': the two beings are disjoined.

The closer the measure of the intensity of appearance of the common part is to the respective values of appearance of the two 'apparents', the more the conjunction of the two beings is there in the world. The intercalary value in this instance is strong. Nevertheless, this value cannot exceed that of the two initial beings, that is, it cannot exceed the weaker of the two initial measurements of intensity. If it reaches the weaker measurement, we have case 1, or the inclusive case. The conjunction is 'borne' by one of the two beings.

In its detail, the question of conjunction is slightly more complicated, because, as we've already remarked, the transcendental values do not directly measure intensities of appearance 'in themselves', but rather differences (or identities). When we speak of the value of appearance of a being, we are really designating a sort of synthetic sublation of the values of transcendental identity between this being in this world, on the one hand, and all the other beings appearing in the same world, on the other. I will not posit directly that the intensity of appearance of Mélisande (one of Bluebeard's wives) is 'very weak' in the opera by Maeterlinck-Dukas. Rather, I will say, on the one hand, that her difference of appearance with respect to Ariadne is very large (in fact, Ariadne sings constantly, while Mélisande almost not at all); on the other, that her difference of appearance with respect to the other wives (Ygraine, Alladine, etc.) is very weak, leading to the 'indistinction', in this opera-world, of her appearance. The conjunction that I will define relates to this differential network. I will thus be able to ask what the measure of the conjunction between two differences is. It is this procedure that draws out the logical 'common' of appearance.

Take, for example, the (very high) transcendental measure of the difference between Mélisande and Ariadne, and the very weak one between Mélisande and Alladine. It is guaranteed that the conjunction, which places the term 'Mélisande' within a double difference, will be very close to the weaker of the two (the one between Mélisande and Alladine). Ultimately, this means that the order of magnitude of the appearance of Mélisande in this world is such that, taken according to her co-appearance with Ariadne, it is barely modified. On the contrary, the transcendental measure of Ariadne's appearance is so enveloping that taken according to its conjunction with any one of the other women it is drastically reduced. What enjoys power has little in common with what appears weakly: weakness can only offer its weakness to the 'common'.

These conjunctive paths of the transcendental cohesion of worlds can be taken in terms of identity as well. If, for example, we say that pages 208 and 211 of this book-world are almost identical (since they repeat the same argument), whereas pages 211 and 214 are identical only in a very weak sense (there is a brutal caesura in the argument), the conjunction of the two transcendental measures of identity (208/211 and 211/214) will certainly lead to the appearance of the lowest value. In the end, this means that pages 276 and 280 are also identical in a very weak sense.

This suggests that the logical stability of a world deploys conjoined identifying (or differential) networks, the conjunctions themselves being deployed from the minimal value (disjunction) up to maximal values (inclusion), passing through the whole spectrum – which depends on the singularity of the transcendental order – of intermediate values (intercalation).

G. The regional stability of worlds: the envelope

Let us take up again, in line with our vulgar phenomenological procedure, the example of disjunction (that is, the conjunction equal to the minimum of appearance). At the moment when I'm lost in the contemplation of the wall inundated by the autumnal red of the virgin ivy, behind me, on the gravel of the path, there's a motorcycle taking off, whose noise, whilst being there in the world, is associated to my vision only by the nil value of appearance. Or again: in this world, the being-there noise of the motorcycle has 'nothing to do' with the being-there 'unfurled-red' of the ivy on the wall.

Notice that I said it's a question of the nil value of a conjunction, and not of a dislocation of the world. The world deploys the 'inappearance' in a world of a One of the two beings-there, and not the appearance of a being (the motorcycle) in a world other than the one which is already there. It is now time to substantiate this point.

In truth, the orientation of the space in question – fixed by the path leading to the façade, the trees bordering it, and the house as what this path moves towards – envelops both the red of the ivy and my gaze (or body), the entire invisible aspect of the world behind me (which nevertheless leads towards it), and finally also the noise of the motorcycle taking off. So that if I turn around, it's not because I imagine there is, between the world and the incongruous noise that disjoins itself from the red of autumn, a sort of abyss interposed between two worlds. No, I simply situate my attention, polarized hitherto by the virgin ivy, in a wider correlation, which includes the house, the path, the fundamental silence of the countryside, the crunch of the gravel, the motorcycle . . .

Moreover, it is in the very movement whereby this correlation is extended that I situate the nil value of conjunction between the noise of the motorcycle and the brilliance of the ivy upon the wall. This conjunction is nil, but only within an infinite fragment of this world that dominates the two terms, as well as many others: this corner of the country in autumn, with its house, path, hills and sky, which the disjunction between the motor and the pure red is powerless to separate from the clouds. Ultimately, the value of appearance of the fragment of world set out by the sky and its clouds, the path and the house, is superior to that of all the disjunctive ingredients – ivy, house, motorcycle, gravel. This is why the synthesis of these ingredients, as operated by the being-there of the corner of the world in which the nil conjunction is indicated, forbids this nullity from being tantamount to a scission of the world, that is, a decomposition of the world's logic.

This entire arrangement can do without my gaze, without my consciousness, without my shifting attention which notes the density of the earth under the liquidity of the sky. The regional stability of the world comes down to this: if you take a random fragment of a given world, the beings that are there in this fragment possess – both with respect to themselves and relative to one other – differential degrees of appearance which are indexed to the transcendental order of this world. The fact that nothing which appears within this fragment, including its disjunctions (i.e. those conjunctions whose value is nil), can break the unity of the world means that the logic of the world guarantees the existence of a synthetic value subsuming all the degrees of appearance of the beings that co-appear in this fragment.

Consequently, we call 'envelope' of a part of the world, that being whose differential value of appearance is the synthetic value appropriate to that part.

The systematic existence of the envelope presupposes that, given any collection of degrees (which measure the intensity of appearance of beings in a part of the world), the transcendental order entails a degree superior or equal to all the degrees in the collection (it subsumes them all); the envelope is the smallest degree to enjoy this property (it 'grips', as closely as possible, the collection of degrees assigned to the different beings-there of the part under consideration).

Such is the case for the elementary experience that has served as our guide. When I turn around in order to acknowledge that the noise of the world is indeed 'of this world', that its site of appearance is 'here' – notwithstanding the fact that it bears no relation to the virgin ivy on the wall – I am not obliged to summon the entire planet, or the sky all the way to the horizon, or even the curve of the hills on the edge of evening. It suffices that I integrate the dominant of a worldly fragment capable of absorbing the motor/ivy disjunction within the logical consistency of appearance. This fragment – the avenue, some trees, the façade . . . – possesses a value of appearance sufficient to guarantee the co-appearance of the disjoined terms within the same world. Of this fragment, we will say that its value is that of the envelope of those beings – strictly speaking, of the degree of appearance of these beings – which constitute its completeness as being-there. This envelope indeed relates to the smallest value of appearance capable of dominating the values of the beings under consideration (the house, the gravel of the path, the red of the ivy, the noise of the motorcycle taking off, the shade of the trees, etc.).

In the final scene of the opera that has served as our guide, Ariadne, having cut the ropes that bind Bluebeard – who lies defeated and dumb – prepares to go 'over there, where they still await me'. She asks the other wives if they wish to leave with her. They all refuse: Sélysette and Mélisande, after hesitating; Ygraine, without even turning her head; Bellangère, curtly; Alladine, sobbing. They prefer to perpetuate their servitude to the man. Ariadne then invokes the very opening of the world. She sings these magnificent lines:

> The moon and the stars brighten all the paths. The forest and the sea call us from afar
>
> and daybreak perches on the vaults of the azure, showing us a world awash with hope.

It's truly the power of the envelope that is here put to work, confronting the feeble values of conservatism, in the castle that opens onto the unlimited night. The music swells, the voice of Ariadne glides on the treble, and all the other protagonists – the defeated Bluebeard, his five wives, the villagers – are signified in a decisive and close-knit fashion by this lyrical transport that is addressed to them collectively. This is what guarantees the artistic consistency of the finale, even though no conflict is resolved in it, no drama unravelled, no destiny sealed. Ariadne's visitation of Bluebeard's castle will have simply served to establish, in the magnificence of song, that beyond every figure and every destiny, beyond things that persevere in their appearance, there is what envelops them and turns them, for all time, into a bound moment of artistic semblance, a fascinating operatic fragment.

H. The conjunction between a being-there and a region of its world

When, distracted by the incongruous noise of the motorcycle taking off on the gravel from my contemplation of the wall awash with the red of the ivy, I turn, and the global unity of the fragment of this world reconstitutes itself, enveloping its disparate ingredients, I'm really dealing with the conjunction between the unexpected noise and the fragmentary totality – the house, the autumn evening – to which the noise seemed, at first, altogether alien. The phenomenological question is simple: what is the value (measured in terms of intensity of appearance) of the conjunction? This is not, as before, the conjunction between the noise of the motorcycle and a singular 'apparent' (the red unfurled on the wall); rather, it is the conjunction of this noise and the global 'apparent', the envelope that is already there, i.e. this fragment of autumnal world. The answer is that the value of the conjunction depends on the value that measures the conjunction between the noise and all the enveloped 'apparents' considered one by one. Let's suppose, for example, that already in the autumn evening, one regularly hears – interrupted, but always recommencing – the whirring of a chainsaw, coming from the forest that blankets the hills. Now, the sudden noise of the motorcycle, whose conjunction with the ivy is measured by the transcendental degree zero, will entertain with this periodic hum a conjunction which might be weak but which is not nil. Moreover, this noise will doubtless be conjoined, in my immediate memory, to a value which in this instance is distinctly higher: to a previous passage of the motorcycle – not skidding, but fast and almost immediately forgotten – which the present noise revives, in accordance with a pairing that the new unity of this fragment of world must envelop.

Now the envelope designates the value of appearance of a region of the world as being superior to all the degrees of appearance it contains; as superior, in particular, to all the conjunctions it contains. Were we to ask ourselves about the value, as being-there, of the conjunction between the noise of the skidding motorcycle and the fragment of autumn set out before the house, we would have to consider, in any case, all the singular conjunctions (the wall and the ivy, the motorcycle and the chainsaw, the second and first passage of the motorcycle . . .) and posit that the new envelope is the one appropriate to all of them. Consequently, the envelope will have to be superior to the minimum (to zero), superior to the value of the conjunction of the noise and the ivy, since the value of the other conjunctions (the motorcycle and chainsaw, for example) is not nil, and the envelope dominates all the local conjunctions.

Conceptually speaking, we will simply declare that the value of the conjunction between an 'apparent' and an envelope is equal to the value of the envelope of all the local conjunctions between this apparent and all the 'apparents' of the envelope in question, considered one by one.

The density of this formulation doubtless calls for another example. In our opera-world, what is the value of conjunction between Bluebeard and that which envelops the series of the five wives (Sélysette, Ygraine, Mélisande, Bellangère and Alladine)? Obviously, it depends on the value of the relation between Bluebeard and each of his wives. The opera's thesis is that this relation is almost invariable, regardless of the wife under consideration (this is, after all, why the five wives are hardly discernible). Consequently, since the value of the conjunction between Bluebeard and the serial envelope of this region of the world ('the wives of Bluebeard') is the envelope of the conjunction between Bluebeard and each of them, this value in turn will not differ greatly from the average value of these conjunctions: since they are close to one another, the one which dominates them in the 'closest' way –

and which is the highest amongst them (the opera suggests that it is the link Bluebeard/Alladine) – is in turn close to all the others.

If we now take into account the fragment of world that comprises the five wives and Ariadne, the situation becomes more complex. What the opera effectively maintains, even in its musical score, is that there's no common measure between the Bluebeard/Ariadne conjunction and the five others. We can't even say that this conjunction is 'stronger' than the others. Were that to be the case, the conjunction between Bluebeard and the envelope of the series of six wives would turn out to be equal to the highest of the local conjunctions, the conjunction with Ariadne. But in actual fact, within the differential network of the opera-world, Ariadne and the other wives are not ordered; they are incomparable. At this point it's necessary to look for a term that would dominate the five very close conjunctions (Bluebeard/ Sélysette, Bluebeard/Mélisande, etc.) as well as the incomparable conjunction Bluebeard/Ariadne. The final impetus of the opera shows that this dominant term is femininity as such, the unstable dialectical admixture of servitude and freedom. It is this admixture, materialized by Ariadne's departure as well as by the abiding of the others, that envelops all the singular conjunctions between Bluebeard and his wives, and finally, through the encompassing power of the orchestra, functions as the envelope for the entire opera.

I. Dependence: the measure of the link between two beings in a world

The system of operations comprising the minimum, the conjunction and the envelope is phenomenologically complete. This principle of completeness comes down to the supposition that every logical relation within appearance (i.e. every mode of consistency of being-there) can be derived from the three fundamental operations.

Vulgar phenomenology, which here serves as our expository principle – much as Aristotle's logic served Kant in the *Critique of Pure Reason* – makes much of relations of causality or dependence of the following type: if such and such an 'apparent' is in a world with a strong degree of existence, then such and such another 'apparent' equally insists within it. Or, alternatively: if such and such a being-there manifests itself, it prohibits such and such another being-there from insisting in the world. And finally, if Socrates is a man, he is mortal. Thus, as far as colour is concerned, the chromatic power of the virgin ivy upon the wall weakens the chalky manifestation of the wall of the façade. Or again, the intensity of Ariadne's presence imposes, by way of contrast, a certain monotony in the song of Bluebeard's five wives.

Can the support for this type of connection – physical causality or, in formal logic, implication – be exhibited on the basis of the three operations that constitute transcendental algebra? The answer is yes.

We will now introduce a derivative transcendental operation, *dependence*, which will serve as the support for causal connections in appearance, as well as for the famous implication of formal logic. *The 'dependence' of an 'apparent' A with regard to another 'apparent' B is the 'apparent' of the greatest intensity that can be conjoined to the first whilst remaining beneath the intensity of the second. Dependence is thus the envelope of those beings-there whose conjunction with the first being, (A), remains lesser in value than their conjunction with the second, (B).* The stronger B's dependence with regard to A, the greater the envelope. This means that there are beings whose degree of appearance is very high in the world under consideration, but whose conjunction with A remains inferior to B.

Let's consider once again the red virgin ivy upon the wall and the house in the setting sun. It's clear, for instance, that the wall of the façade, conjoined to the ivy that covers it, produces an intensity which remains inferior to that of the house as a whole. Consequently, this wall will enter into the dependence of the house with regard to the virgin ivy. But we can also consider the gilded inclination of the tiles beneath the ivy: its conjunction with the ivy is not nil, and remains included in (and therefore inferior to) the intensity of the appearance of the house as a whole. The dependence of the house with regard to the ivy will envelop these two terms (the wall, the roof) and many others. It is thus that even the far-away whirring of the chainsaw will be part of it. For as we've said, the conjunction of the chainsaw with the red of the ivy was equal to the minimum, and the minimum, as the measure of the inapparent, is surely inferior to the value of appearance of the house as such.

In effect, for a reason that can only be fully illuminated under the stark light of formalization, the dependence of the being-there 'house' with regard to the being-there 'red virgin ivy' will be the envelope of the entire autumnal world.

Is the word 'dependence' pertinent here? Definitely. For if a being – 'strongly' depends on A – i.e. the transcendental measure of its dependence is high – it is because one is able to conjoin 'almost' the entire world to A whilst nevertheless remaining beneath the value of appearance of B. In brief, if something general enough holds for A, then it holds a fortiori for B, since B is considerably more enveloping than A. Thus what holds (in the global terms of appearance) for the virgin ivy – one can see it from afar, it glimmers with the reflections of the evening, etc. – holds at once for the house, whose dependence with regard to the ivy is very high (maximal, in fact). 'Dependence' means that the predicative or descriptive situation of A holds almost entirely for B, once the transcendental value of dependence is high.

It is possible to anticipate some obvious properties of dependence in the light of the foregoing discussion. Specifically, the property whereby the dependence of a degree of intensity with relation to itself is maximal; since the predicative situation of being A is *absolutely* its own, the value of this 'tautological' dependence must necessarily be maximal. A formal exposition will deduce this property, and some others, from the sole concept of dependence.

Besides dependence, another crucial derivation concerns negation. Of course, we have already introduced a measure of the inapparent as such: the minimum. But are we in a position to derive, on the basis of our three operations, the means to think, within a world, the negation of a being-there of this world? This question warrants a complete discussion in its own right.

J. The reverse of an apparent in the world

We shall show that, given a degree of appearance of a being, we can define the reverse of this degree, and therefore the support for logical negation (or for negation *in appearance*) as a simple consequence of our three fundamental operations.

First of all, what is a degree of appearance which is 'external' to another given degree? It is a degree whose conjunction with the given degree is equal to zero (to the minimum). In our example, this is the case with the degree of appearance of the motorcycle noise with respect to that of the red of the virgin ivy.

Now, what is the region of the world external to a given 'apparent'? It is the region that assembles all those 'apparents' whose degree of appearance is external to the degree of appearance of the initial being-there. Thus, with regard to the red upon the autumnal wall, this region would include the disparate collection of degrees of noise belonging to the skidding motorcycle, but also the trees upon the hill behind me, the periodic whirring of the chainsaw, perhaps even the whiteness of the gravel, or the vanishing form of a cloud, and so on. But doubtless this is not the case for the stony wall, too implicated by the ivy, or for the roof-tiles struck with the rays of the setting sun: these data are not 'without relation' to the colour of the ivy, their conjunction with it does not amount to nil.

Finally, once we're given the heterogeneous set of beings that are there, in the world – but which in terms of their appearance have nothing in common with the scarlet ivy – what is it that synthesizes their degrees of appearance and dominates all their measures in the closest possible way? The envelope of the set. In other words, that being whose degree of appearance is superior or equal to those of all the beings that are phenomenologically foreign to the initial being (in this case, the virgin ivy). This envelope will prescribe with precision the reverse of the virgin ivy, in the world 'an autumn evening in the country'.

We shall call 'reverse' of the degree of appearance of a being-there in a world, the envelope of that region of the world comprising all the beings-there whose conjunction with the first has a value of zero (the minimum).

Given an 'apparent' in the world (the gravel, the trees, the cloud, the whirring of the chainsaw . . .), its conjunction with the scarlet ivy is always transcendentally measurable. We always know whether its value is or is not the minimum, a minimum whose existence is required by every transcendental order. Finally, given all the beings whose conjunction with the ivy is nil, the existence of the envelope of this singular region is guaranteed by the principle of the regional stability of worlds. Now, this envelope is by definition the reverse of the scarlet ivy. Therefore it's clear that the existence of the reverse of a being is really a logical consequence of the three fundamental parameters of being-there: minimality, conjunction and the envelope.

It's remarkable that what will serve to sustain negation in the order of appearance is the first consequence of the transcendental operations, and in no sense represents an initial parameter. Negation, in the extended and 'positive' form of the existence of the reverse of a being, is a result. We can say that once the being of being-there – i.e., appearance as constrained by the logic of a world – is at stake, the reverse of a being exists, in the sense that there exists a degree of appearance 'contrary' to its own.

Once again, it's worth following this derivation closely.

Take the character of Ariadne, at the very end of *Bluebeard and Ariadne*, when she leaves by herself – the other wives having refused to be freed from the tie of love and slavery that binds them to Bluebeard. At this point in the opera, what is the reverse of Ariadne? Bluebeard, more fascinated than ever by the splendid freedom of the one he was not able to enslave, maintains a silence about which it can be argued that it is internal to the explosion of feminine song, so that the value of the conjunction Bluebeard/Ariadne is certainly not nil. The conjunction of the surrounding villagers – who have captured then subsequently freed Bluebeard, who no longer obey anyone but Ariadne, and who tell her: 'Lady, truly, you are too beautiful, it's not possible . . .' – is certainly not equal to zero either. The Midwife is like an exotic part of Ariadne herself, her body without concept. In fact, at the very moment of the extreme declaration of freedom, when Ariadne sings 'See, the door is open and the country is blue', those who subjectively have nothing in common with Ariadne, who make up her exterior, her absolutely heterogeneous feminine 'ground', are Bluebeard's women, who can only think the relationship to man in the categories of conservation and identity. They thereby manifest their radical foreignness vis-à-vis the imperative to which Ariadne subjects the new feminine world – the world that opens up, contemporaneous with Freud, at the beginning of the century (the opera dates from 1906). Bluebeard's women manifest this foreignness through their refusal, their silence or their anxiety. Consequently, it is musically evident that the reverse of Ariadne's triumphal song, with which the men (the villagers and Bluebeard) paradoxically identify, is to be sought in the five wives: Ygraine, Mélisande, Bellangère, Sélysette and Alladine. And since the envelope of the group of the five wives is already given – as we've noted – by the degree of existence of Alladine, which is very slightly superior to the degree of the four others, we can conclude the following: in the world of the opera's finale, the reverse of Ariadne is Alladine.

The proof is provided in the staging of this preferential negation. I quote from the very end of the libretto:

ARIADNE: Will I go alone, Alladine?

At the sound of these words, Alladine runs to Ariadne, throws herself in her arms, and, wracked by convulsive sobs, holds her tightly and feverishly for a long while.

Ariadne embraces her in turn and disentangles herself gently, still in tears.

Stay too, Alladine . . . Goodbye, be happy . . .

She moves away, followed by the Midwife. – The wives look at each other, then look at Bluebeard, who is slowly raising his head. – A silence ensues.

The end

We can see that the opera-world attains its silent border, or the explosion just before silence, when the solitude of this woman, Ariadne, separates itself in tears from its feminine reverse.

Dukas, who wrote a strange and vaguely sarcastic note about his own opera, which was published in 1936 after his death, was perfectly well aware that the group of Bluebeard's five wives constituted the negative of Ariadne. As he wrote, Ariadne's relationship to these wives is 'clear if one is willing to reflect that it rests on a *radical* opposition, and that the whole subject is based on Ariadne's confusion of her own desire for freedom in love with the scant need for it felt by her companions, born slaves of the desire of their opulent torturer'. And, as he adds, referring to the final scene we have just quoted: 'It is there that the absolute opposition between Ariadne and her companions will become pathetic, through the collapse of the freedom that she had dreamed for them all.'

Dukas will declare that Alladine synthesizes this feminine reverse of Ariadne, this absolute and latent negation, in a manner adequate to the effects of the art of music: indeed, he writes that Alladine, at the moment of separation, is 'the most touching'.

K. There exists a maximal degree of appearance in a world

This is a consequence that combines the (axiomatic) existence of a minimum, which is responsible for measuring the non-appearance of a being in a world, and the (derived) existence of the reverse of any given transcendental degree. What, in effect, can measure the degree of appearance which is the reverse of the minimal degree? What is the value of the reverse of the unapparent? Well, its value is that of the 'apparent' as such, the indubitable 'apparent'; in short, the apparent whose being-there in the world is absolutely attested to. Such a degree is necessarily maximal. This is because there cannot be a degree of appearance superior to the one that validates appearance as such.

The transcendental maximum is attributed to the being that is absolutely there.

For example, the number 633 'inappears' with regard to the pagination of this book. Its transcendental value in the world 'pages of this book' is nil. If we look for the reverse of this measure, we shall first find all of those pages which themselves are in the book, and whose conjunction with 633 is consequently and necessarily nil (they cannot discuss the same thing, contradict it, return to it, etc.), because it is not of the book. But what envelops all the numbers of the book's pages? It is the 'number of pages' of the book, which is really the number affecting the last page. Let's say that it's 256. We can then clearly see that the reverse of the minimum of appearance, affecting the number 633 as 'zero-in-terms-of-the-book', is none other than 256, the maximum number of pages of the book. In fact, 256 is the 'number of the book' in the sense that every number less than or equal to 256 marks a page. It is the transcendental maximum of pagination and the reverse of the minimum, which instead indexes every number that is not of the book (in fact, every number greater than 256).

The existence of a maximum (here deduced as the reverse of a minimum) is a worldly principle of stability. Appearance is not infinitely amendable; there is no infinite ascension towards the light of being-there. The maximum of appearance distributes, unto the beings indexed to it, the calm and equitable certainty of their worldliness.

This is also because there is no Universe, only worlds. In each and every world, the immanent existence of a maximal value for the transcendental degrees signals that *this* world is never *the* world. The power of localization held by the being of a world is determinate: if a being appears in this world, this appearance possesses an absolute degree; this degree marks, for a given world, the being of being-there.

L. What is the reverse of a maximal degree of appearance?

There is no doubt that this point is better clarified by formal exposition than by the artifices of phenomenology. The limitations of phenomenology notwithstanding, it is interesting to enter the problem by way of the following remark: the conjunction between the maximum – the existence of which we have just established – and any transcendental degree is equal to the latter. That the reverse of the maximum is the minimum is but a consequence of this remark.

Take the world 'end of an autumn afternoon in the country'. The degree of maximal appearance measures appearance as such, i.e. the entire world to the extent that it allows for a measurement of appearance. We can say that the maximum degree fixes the 'there' of being-there in its immovable certainty. In short, it is the measure of the autumnal envelopment of the entire scene, its absolute appearance, without the cut provided by any kind of witness. What the poets seek to name as the 'atmospheric' quality of the landscape, or the painters as general tonality, here subsumes the singular chromatic gradations and the repetition of lights and shades.

It's obvious that what this enveloping generality has in common with a singular being-there of the world is precisely that this being is *there*, with the intensity proper to its appearance. Thus the red of the ivy, which the setting sun strikes horizontally, is an intense figure of the world. But this intensity, when related to the entire autumnal scene that includes it and conjoined to this total resource of appearance, is simply identified, repeated, restored to itself. As a result, it's true that the conjunction of a singular intensity of appearance and of maximal intensity simply returns the initial intensity. Conjoined to the autumn, the ivy is its red, which was already there as 'ivy-in-autumn'.

Likewise, in the finale of the opera, we know that the femininity-song that rises from Ariadne, in the successive waves of music – after the sad 'be happy' that she bequeaths to the voluntary servitude of the other wives – is the supreme measure of artistic appearance in this opera-world. Which is to say that, once related back to this element that envelops all the dramatic and aesthetic components of the spectacle, once conjoined to its transcendence which carries the ecstatic and grave timbre of the orchestra, the wives, Ariadne and Bluebeard are simply the captive repetition of their own there-identity, the scattered material for a global supremacy which has been declared at last.

Consequently, the equation ('The conjunction of the maximum and a degree is equal to this degree') is phenomenologically unimpeachable. But if this is indeed the case, the fact that the reverse of the supreme measure – of the maximum transcendental degree – is also the inapparent is itself a matter of course. For this reverse, by definition, must have nothing in common with that of which it is the reverse; its conjunction with the maximum must be nil. But this conjunction, as we have just seen, is nothing but the reverse itself. It is therefore for the reverse that the degree of appearance in the world is nil; it is the reverse that 'unappears' in this world.

How could anything at all within the opera not bear any relation to the ecstatic finale, when precisely all the ingredients of the work – themes, voices, meaning, characters – relate to it and insist within it with their latent identity? Only what has never appeared in this opera can have a conjunction with its finale equal to zero. Therefore, the only transcendental degree capable of figuring the reverse of the skies opened up in this final moment by Dukas' orchestra is indeed the minimal degree.

It is thereby guaranteed that, in any transcendental whatsoever, the reverse of the maximum is the minimum.

CHAPTER 17
HEGEL AND THE WHOLE

A. Hegel and the question of the Whole

Hegel is without doubt the philosopher who has gone farthest in the interiorization of Totality into every movement of thought, even the smallest. One could argue that whereas we locate the starting point of a transcendental theory of worlds in the statement 'There is no Whole', Hegel guarantees the inception of the dialectical odyssey by positing that 'There is nothing but the Whole.' It is of the greatest interest to examine the consequences of an axiom so radically opposed to the inaugural axiom of our own work on the logics of appearing. But this interest cannot reside in a simple extrinsic comparison, or in a comparison of results. What is decisive here is following the movement of the Hegelian idea, that is, to accompany it at the very moment in which it explicitly prescribes the method of thinking.

In our case, the inexistence of the Whole fragments the exposition of thought by means of concepts which, however tightly linked, all lead back to the fact that situations, or worlds, are disjoined, or to the assertion that the only truth is a local one. As we shall see, this culminates in the complex question of the plurality of eternal truths. For Hegel, totality as self-realization is the unity of the True. The True is 'self-becoming' and must be thought 'not only as substance, but also and at the same time as subject'.[1] Which is to say that the True gathers its immanent determinations – the stages of its total unfolding – in what Hegel calls the absolute idea. If the difficulty, for us, is that of not slipping into relativism (since there are truths), the difficulty for Hegel, since truth is the Whole, is that of not slipping either into the (subjective) mysticism of the One or into the (objective) dogmatism of Substance. Regarding the first, whose principal advocate is Schelling, he will say that the one 'who wants to find himself beyond and immediately within the absolute, has no other knowledge before himself than that of the empty negative, the abstract infinite'.[2] Of the second, whose principal advocate is Spinoza, he will say that it remains 'an extrinsic thought'. Of course, Spinoza's 'true and simple insight' – that 'determinacy is negation' – 'grounds the absolute unity of substance'.[3] Spinoza saw perfectly that every thought must presuppose the Whole as containing within itself, by self-negation, all determinations. But he masked the *subjective* absoluteness of the Whole, which alone guarantees integral immanence: 'its substance does not itself contain the absolute form, and the knowing of this substance is not an immanent knowing'.[4]

Ultimately, the Hegelian challenge can be summed up in three principles:

- The only truth is that of the Whole.
- The Whole is a self-unfolding, and not an absolute-unity external to the subject.
- The Whole is the immanent arrival of its own concept.

This means that the thought of the Whole is the effectuation of the Whole itself. Therefore, what exhibits the Whole within thought is nothing other than the path of thinking, that is to say its method. Hegel is the methodical thinker of the Whole. It is indeed with regard to this point that he brings his immense metaphysico-ontological book, the *Science of Logic* to a close:

> The method is the pure concept that relates itself only to itself; it is therefore the *simple self-relation* that is *being*. But now it is also *fulfilled being*, the *concept that comprehends* itself, being as the *concrete* and also absolutely *intensive* totality. In conclusion there remains only this to be said about this Idea, that in it, first, the *science of logic* has grasped its own concept. In the sphere of *being*, the beginning of its *content*, its concept appears as a knowing in a subjective reflection external to that content. But in the Idea of absolute cognition the concept has become the Idea's own content. The Idea is itself the pure concept that has itself for subject matter and which, in running itself as subject matter through the totality of its determinations, develops itself into the whole of its reality, into the system of Science, and concludes by apprehending this process of comprehending itself, thereby superseding its standing as content and subject matter and cognizing the concept of Science.[5]

This text calls for three remarks.

(a) Against the idea (which I uphold) of a philosophy perennially conditioned by external truths (mathematical, poetic, political, etc.), Hegel brings the idea of an unconditionally autonomous speculation to its culmination: 'the pure concept that is in relation only to itself' articulates at once, in its simple (and empty) form, the initial category, that of being. To place philosophy under the immanent authority of the Whole is also to render possible and necessary its self-founding, since it must be the exposition *of* the Whole, identical to the Whole *as* exposition (of itself).

(b) However, the movement of this self-founding goes from (apparent) exteriority to (true) interiority. The beginning, because it is not yet the Whole, seems foreign to the concept: 'In [. . .] *being* [. . .] its concept appears as a knowing [. . .] external to that content.' But through successive subsumptions, thinking appropriates the movement of the Whole as constituting its own being, its own identity: 'in the Idea of absolute cognition the concept has become the Idea's own content'. The absolute idea is 'itself the pure concept that has itself for subject matter and which [runs] itself [. . .] through the totality of its determinations [. . .] into the system of Science'. Moreover, it is not only the exposition of this system, it is its completed reflection and ends up 'cognizing the concept of Science'.

Here one can see that the axiom of the Whole leads to a figure of thought as the saturation of conceptual determinations – from the exterior toward the interior, from exposition toward reflection, from form toward content – as one comes to possess, in Hegel's vocabulary, 'fulfilled being' (*das erfüllte Sein*) and the 'concept comprehending itself'. This is absolutely opposed to the axiomatic and egalitarian consequences of the absence of the Whole. For us it is impossible to order worlds hierarchically, or to saturate the dissemination of multiple-beings. For Hegel, the Whole is also a norm; it provides the measure of where thought finds itself; it configures Science as system.

Of course, we share with Hegel a conviction about the identity of being and thought. But for us this identity is a local occurrence, and not a totalized result. We also share with Hegel the conviction of a universality of the True. But for us this universality is guaranteed by the singularity of truth-events, and not by the fact that the Whole is the history of its immanent reflection.

(c) Hegel's inaugural word is 'being as concrete totality' (*konkrete Totalität*). The axiom of the Whole comes down to distributing thought between purely abstract universality and the 'intensive-pure-and-simple' which characterizes the concrete; between the Whole as form and the Whole as internalized content. The upshot of the theorem of the non-Whole is an entirely different distribution of thought, according to a threefold register: the thinking of the multiple (mathematical ontology), the thinking of appearance (logic of worlds); and true-thinking (post-evental procedures).

Of course, triplicity is also a major Hegelian theme. But for Hegel it is the triple of the Whole: the immediate, or the-thing-according-to-its-being; mediation, or the-thing-according-to-its-essence; the surmounting of mediation, or the-thing-according-to-its-concept. Or the beginning (the Whole as the pure edge of thought); patience (the negative labour of internalization); and the result (the Whole in and for itself).

The triple of the non-Whole, which we propose, goes as follows: indifferent multiplicities, or ontological unbinding; worlds of appearance, or the logical link; procedures of truth, or subjective eternity.

Hegel remarks that the thoroughgoing cognition of the triple of the Whole makes four: this is because the Whole itself, as the immediacy-of-the-result, is still beyond its dialectical construction. Similarly, in order for truths (3) to supplement the worlds (2) of which the pure multiple is being (1), we need a vanishing cause, which is the exact opposite of the Whole: an abolished flash, which we call the event, and which counts as 4.

B. Being-there and the logic of the world

Hegel thinks with altogether unique incisiveness the correlation between the local externalization of being (being-there) on the one hand, and the logic of determination as the coherent figure of the situation of being on the other. This is one of the first dialectical moments of the *Science of Logic*; one of those moments that fix the very style of thinking.

First of all, what is being-there? It is that being which is determined by its coupling with what it is not. Just as, for us, multiple-being separates itself from its pure being once it is assigned to a world, for Hegel, being-there 'is not simple being, but being-there'. He then establishes a gap between pure being ('simple being') and being-there, a gap that comes down to the fact that being is determined by what within it, it is not, and therefore by non-being: 'According to its becoming, being-there is in general being with non-being, but in such a way that this non-being is assumed in its simple unity with being; being-there is being determined in general.'[6] We can pursue this parallel further. For us, once it is posited – not only in the mathematical rigidity of its multiple-being, but also in and through its worldly localisation – being is given simultaneously as that which is other than itself and other than others. Whence the necessity of a logic that could integrate and confer consistency upon these differentiations. For Hegel too, the immanent emergence of determination – that is, of the specified negation of a being-there – means that being-there becomes being-other. With regard to this point, Hegel's text is quite remarkable:

> [N]on-being is not negative determinate being in general, but another, and more specifically – seeing that being is differentiated from it – at the same time a *relation* to its negative determinate being, a being-for-other. Hence being in-itself is, first, a negative relation to the negative determinate being, it has the otherness outside it and is opposed to it; in so far as something is *in itself* it is withdrawn from otherness and being-for-other. But secondly it has also present in it non-being itself, for it is itself the *non-being* of being-for-other. But being-for-other is, first, a negation of the simple relation of being to itself which, in the first instance, is supposed to be determinate being and something; in so far as something is in another or is for another, it lacks a being of its own. But secondly, it is not negative determinate being as pure nothing; it is negative determinate being which points to being-in-itself as to its own being which is reflected into itself, just as, conversely, being in itself points to being-for-other.[7]

Of course, the assertion that being-there is essentially 'being-for-other' requires a logical set-up that will lead – via the exemplary dialectic between being-for-another-thing and being-in-itself – toward the concept of reality. Reality is in effect the moment of the unity of being-in-itself and of being-other, or the moment in which determined being possesses in itself the ontological support of every difference from the other; what Hegel calls being-for-another-thing. And for us too, the 'real' being is the one which, locally appearing (within a world), is at the same time its own multiple-identity – the identity defined by rational ontology – and the various degrees of its difference from other beings in the same world. Thus we agree with

Hegel that the moment of the reality of a being is that in which being, locally effectuated as being-there, is identity with itself and with others as well as difference from itself and from others. Hegel's formula is superb, declaring that 'Being-there as reality, is the differentiation of itself into being-in-itself and being-for-other.'[8]

The title of Hegel's book alone suffices to prove that ultimately what regulates all this is a logic – the logic of the actuality of being. This is accompanied by the affirmation according to which, on the basis of this being-there, 'determinacy will no longer detach itself from being', for – this is the decisive point – 'the true that now finds itself as ground is this unity of non-being with being'.[9] And in effect, as far as we're concerned, what is exposed to thought in the (transcendental) logic of the appearance of beings is a regulated play of multiple-being 'in itself' and of its variable differentiation. Logic, qua consistency of appearance, organizes the aleatory unity – under the law of the world – of the mathematical capture of a being and the local evaluation of its relations with itself as well as others.

If our speculative agreement with Hegel is so manifest here, it is obviously because for him being-there remains a category that is still very far from being saturated, and very far from attaining the internalization of the Whole. As is so often the case, we will admire in Hegel the power of local dialectics, the precision of the logical fragments in which he articulates some fundamental concepts (in this instance, being-there and being-for-another).

Note that we could also have anchored our comparison in the dialectic of the phenomenon, rather than in that of being-there. Unlike us, in effect, Hegel does not identify being-there (the initial determination of being) with appearance (which for him is a determination of essence). Nonetheless, the logical constraint that leads from being-there to reality is practically the same as the one that leads from appearance to 'the essential relation'. Just as we posit that the logical legislation of appearance is the constitution of the singularity of a world, Hegel posits that:

1. Essence appears, and becomes real appearance.

2. Law is essential appearance.

The idea is a profound one, and it has inspired us. We must understand, at the same time, that appearance, albeit contingent with regard to the multiple composition of beings, is absolutely real; and that the essence of this real is purely logical.

However, unlike Hegel, we do not posit the existence of a 'kingdom of laws', and even less that 'the existent world in and for itself is the totality of existence; there is nothing else outside of it'.[10] For us, it is of the essence of the world not to be the totality of existence, and to endure, outside of itself, the existence of an infinity of other worlds.

C. Hegel cannot accept a minimal determination

For Hegel, there can be neither a minimal (or null) determination of the identity between two beings, nor an absolute difference between two beings. On this point Hegel's doctrine is thus the exact opposite of our own, which instead deploys the absolute intra-worldly difference between two beings from the 'null' measure of their identity. This opposition between dialectical logic and the logic of worlds is illuminating because it is constructive, as is every opposition (*Gegensatz*) for Hegel. For him, in effect, opposition is nothing less than 'the unity of identity and diversity'.[11]

The question of a minimum of identity between two beings, or between a being and itself, cannot have a meaning for a thought that assumes the being of Whole, for if there is a Whole there is no non-apparent as such. A being can fail to appear in a given world, but it is inconceivable that it would not appear in the Whole. This is why Hegel always insists on the immanence and proximity of the absolute in any given being. This means that the being-there of every being consists in having to appear as a moment of the Whole. For Hegel, appearance is never measurable by zero.

Of course, there can be variable intensities. But beneath this variation of appearance there is always a fixed determination that affirms the thing as such in accordance with the Whole.

Consider this passage, at once sharp and subtle, which is preoccupied with the concept of magnitude:

A magnitude is usually defined as that which can be *increased* or *diminished*. But to increase means to make the magnitude *more*, to decrease, to make the magnitude *less*. In this there lies a *difference* of magnitude as such from itself and magnitude would thus be that of which the magnitude can be altered. The definition thus proves itself to be inept in so far as the same term is used in it which was to have been defined. . . . In that imperfect expression, however, one cannot fail to recognize the main point involved, namely the indifference of the change, so that the change's own *more* and *less*, its indifference to itself, lies in its very concept.[12]

The difficulty here derives directly from the inexistence of a minimal degree, which would permit the determination of what possesses an effective magnitude. Hegel is then bound to posit that the essence of change in magnitude is Magnitude as the element 'in itself' of change. Or that far from taking root in the localized prescription of a minimum, the degrees of intensity (the more and the less) constitute the surface of change, considered as the immanent power of the Whole within each thing. In my own work, I subordinate appearance as such to the transcendental measure of the identities between a being and all the other beings that are-there within a determined world. Hegel instead subordinates this measure (the more/less, *Mehr Minder*) to the absoluteness of the Whole, which governs the change within each thing and elevates it to the level of concept.

In my own doctrine, the degree of appearance of a being finds its real in minimality (the zero), which alone authorizes the consideration of its magnitude. For Hegel, on the contrary, the degree has its real in the (qualitative) change that avers the existence of the Whole, consequently there is no conceivable minimum of identity.

Now, that there exists in every world an absolute difference between beings (in the sense of a null measure of the intra-worldly identity of these beings or of a minimal degree of identity of their being-there) is yet another thing that Hegel is not going to allow. He calls this thesis (which he considers to be false) 'the proposition of diversity'. It declares that 'Two things are not perfectly equal.' In his eyes the essence of this thesis is to produce its own 'dissolution and nullity'. Here is Hegel's refutation:

> This involves the dissolution and nullity of the *proposition of diversity*. Two things are not perfectly equal; so they are at once equal and unequal; equal, simply because they are things, or just two, without further qualification – for each is a thing and a one, no less than the other – but they are unequal *ex hypothesi*. We are therefore presented with this determination, that both moments, equality and inequality, are different in *One and the same thing*, or that the difference, while falling asunder, is at the same time one and the same relation. This has therefore passed over into *opposition*.[13]

We encounter here the classical dialectical movement whereby Hegel sublates identity in and by difference itself. From the inequality between two things we derive the immanent equality for which this inequality exists. For example, things only exhibit their difference in so far as each is One by differentiating itself from the other, and therefore – from this vantage point – is the same as the other.

This is precisely what the minimality clause, as the first moment of the phenomenology of being-there, renders impossible for us. Of course, we do not adopt, any more than Hegel, 'the proposition of diversity'. It is possible that in a given world two beings may appear to be absolutely equal. Neither do we proceed to a sublation of the One of the two beings; we do not exhibit anything as 'One and the same thing': it might be the case be that in a given world two beings will appear as being absolutely unequal. There can be Two-without-One (I am convinced that this is the great problem of amorous truths).

All of this follows from the fact that, for us, the clause of the non-being of the Whole irreparably disjoins the logic of being-there (degrees of identity, theory of relations) from the ontology of the pure multiple (the mathematics of sets). Whereas Hegel's aim, as prescribed by the axiom of the Whole, is to attest, for any given category (in this instance, the equality of beings), its unified onto logical character.

D. The appearance of negation

Hegel confronts with his customary impetuousness the centuries-old problem whose obscurity we have already underlined: what becomes, not of the negation of being, but of the negation of being-there? How can negation appear? What is negation, not in the guise of Nothingness, but in that of a non-being within a world, and in accordance with the logic of this world? In Hegel's post-Kantian vocabulary, the most radical form of this question will be the following: what becomes of the phenomenal character of the negation of a phenomenon?

For Hegel, the phenomenon is 'essence in its existence', that is, to adopt his vocabulary, a being-determined-in-its-being (a pure multiplicity) in so far as it is there, in a world. Consequently, the negation of a phenomenon thus conceived will constitute an essential negation of existence. In effect, it's easy to see how Hegel will make the fact that essence is at once internal to the phenomenon but also alien to it (because the phenomenon is essence, but only in so far as the essence exists) 'labour' within the phenomenon itself. We will therefore be able to observe the inessential aspect of phenomenality (existence as pure external diversity) enter into contradiction with the essence whose phenomenon is existence, the immanent unity of this diversity.

Thus, the negation of the phenomenon will be its subsisting-as-one *within* existential diversity. This is what Hegel calls the *law* of the phenomenon.

The solution of the problem is therefore the following: the negation of the phenomenon is to be found in the fact that every phenomenon has a law. One can clearly see here that (as is the case with our own concept of the reverse) negation itself remains a positive and intra-worldly given.

Here is how Hegel articulates the negative passage from phenomenal diversity to the unity of law:

> The phenomenon is at first existence as *negative* self-mediation, so that the existent is mediated with itself through *its own non-subsistence*, through an other, and, again, through the *non-subsistence of this other*. In this is contained *first*, the mere illusory being and the vanishing of both, the unessential phenomenon; *secondly*, also their *permanence* or *law*; for *each* of the two *exists* in this sublating of the other; and their positedness as their negativity is at the same time the *identical, positive* positedness of both. This permanent subsistence which the phenomenon has in law, is therefore, conformable to its determination, opposed, *in the first place*, to the *immediacy* of being which existence has.[14]

It's obvious that the phenomenon, as the non-subsisting of essence, is nothing but 'the being and the vanishing', the appearing and the disappearing. But it nonetheless supports the permanence of the essence of which it is existence, as its internal other. This proper negation of phenomenal non-subsisting by the permanence of the essence within it is the law. Not simply essence, but the essence that has become the law of the phenomenon, and thereby the positivity of appearing-disappearing.

Thus the sun-drenched vine in the autumn evening is the pure phenomenon for the essential 'autumn' that it harbours within it, the autumn as the compulsory chemistry of the leaves. Its appearing-red is certainly the inessential aspect of this vegetable chemistry, but it also attests to its permanence as the invariable negation of its own fugacity. Finally, the autumn law of plants, the chemistry that rules that at a given temperature a given pigmentation of the leafage is necessary, is the immanent negation, on the wall of the house, of the phenomenon 'red of the vine'. It is the invisible invariable of the fugacity of the visible. As Hegel says, 'the realm of laws is the *stable* image of the phenomenal world'.[15]

What we must concede to Hegel can be summarized in two points:

1. The negation of a phenomenon cannot be its annihilation. This negation must itself be phenomenal; it must be a negation *of* the phenomenon. It must touch upon what is apparent in appearance, upon the existence of appearance, and not be carried out as a simple suppression of its being.

   In the positivity of the law of the phenomenon, Hegel perceives intra-worldly negation. Obviously, I'm proposing an entirely different concept, that of the reverse of a being-there. Or, more precisely: the reverse of a transcendental degree of appearance. But Hegel and I agree upon the affirmative reality of 'negation', once one decides to operate according to a logic of appearance. There is a being-there of the reverse, just like there is a being-there of law. Law and reverse are by no means related to Nothingness.

2. Phenomenal negation is not classical. In particular, the negation of negation is not equivalent to affirmation. For Hegel, law is the negation of the phenomenon, but the negation of the law in no way brings back the phenomenon. In the *Science of Logic*, this second negation in fact opens onto the concept of actuality.

   Similarly, if Alladine is the reverse of Ariadne, the reverse of Alladine is not Ariadne. Rather, as we've suggested, it is the feminine-song grasped in its own accord.

The similarities, however, stop there. For in Hegel, the negation of the phenomenon is invariably the effectuation of the contradiction that constitutes the phenomenon's immediacy. If law comes about as the negation of the phenomenon, if, as Hegel says, 'the phenomenon finds its contrary in the law, which is its negative unity',[16] it is ultimately because the phenomenon contains the contradiction of essence and existence. The law is the unity of essence returning through negation in the dispersion of its own existence. For Hegel, there is an appearance of negation, because appearance, or existence, is internally its other, essence. Or: negation is here, since the 'here' is already negation.

We cannot be satisfied with this axiomatic solution, which places the negative at the very origin of appearance. As I've said, negation for us is not primitive but derivative. 'Reverse' is a concept constructed on the basis of three fundamental transcendental operations: the minimum, the conjunction and the envelope.

It follows that the existence of the reverse of a degree of appearance has nothing to do with an immanent dialectic between being and being-there, or between essence and existence. That Alladine is the reverse of Ariadne relates to the logic of this singular world which is the opera *Ariadne and Bluebeard*, and could not be directly drawn from Ariadne's being-in-itself. More generally, the reverse of an apparent is a singular worldly exteriority whose envelope is determined, and which cannot be drawn from the consideration of the being-there taken in terms of its pure multiple being. In other words, the reverse is indeed a logical category (and is therefore relative to the worldliness of beings); it is not an ontological category (which would be linked to the intrinsic multiple composition of beings, or, if you will, to the mathematical world).

Great as its conceptual beauty may be, we cannot accept the declaration that opens the section of the *Science of Logic* entitled 'The World of Appearance and the World-in-Itself':

> The existent world tranquilly raises itself to the realm of laws; the null content of its varied being-there has its subsistence in an *other*; its subsistence is therefore its dissolution. But in this other the phenomenal also coincides *with itself*; thus the phenomenon in its changing is also an enduring, and its positedness is law.[17]

No, the phenomenal world does not 'raise itself up' to any realm whatsoever. Its 'varied being-there' has no separate subsistence that would represent its negative effectuation. Existence only results from the contingent logic of a world that nothing sublates, and in which, in the guise of the reverse, negation appears as pure exteriority.

From the red of the vine set upon the wall, one will never draw – even as its law – the autumnal shadow on the hills, which envelops the transcendental reverse of this vine.

CHAPTER 18
LANGUAGE, THOUGHT, POETRY[1]

In the world today there are a staggering number of truly remarkable poets. This is particularly true here in Brazil. But – at least in Europe – who is aware of these poets? Who reads them? Who learns them by heart?

Poetry, alas, grows more and more distant. What commonly goes by the name of 'culture' forgets the poem. This is because poetry does not easily suffer the demand for clarity, the passive audience, the simple message. The poem is an intransigent exercise. It is devoid of mediation and hostile to the media. The poem resists the democracy of polls and television – and is always already defeated.

The poem does not consist in communication. The poem has nothing to communicate. It is only a saying, a declaration that draws authority from itself alone.

Let us listen to Rimbaud:

Ah ! la poudre des saules qu'une aile secoue!
Les roses des roseaux dès longtemps dévorées!

Ah! The pollen of willows which a wing shakes!
The roses of the reeds, long since eaten away![2]

Who speaks? What world is being named here? What elicits this abrupt entry into the partition of an exclamation? Nothing in these words is communicable; nothing is destined in advance. No opinion will ever coalesce around the idea that reeds bear roses, or that a poetic wing rises from language to disperse the willows' pollen.

The singularity of what is declared in a poem does not enter into any of the possible figures of interest.

The action of the poem can never be general, nor can it constitute the conviviality of a public. The poem presents itself as a thing of language, encountered – each and every time – as an event. Mallarmé says of the poem that 'made, existing, it takes place all alone'.[3] This 'all alone' of the poem constitutes an authoritarian uprising within language. This is why the poem neither communicates nor enters into general circulation. The poem is a purity folded in upon itself. The poem awaits us without anxiety. It is a closed manifestation. It is like a fan that our simple gaze unfolds. The poem says:

Sache, par un subtil mensonge
Garder mon aile dans ta main.

Learn, through a subtle stratagem
How to guard my fragile wing in your hand.[4]

It is always a 'subtle lie' that binds us to the encounter of the poem. As soon as we've encountered and unfolded it, we act as if it had been destined for us all along. And it is thus, guarded by this wing that we clutch in our hand, that we regain our trust in the native innocence of words.

Folded and reserved, the modern poem harbours a central silence. This pure silence interrupts the ambient cacophony. The poem injects silence into the texture of language. And, from there, it moves towards an unprecedented affirmation. This silence is an operation. In this sense, the poem says the opposite of what Wittgenstein says about silence. It says: 'This thing that cannot be spoken of in the language of consensus; I create silence in order to say it. I isolate this speech from the world. And when it is spoken again, it will always be for the first time.'

This is why the poem, in its very words, requires an operation of silence. We can say the following of poetry:

Du doigt que, sans le vieux santal
Ni le vieux livre, elle balance
Sur le plumage instrumental
Musicienne du silence.

Which, without the old, worn missal
Or sandalwood, she balances
On the plumage instrumental
Musician of silences.[5]

The music of silence: a reserved and refolded word, the poem is what Mallarmé called 'restrained action'. He already opposed it to this other use of language, which governs us today: the language of communication and reality, the confused language of images; a mediated language which is the province of the media; the language Mallarmé described as that of *universal reportage*.

Yes, the poem is first of all this unique fragment of speech subtracted from universal reporting. The poem is a halting point. It makes language halt within itself. Against the obscenity of 'all seeing' and 'all saying' – of showing, sounding out and commenting everything – the poem is the guardian of the decency of speech. Or of what Jacques Lacan called the ethics of 'well-saying'.

In this sense, the poem is language's delicacy towards itself; it is a delicate *touch* of the resources of language. But as Mallarmé had already remarked, our era is in every respect a stranger to delicacy. I quote: 'they behave with little delicacy, disgorging, in loud revelry, the vast expanse of human incomprehension'.[6]

Thus we can say that the poem is language itself, in its solitary exposition as an exception to the noise that has usurped the place of comprehension.

What are we to say then of what the poem *thinks*? The poem is the musician of its own silence. It is the delicate guardian of language. But what is its destiny for thought? Does a thought of the poem exist, a poem-thought?

I say a 'thought' and not a 'knowledge'. Why?

The word 'knowledge' must be reserved for what relates to an object, the object of knowledge. There is knowledge when the real enters experience in the form of an object.

But – and this point is crucial – the poem does not aim at, presuppose or describe an object. The poem has no relation to objectivity. Consider the following verses:

Comme sur quelque vergue bas
Plongeante avec la caravelle
Ecumait toujours en ébats
Un oiseau d'annonce nouvelle

Qui criait monotonement
Sans que la barre ne varie
Un inutile gisement
Nuit, désespoir et pierrerie
Par son chant reflété jusqu'au
Sourire du pâle Vasco.

As upon some yardarm low
Plunging with the caravel

A bird announcing tidings new
Gaily skimmed the foaming swell

And though the tiller never varied
Forever wailed in piercing tones
Of a motherlode deep buried
Night, despair and precious stones

Reflected by its song unto
The smile of some forsaken Vasco.[7]

What these verses seem to recount is certainly not the objectivity of Vasco da Gama's discovery of new territories. And the messenger, the desiring bird, does not (and will never) take the figure of an object the experience of which could be shared.

The poem contains no anecdotes, no referential object. From beginning to end, it declares its own universe.

Not only does the poem not have an object, but a sizeable part of its *operation* aims precisely at denying the object; at making it so that thought no longer relates to the object. The poem wants thought to declare what there is through the *deposition* of every supposed object. This is the heart of the poetic experience conceived as an experience of thought: to gain access to an ontological affirmation that does not set itself out as the apprehension of an object.

In general, the poem attains this result by means of two contrary operations, which I will call 'subtraction' and 'dissemination'.

Subtraction organizes the poem around a direct concern with the retreat of the object: the poem is a negative machinery, which utters being, or the idea, at the very point where the object has vanished.

Mallarmé's logic is subtractive. At the point where objective reality (the setting sun) disappears, the poem brings forth what Mallarmé calls the 'pure notion'. This is a kind of pure, disobjectified and disenchanted thinking of the object. A thinking that is now *separate* from any givenness of the object. The emblem of this notion is often the star, the constellation, which resides 'on some vacant and superior surface', which is 'cold from forgetting and obsolescence'.[8]

The poem's operation aims at passing from an objective commotion, the solar certainty ('firebrand of glory, bloody mist, gold, spume!'[9]), to an inscription that *gives* us nothing, since it is inhuman and pure, 'scintillations of the one-and-six',[10] and bears the marks of a mathematical figure, 'a Constellation numbering the successive astral shock of a total count in the making'.[11]

Such is the subtractive operation of the poem, which forces the object to undergo the ordeal of its lack.

Dissemination, for its part, aims to dissolve the object through an infinite metaphorical distribution. Which means that no sooner is it mentioned than the object migrates elsewhere within meaning; it disobjectifies itself by becoming something other than it is. The object loses its objectivity, not through the effect of a lack, but through that of an excess: an excessive equivalence to other objects.

This time, the poem loses the object in the pure multiple.

Rimbaud excels in dissemination. He sees 'very clearly a mosque instead of a factory'.[12] Life itself, like the subject, is other and multiple; for instance, 'this gentleman does not know what he is doing: he is an angel'.[13] And this family is 'a pack of dogs'.[14]

Above all, the desire of the poem is a kind of migration among disparate phenomena. The poem, far from *founding* (*fonder*) objectivity, seeks literally to *melt* (*fondre*) it down.

Mais fondre où fond ce nuage sans guide
– Oh, favorisé de ce qui est frais!
Expirer en ces violettes humides
Dont les aurores chargent ces forêts?

But to dissolve where that melting cloud is melting
– Oh! favoured by what is fresh!
To expire in those damp violets
Whose awakening fills these woods?[15]

Thus the object is seized and abolished in the poetic hunger of its subtraction, and in the poetic thirst of its dissemination.

As Mallarmé will say:

Ma faim qui d'aucun fruit ici ne se régale
Trouve en leur docte manque une saveur égale.

Oh no fruits here does my hunger feast
But finds in their learned lack the self-same taste.[16]

The fruit, subtracted, nevertheless appeases hunger, which is here the expression of an objectless subject.

And Rimbaud, concluding the 'Comedy of Thirst', will spread this thirst over the whole of nature:

Les pigeons qui tremblent dans la prairie
Le gibier, qui court et qui voit la nuit,
Les bêtes des eaux, la bête asservie,
Les derniers papillons! . . . ont soif aussi.

The pigeons which flutter in the meadow,
The game which runs and sees in the dark,
The water animals, the animal enslaved,
The last butterflies! . . . also are thirsty.[17]

Rimbaud here turns thirst into the dispersion of every subject, as well as every object.

The poem introduces the following question into the domain of language: what is an experience without an object? What is a pure affirmation that constitutes a universe whose right to being, and even probability, nothing guarantees?

The thought of the poem only begins after the complete disobjectification of presence.

That is why we can say that, far from being a form of knowledge, the poem is the exemplary instance of a thought obtained in the retreat and subtraction from everything that sustains the faculty of knowledge.

No doubt this is why the poem has always *disconcerted* philosophy.

You are all familiar with the proceedings instituted by Plato against painting and poetry. Yet if we follow closely the argument of Book X of the *Republic*, we notice a subjective complication, a certain awkwardness in the midst of this violent gesture that excludes the poets from the City.

Plato manifestly oscillates between a will to *repress* poetic seduction and a constant *temptation* to return to the poem.

The stakes of this confrontation with poetry seem immense. Plato does not hesitate to write that 'we were entirely right in our organization of the city, and especially, I think, in the matter of poetry'.[18] What an astounding pronouncement! The fate of politics tied to the fate of the poem! The poem is here accorded an almost limitless power.

Further on, all sorts of signs point to the temptation. Plato recognizes it is only 'by force', βια, that one can separate oneself from the poem. He admits that the defenders of poetry may 'speak in its favour without poetic meter'.[19] He thereby calls prose to the rescue of poetry.

These oscillations justify the statement that, for philosophy, poetry is the precise equivalent of a *symptom*.

Like all symptoms, this symptom insists. It is here that we touch upon the secret of Plato's text. It could be thought that as the founder of philosophy, Plato *invents* the conflict between the philosopher and the poet. Yet this is not what he says. On the contrary, he evokes a more ancient, even immemorial, conflict: 'παλαια τιζ διαφορα φιλοσοφια τε και ποιητικη': 'there is from old a quarrel between philosophy and poetry'.[20]

What does this antiquity of the conflict refer to? Often, the reply is that philosophy desires truth; that the poem is an imitation, a semblance, which distances truth. But I think this is a feeble idea. For true poetry is not imitation. The thought of the poem is not a mimesis.

The thesis of imitation – of the illusory and internal character of the mimetic – is not, in my view, the most fruitful avenue for us. What imitation can we perceive in Rimbaud's mysterious declaration:

Ô saisons, ô châteaux!
Quelle âme est sans défauts?

O seasons, O towers!
What soul is blameless?[21]

The poem possesses no imitative rule. The poem is separate from the object. We could even say that it is the naming without imitation *par excellence*. Mallarmé goes so far as to say, in the poem itself, that it is nature which is unable to imitate the poem. It is thus that the Faun, asking himself if the wind and water bear the trace of his sensual memory, ends up abandoning this search, remarking that the power of wind and water is inferior to that of his sole flute:

Suffoquant de chaleur le matin frais s'il lutte
Ne murmure point d'eau que ne verse ma flûte
Au bosquet arrosé d'accords; et le seul vent
Hors des deux tuyaux prompt à s'exhaler avant

Qu'il disperse le son dans une pluie aride,
C'est à l'horizon pas remué d'une ride
Le visible et serein souffle artificiel
De l'inspiration, qui regagne le ciel.

Of stifling heat that suffocates the morning
Save from my flute, no waters murmuring
In harmony flow out into the groves;
And the only wind on the horizon no ripple moves
Exhaled from my twin pipes and swift to drain
The melody in arid drifts of rain
Is the visible, serene and fictive air
Of inspiration rising as if in prayer.[22]

Far from the poem being an imitation, it is rather the deployment of objects in reality that fails to equal the poem.

In fact, Plato's principal argument is that the poem ruins discursiveness (διανοια in Greek).

What is philosophically opposed to the poem is not philosophy itself directly, but *dianoia*, the discursive thinking that connects and argues; a thinking whose paradigm is mathematical.

Plato points out that the remedies that have been found against the poem are 'measure, number, weight'. In the background of this conflict, we find these two extremes of language: the poem, which aims at object-less presence, and mathematics, which produces the cipher of the Idea.

Plato invites geometers in through the main door, so that the poets may leave the premises by the servant's entrance.

What disconcerts philosophy, what makes the poem into a symptom of philosophy, is not illusion and imitation. Rather, it's the fact that the poem might indeed be a thought without knowledge, or even this: a properly incalculable thought.

Dianoia is the thinking that crosses; it is crossing of the thinkable.

The poem does not cross. Wholly affirmative, it holds itself on the threshold of what is, withdrawing or dispersing the objects that encumber it.

But is this movement not *also* that of Platonic philosophy, when it attains the supreme principle of all that is?

Plato guarantees thought's *grasp* of being through the interpolation of knowledge and the objects of knowledge. The Idea is the intelligible exposition of the experience of the object; of objective experience *in its entirety*. For there are, as we know, Ideas of hair, the horse, and mud, just as there are Ideas of movement, rest and justice.

But beyond all Ideas of the object, beyond ideal objectivity, there is the Good, or the One, which is not an Idea; which is, according to Plato's expression, beyond substance, beyond ideal being-there.

Are this One and this Good not subtracted from intelligible objectivity? And even if they can be *thought*, is it not impossible to know them? What's more, in order to speak about them, is it not necessary to make use of the metaphor of the sun, of the myth of the dead returned to the earth, in short, of the resources of the poem? To sum up: in order to *pass beyond* the givenness of being as it occurs in accordance with the experience of objects, *dianoia* is insufficient. The great disobjectifying operations of the poem – subtraction and dissemination – are required. The argumentative crossing founders as soon as it is faced with the principle of being qua being.

It might then be the case that the poem disconcerts philosophy because the operations of the poem *rival* those of philosophy; that the philosopher has always been the envious rival of the poet. In other words: the poem is a thought which is nothing aside from its act, and which therefore has no need also to be the thought of thought. Now, philosophy establishes itself in the desire of thinking thought. But it is always unsure if thought *in actu*, the thought that can be sensed, is not more real than the thought of thought.

The ancient discord evoked by Plato opposes, on the one hand, a thought that goes straight to presence, and, on the other, a thought that takes, or wastes, the time needed to think itself. This rivalry sheds light on the symptom, the painful separation, the violence and the temptation.

But the poem is no more tender toward philosophy than is philosophy toward the poem. It is not tender toward *dianoia*: 'You, mathematicians, expire,'[23] Mallarmé says abruptly. Nor is it tender with regard to philosophy itself: 'Philosophers,' Rimbaud says, 'you belong to your West.'[24]

Conflict is the very essence of the relationship between philosophy and poetry. Let's not pray for an end to this conflict. For such an end would invariably mean either that philosophy has abandoned argumentation or that poetry has reconstituted the object.

Now, to abandon the rational mathematical paradigm is fatal for philosophy, which then turns into a failed poem. And to return to objectivity is fatal for the poem, which then turns into a didactic poetry, a poetry lost in philosophy.

Yes, the relationship between philosophy and poetry must remain, as Plato says, μεγαζ δ αγων, a mighty quarrel.

Let us struggle then, partitioned, split, unreconciled. Let us struggle for the flash of conflict, we philosophers, always torn between the mathematical norm of literal transparency and the poetic norm of singularity and presence. Let us struggle then, but having recognized the *common task*, which is to think what was unthinkable, to say what it is impossible to say. Or, to adopt Mallarmé's imperative, which I believe is common to philosophy and poetry: 'There, wherever it may be, deny the unsayable – it lies.'[25]

NOTES

Chapter 1

1. [Abraham Fraenkel, Yehoshua Bar-Hillel and Azriel Levy, *Foundations of Set-Theory*, 2nd revised edition (Amsterdam: North-Holland, 1973), pp. 331–2.]

2. [Ibid., p. 332.]

3. [Pascal Engel, 'Platonisme mathématique et antiréalisme' in *L'objectivité mathématique. Platonisme et structures formelles*, ed. M. Panza and J.-M. Salanskis (Paris: Masson, 1995), pp. 133–46.]

4. [*Foundations of set-Theory*, p. 332.]

5. [Ibid., p. 332.]

6. [Ibid., p. 332.]

7. [Descartes, 'Rules for the Direction of the Mind', in *The Philosophical Works of Descartes, Volume 1*, trans. E. S. Haldane and G. R. T. Ross (Cambridge: Cambridge University Press, 1967), p. 5.]

8. [Spinoza, *Ethics*, in *A Spinoza Reader*, ed. and trans. Edwin Curley (Princeton: Princeton University Press), p. 114.]

9. [Immanuel Kant, *Critique of Pure Reason*, trans. Norman Kemp Smith (London: Macmillan, 1993), p. 19.]

10. [*Hegel's Science of Logic*, trans. A. V. Miller (Atlantic Highlands, NJ: Humanities Press, 1989), pp. 241–3.]

11. [Lautréamont, *Maldoror and Poems*, trans. P. Knight (Harmondsworth: Penguin, 1978), pp. 92–5.]

12. [Stéphane Mallarmé, 'A Throw of the Dice' in *Collected Poems*, trans. Henry Weinfield (Berkeley: University of California Press, 1994), p. 144.]

13. [Stéphane Mallarmé, 'II. Scène. La Nourice-Hérodiade', *Collected Poems*, p. 30.]

14. [Stéphane Mallarmé, 'Funeral Toast', *Collected Poems*, p. 45.]

15. [Stéphane Mallarmé, 'Several Sonnets', *Collected Poems*, p. 67.]

16. [*The Seminar of Jacques Lacan*, ed. Jacques-Alain Miller, trans. Bruce Fink (New York: Norton, 1998), p. 119.]

17. [Ludwig Wittgenstein, *Tractatus Logico-Philosophicus*, trans. D. F. Pears and B. F. McGuiness (London: Routledge, 1992), p. 65.]

18. [Ludwig Wittgenstein, *Remarks on the Foundations of Mathematics* (Oxford: Basil Blackwell, 1978), III-81, p. 210. Translation modified.]

19. [Alain Badiou, *Le Nombre et les nombres* (Paris: Seuil, 1990).]

Notes

20. [Alain Badiou, *L'être et l'événement* (Paris: Seuil, 1988).]
21. [On the relation between mathematics and the concept of 'gesture', see Gilles Châtelet, *Les enjeux du mobile* (Paris: Seuil, 1993).]
22. [Stéphane Mallarmé, *Igitur*, in *Oeuvres Complètes* (Tours: Gallimard, Bibliothèque de la Pléiade, 1965), p. 434.]
23. [Ibid., p. 434.]
24. ['O binomio de Newton é tão belo', Fernando Pessoa, *Poesias de Álvaro de Campos*, in *Obra Poetica* (Rio de Janeiro: Editora Nova Aguilar, 1995).]

Chapter 2

1. The actual state of the relations between philosophy and mathematics is dominated by three tendencies: (1) the grammarian and logical analysis of statements, which makes of the discrimination between meaningful and meaningless statements what is ultimately at stake in philosophy; here, mathematics, or rather formal logic, have a paradigmatic function (as model of the 'well-formed language'); (2) the epistemological study of concepts, most often grasped through their history, with a pre-eminent role accorded to original mathematical texts; here, philosophy provides a sort of latent guide for a genealogy of the sciences; (3) a commentary on contemporary 'results', by way of analogical generalizations whose categories are borrowed from classical philosophemes. In none of these three cases is philosophy *as such* put under the condition of mathematical eventality. I will set apart four French philosophers from these aforementioned tendencies: Jean Cavaillès, Albert Lautman, Jean-Toussaint Desanti, and myself. Although operating from very different perspectives, and on a discontinuous philosophical 'terrain', these four authors have pursued an intellectual project that treats mathematics neither as a linguistic model, nor as an (historical and epistemological) object, nor as a matrix for 'structural' generalizations, but rather as a singular site of thinking, whose events and procedures must be retraced from *within* the philosophical act.
2. [Ludwig Wittgenstein, *Remarks on the Foundations of Mathematics* (Oxford: Basil Blackwell, 1978), §52, V–52–3, pp. 301–2.]
3. [Plato, *The Republic*, Book VI, 511, c-d. From the translation by the author.]
4. [*Hegel's Science of Logic*, trans. A. V. Miller (Atlantic Highlands, NJ: Humanities Press, 1989), Vol. I, Book I, Section 2, Ch. 2, (c), pp. 241–3.]
5. [*Hegel's Science of Logic*, p. 240.]
6. [*Hegel's Science of Logic*, p. 242. Translation modified.]

Chapter 3

1. [Martin Heidegger, 'Sketches for a History of Being as Metaphysics', in *The End of Philosophy*, trans. Joan Stambaugh (New York: Harper and Row, 1973), p. 55. Translation modified.]

2. [Martin Heidegger, *Introduction to Metaphysics*, trans. Ralph Mannheim (New Haven: Yale University Press, 1980), p. 38. Translation modified.]

3. [Martin Heidegger, *Introduction to Metaphysics*, trans. Ralph Mannheim (New Haven: Yale University Press, 1980), p. 38. Translation modified.]

4. [Lucretius, *De Rerum Natura*, trans. W. H. D. Rouse and M. F. Smith, 2nd revised edition (Cambridge, MA: Harvard University Press, 1982), 1.1002–8, p. 83.]

5. [Plato, *Parmenides*, 143e-44b. From the author's translation.]

6. [*De Rerum Natura*, 1.445–69, p. 39.]

7. [*The Republic*, Book VI, 511c. From the author's translation.]

8. [*De Rerum Natura*, 1.887–912, pp. 75–6. Translation modified.]

Chapter 4

1. [Paul Benacerraf and Hilary Putnam, *Philosophy of Mathematics: Selected Readings* (Oxford: Basil Blackwell, 1964), p. 15.]

2. [Abraham Fraenkel, Yehoshua Bar-Hillel and Azriel Levy, *Foundations of Set-Theory*, 2nd rev. ed. (Amsterdam: North-Holland, 1973), p. 332.]

3. [Kurt Gödel, 'What is Cantor's Continuum Problem?', in *Philosophy of Mathematics*, p. 272.]

4. [Ludwig Wittgenstein, *Tractatus Logico-Philosophicus*, trans. by D. F. Pears and B. McGuinness (London: Routledge, 1992), p. 65.]

Chapter 5

1. [Cf. *Litre et l'événement* (Paris: Seuil, 1988), pp. 149–60.]

2. [Cf. Gilles Châtelet, *Les enjeux du mobile* (Paris: Seuil, 1993).]

3. [G. w. Leibniz, 'Monadology', in *Philosophical Writings*, ed. G. H. R. Parkinson, trans. M. Morris and G. H. R. Parkinson (London: J. M. Dent & Sons, 1990), p. 190.]

Chapter 6

1. [This essay was written as a reply to articles by Arnaud Villani and José Gil in *Futur anterieur* 43, both of which were fierce attacks on Badiou's presentation of Deleuze in his *Deleuze: The Clamor of Being* (Minnesota: Minnesota University Press, 2001). We thank the editors of *multitudes*, and in particular Éric Alliez and Maurizio Lazzarato, for allowing us to publish this translation of Badiou's essay.]

Notes

2. [Alain Badiou, *Le Nombre et les nombres* (Paris: Seuil, 1990).]

3. [See Gilles Deleuze and Felix Guattari, *What is Philosophy?*, trans. H. Tomlinson and G. Burchill (London: Verso, 1994), pp. 151–3.] I say strange, rather than false or incorrect. I do not register any incorrectness in this text, only a bizarre torsion, an impracticable vantage point that makes it impossible to understand what is at stake or what we are dealing with. (The situation is inverted when it comes to my own writings on Deleuze, which my critics claim to understand only too well, suspecting as they do that this clarity is precisely what fails to do justice to the miraculous and indefinite subtleties of Deleuze's own texts. But I hold that philosophy, though certainly compelled toward difficulty, must shun every sort of obscure profundity. Nothing is profound to one who forbids himself the refuge of the virtual.) Thus, I consider Deleuze's note in *What is Philosophy?* – whose obviously amicable and attentive intention I welcomed – as one more enigmatic aspect (there are others, of course) of Deleuze's take on multiplicities. I am, moreover, delighted to have provided him with the occasion. But I would be grateful to anyone who could clarify this textual fragment for me, and explain what relation it bears to *Being and Event*. This is a genuine invitation, wholly devoid of irony.

4. It seems likely that Deleuze's self-criticism with regard to the doctrine of simulacra relates to the far too immediately Nietzschean form of anti-Platonism displayed in *Difference and Repetition*. But the profound theme enveloped by this doctrine is maintained in its entirety right up to the last works. Deleuze says: the difference between actual beings is modal, only the unity of the virtual (running through the 'great circuit') is wholly real. There are dozens of explicit passages on this point. That this unity is that of Relation, or of Difference if you wish, does nothing but accentuate the ontological impact of the thesis. For Heidegger too, being is said as difference (of Being and beings). But Forgetting lies in no longer thinking that it is Being, and not beings, which is the differentiator of this difference. Likewise, for Deleuze, the philosophical blunder lies in believing that it is actual differences that allow us to ascend analogically to Difference, whereas in fact noetic intuition is only complete when it pushes its movement all the way up to the point where it impersonally identifies itself with the differentiating and immanent power of the Virtual. The essence of the actual is actualization, but the essence of actualization is Life. Now, there is no essence of Life (of the Vi[r]t[u]al): therefore, Life is necessarily the pre-philosophical One of every philosophy. In this respect, and taking into account Deleuze's consistency on this essential point, the theme of an affirmative surge of simulacra is to my mind more convincing in *Difference and Repetition* than in its later formulations, because it is more adequate to the theme of univocity, as well as to the critique of 'Platonism'. Deleuze is never more at ease than when he manages to fuse, in a single point, Nietzsche, Bergson and Spinoza. This is the case every time he thinks of the immanent relation between the differentiating power of the One and its modal expressions.

   Incidentally, I am astonished by the scant attention paid by most of Deleuze's disciples (with the notable exception of Éric Alliez) to the philosophical genealogy constructed by the latter. We find them more embarrassed than empowered by these constant didactic references to Nietzsche, Bergson, Whitehead, the Stoics, and Spinoza in particular. Doubtless, it is because they are far more preoccupied with making Deleuze seem 'modern', according to their understanding of the term; an understanding which invariably contains an obscure dose of fashionable anti-philosophy. No doubt this is the reason why they 'prefer' the books written with Guattari, in which some 'modern' touches can be glimpsed, which accounts for my correspondingly lesser interest in these texts. A reading of the brief *Foucault* suffices to confirm the degree of sovereign intensity with which Deleuze returns – unchanged – to his initial intuitions.

Allow me to reiterate that in my eyes one of Deleuze's cardinal virtues is not to have used, under his own name, almost any of the 'modern' deconstructionist paraphernalia, and to have been an unrepentant metaphysician (as well as a physicist – in the pre-Socratic sense of the term).

Chapter 7

1. [Spinoza, *Ethics*, in *A Spinoza Reader*, ed. and trans. Edwin Curley (Princeton, NJ: Princeton University Press, 1994), p. 109.]

2. [*Ethics*, p. 100.]

3. [*Ethics*, p. 119.]

4. [*Ethics*, Book I, Definition 6, p. 85.]

5. [*Ethics*, p. 85.]

6. [*Ethics*, p. 85.]

7. [Spinoza to De Vries, Letter 9, *A Spinosa Reader*, p. 81.]

8. [*Ethics*, p. 105.]

9. [*Ethics*, p. 100.]

10. [Spinoza to Schuller and Tschirnhaus, Letter 64, *A Spinosa Reader*, p. 271.]

11. [Spinoza to Oldenburg, Letter 32, *A Spinoza Reader*, p. 82.]

12. [*Ethics*, p. 97.]

13. [*Ethics*, p. 124.]

14. [*Ethics*, p. 155.]

15. [*Ethics*, p. 132.]

16. [*Ethics*, p. 86.]

17. [*Ethics*, p. 116.]

18. [*Ethics*, p. 132.]

19. [*Ethics*, p. 119.]

20. [*Ethics*, p. 101.]

21. [*Ethics*, p. 123.]

22. [*Ethics*, p. 263.]
23. [*Ethics*, p. 133.]
24. [*Ethics*, p. 132.]
25. [*Ethics*, p. 143.]
26. [*Ethics*, p. 143.]
27. [*Ethics*, Book II, Proposition 40, Scholium 1, p. 139. Translation modified.]
28. [*Ethics*, p. 144.]
29. [*Ethics*, p. 246.]
30. [*Ethics*, Book II, Proposition 40, Scholium 2, p. 141.]
31. [*Ethics*, Book V, Proposition 23, Scholium, p. 256.]
32. [*Ethics*, Book V, Proposition 40, Scholium, p. 141.]
33. [*Ethics*, Book II, Proposition 44, Corollary 2, Demonstration, p. 144.]

Chapter 8

1. [Lucretius, *De Rerum Naturae*, trans. W. H. D. Rouse and M. F. Smith (Cambridge, MA: Harvard University Press, 1982), 1.995, p. 83. Translation modified.]

Chapter 9

1. This paper was presented in 1991, on the invitation of the board of directors of the École de la Cause freudienne, in the lecture hall of that institution. It was published in the journal *Actes* – whose subtitle is *Revue de l'École de la Cause freudienne* – at the end of 1991. It has also appeared in Italian translation in the journal *Agalma*, published in Rome.
2. [Stéphane Mallarmé, *Igitur* in *Oeuvres Complètes* (Tours: Gallimard, Bibliothèque de la Pléiade, 1965), p. 451.]
3. [Jeff Paris and Leo Harrington, 'A Mathematical Incompleteness in Peano Arithmetic', in *Handbook of Mathematical Logic*, ed. J. Barwise (Amsterdam: North-Holland, 1977), pp. 1133–42.]
4. [René Guitart has since published two books on the practice of mathematics and its relation to both philosophy and psychoanalysis: *Evidence et étrangeté* (Paris: PUF, 2000) and *La pulsation mathématique* (Paris: L'Harmattan, 2000).]
5. [Paul J. Cohen, *Set Theory and the Continuum Hypothesis* (New York: W. A. Benjamin, 1966).]
6. [Stéphane Mallarmé, 'Other Poems and Sonnets' in *Collected Poems*, trans. Henry Weinfield (Berkeley: University of California Press, 1994), p. 79.]

7. [*Le Bel indifférent* is the title of a brief play written for Edith Piaf by Jean Cocteau in 1939.]

8. [Stéphane Mallarmé, 'Letter of May 27, 1867', in *Selected Letters*, ed. and trans. R. Lloyd (Chicago: University of Chicago Press, 1988), p. 77.]

9. [Samuel Beckett, *Three Novels: Molloy, Malone Dies, The Unnameable* (New York: Grove, 1991), p 350.]

10. [*Three Novels*, p. 13.]

11. [Samuel Beckett, *How It Is* (New York: Grove, 1988), p. 130.]

12. [Stéphane Mallarmé, 'Prose (for des Esseintes)', *Collected Poems*, p. 46. Translation modified.]

Chapter 10

1. This paper was originally delivered in Montpellier, in autumn 1991, at the invitation of the Department of Psychoanalysis of the Paul-Valéry University, chaired by Henri Rey-Fleaud.

2. [On the Lacanian notion of a *sujet supposé savoir*, see Dylan Evans, *An Introductory Dictionary of Lacanian Psychoanalysis* (London: Routledge, 1996), pp. 196–8.]

3. [Jacques Lacan, *Le Séminaire – Livre XVII: L'envers de la psychanalyse*, ed. J.-A. Miller (Paris: Seuil, 1991).]

4. [*Le Séminaire – Livre XVII*, p. 58.]

5. [Jacques Lacan, *Le Séminaire – Livre XIX: . . . Ou pire*. This seminar remains unpublished. However, a version of the text, edited by Jacques-Alain Miller, appeared in *Scilicet* 5, 1975 and has since been reprinted in *Autres Écrits* (Paris: Seuil, 2001).]

6. [Jacques Lacan, *Le Séminaire – Livre XVII: L'envers de la psychanalyse*, ed. J.-A. Miller (Paris: Seuil, 1991).]

7. [*The Seminar of Jacques Lacan – Book I: Freud's Papers on Technique 1953–1954*, ed. J.-A. Miller, trans. J. Forrester (New York: Norton, 1991), p. 271.]

8. [*The Seminar of Jacques Lacan – Book XX: Encore*, ed. J.-A. Miller, trans. B. Fink (New York: Norton, 1998), p. 97.]

9. [Samuel Beckett, *Three Novels: Molloy, Malone Dies, The Unnameable* (New York: Grove, 1991), p. 414.]

Chapter 11

1. [Immanuel Kant, *Critique of Pure Reason*, trans. Norman Kemp Smith (London: Macmillan, 1993), B131, p. 152. Translation modified.]

2. [*Critique of Pure Reason*, B132, p. 153.]

3. [*Critique of Pure Reason*, B134, p. 154.]

4. [*Critique of Pure Reason*, B135, p. 154.]

5. [*Critique of Pure Reason*, B138, p. 157.]

6. [*Critique of Pure Reason*, A94/B128, p. 128.]

7. [*Critique of Pure Reason*, A158/B197, p. 194.]

8. [*Critique of Pure Reason*, A108, p. 137.]

9. [*Critique of Pure Reason*, A107, p. 136.]

10. [*Critique of Pure Reason*, A107, p. 136.]

11. [*Critique of Pure Reason*, A109, p. 137.]

12. [*Critique of Pure Reason*, A 109, p. 137.]

13. [*Critique of Pure Reason*, A109, p. 137. Translation modified.]

14. [*Critique of Pure Reason*, A350, p. 334.]

15. [*Critique of Pure Reason*, A105, p. 135.]

16. [Martin Heidegger, *Kant and the Problem of Metaphysics*, trans. R. Taft (Bloomington and Indianapolis: Indiana University Press, 1990), p. 118. Translation modified.]

17. [*Critique of Pure Reason*, B138, pp. 156–7.]

Chapter 13

1. [See Alain Badiou, *L'être et l'événement* (Paris: Seuil, 1988), pp. 109–19.]

2. [See Alain Badiou, 'La politique comme pensée: l'oeuvre de Sylvain Lazarus' in *Abrégé de Métapolitique* (Seuil, 1998) and Sylvain Lazarus, *Anthropologie du Nom* (Seuil, 1997).]

3. [See 'Qu'est-ce que l'amour' in *Conditions* (Paris: Seuil, 1992); translated as 'What is Love?' by J. Clemens in *Umbr(a): A Journal of the Unconscious*, No. 1, 1996; reprinted in R. Salecl (ed.), *Sexuation* (Duke University Press, 2000), pp. 263–81.]

4. [This is the name for the political enterprise jointly undertaken by militants of the *Organisation politique*, of which Badiou is a member, and informal groups of 'illegal' immigrant workers.]

Chapter 14

1. [Immanuel Kant, 'Preface to the Second Edition', *Critique of Pure Reason*, trans. Norman Kemp Smith (London: MacMillan, 1993), Bviii, p. 17.]

2. [*Critique of Pure Reason*, Bix, p. 18.]

3. [See Claude Imbert, *Pour une histoire de la logique. Un héritage platonicien* (Paris: PUF, 2000).]

4. [Martin Heidegger, *Introduction to Metaphysics*, trans. G. Friedman and R. Polt (New Haven: Yale University Press, 2000), p. 126.]

5. [*Introduction to Metaphysics*, p. 127.]

6. [Aristotle, *Metaphysics* 1005a28-29, in *The Basic Works of Aristotle*, trans. W. D. Ross (New York: Random House, 2001), p. 736.]

7. [*Metaphysics* 1006a1-2, p. 737.]

8. [*Metaphysics* 1011b24-25, p. 749.]

9. [See 'L'orientation aristotélicienne et la logique', in *Court Traité d'Ontologie Transitoire* (Paris: Seuil, 1998), pp. 111-18.]

10. [*Citra* is Latin for 'on the nearer side' or 'on this side of'.]

11. [See Section 1, 'Mathematics is Ontology', especially 'The Question of Being Today' and 'Platonism and Mathematical Ontology'.]

12. [*Critique of Pure Reason*, A427/B455, p. 396.]

13. [Samuel Eilenberg and Saunders Mac Lane, 'General theory of natural equivalences' in *Transactions of the American Mathematical Society* 58 (1945), pp. 231-94.]

Chapter 15

1. [See Immanuel Kant, *Critique of Pure Reason*, trans. by Norman Kemp Smith (London: MacMillan, 1993), A66/B91-B116, pp. 103-19.]

2. [*Critique of Pure Reason*, A57/B81, pp. 96-7.]

3. [*Critique of Pure Reason*, A57/B81, pp. 96-7. Translation modified.]

4. [*Critique of Pure Reason*, A66/B91, p. 104.]

Chapter 16

1. [Alexandre Koyré, *From the Closed World to the Infinite Universe* (Baltimore: John Hopkins Press, 1968).]

2. [John, I.5]

3. [Badiou is referring here to the brief Scholium 1 ('L'existence et la mort') of Chapter 2 ('L'objet') of *Logiques des mondes* (Paris: Seuil, forthcoming). A version of this text has recently appeared in English translation: 'Existence and Death', trans. Nina Power and Alberto Toscano, *Discourse, Special Issue: 'Mortals to Death'*, ed. Jalal Toufic, 24.1 (Winter 2002): 63-73.]

Chapter 17

1. [G. W. F. Hegel, 'Preface', *Phenomenology of spirit*, trans. A. V. Miller (Oxford: OUP, 1977), 18, p. 10. Translation modified.]
2. [*Hegel's Science of Logic*, trans. A. V. Miller (Atlantic Highlands, NJ: Humanities Press, 1989), pp. 841–2. Translation modified.]
3. [*Science of Logic*, 'Remark on the Philosophy of Spinoza and Leibniz', Volume I, Book II, Section 3, Ch. 1., C, p. 536. Translation modified.]
4. [*Science of Logic*, p. 536. Translation modified.]
5. [*Science of Logic*, Volume II, Section 3, Ch. 3, pp. 842–3. Translation modified.]
6. [*Science of Logic*, Volume I, Book I, Section 1, Ch. 2, A(a), p. 110.]
7. [*Science of Logic*, Volume I, Book I, Section 1, Ch. 2, B(a), p. 120.]
8. [*Science of Logic*. Translated from the author.]
9. [*Science of Logic*. Translated from the author.]
10. [*Science of Logic*. Translated from the author.]
11. [*Science of Logic*, Volume 1, Book II, Section 1, Ch. 2, B(c), p. 424.]
12. [*Science of Logic*, Volume I, Book I, Section 2, 'Remark', p. 186. Translation modified.]
13. [*Science of Logic*, Volume I, Book II, Section 1, Ch. 2, B(b), p. 423. Translation modified.]
14. [*Science of Logic*, Volume I, Book II, Section 2, Ch. 2, A, p. 502. Translation modified.]
15. [*Science of Logic*, p. 503. Translation modified.]
16. [*Science of Logic*, B, p. 506. Translation modified.]
17. [*Science of Logic*, p. 505. Translation modified.]

Chapter 18

1. [This paper was originally delivered at Fumec, Belo Horizonte, Brazil in 1993.]
2. [Arthur Rimbaud, *Collected Poems*, ed. and trans. Oliver Bernard (Harmondsworth: Penguin, 1986), p. 202.]
3. ['il a lieu tout seul: fait, étant', Stéphane Mallarmé, 'Quant au livre', in *Oeuvres Complètes* (Tours: Gallimard, Bibliothèque de la Pléiade, 1965), p. 372.]
4. [Stéphane Mallarmé, 'Another Fan' ('Autre Éventail'), in *Collected Poems*, trans. Henry Weinfield (Berkeley: University of California Press, 1994), p. 50.]
5. [Mallarmé, 'Saint' ('Sainte'), *Collected Poems*, p. 43.]
6. [Ils agissent peu délicatement, que de déverser, en un chahut, la vaste incomprehension humaine.' Mallarmé, 'Mystery in Literature' (Le mystère

dans les lettres'), in *Mallarmé in Prose*, ed. Mary Ann Caws (New York: New Directions, 2001), p. 47. Translation modified.]

7. [Stéphane Mallarmé, 'Homage' ('Hommage'), *Collected Poems*, p. 76.]

8. ['sur quelque surface vacante et superiéure' / 'froide d'oubli et de désuétude', Mallarmé, 'A Throw of the Dice' ('Un coup de dés'), *Collected Poems*, p. 144. Translation modified.]

9. ['tison de gloire, sang par écume, or, tempête', Mallarmé, 'Several Sonnets, III' ('Plusieurs Sonnets, III'), *Collected Poems*, p. 68.]

10. ['de scintillation sitôt le septuor', Mallarmé, 'Several Sonnets, IV' ('Plusieurs Sonnets, IV'), *Collected Poems*, p. 69.]

11. ['cette Constellation qui énumère le heurt successif sidéralement d'un compte total en formation', Mallarmé, 'A Throw of the Dice' ('Un coup de dés'), *Collected Poems*, p. 145. Translation modified.]

12. ['très franchement une mosquée à la place d'une usine', Rimbaud, 'Ravings II:Alchemy of the Word' ('Délires II: Alchimie du verbe'), *A Season in Hell*, in *Collected Poems*, p. 329.]

13. ['ce Monsieur qui ne sait ce qu'il fait: il est un ange', Rimbaud, *Collected Poems*, p. 334.]

14. ['une nichée de chiens', Rimbaud, *Collected Poems*, p. 334.]

15. [Rimbaud, 'Comedy of Thirst' ('La comédie de la soif'), *Collected Poems*, p. 212. Translation modified.]

16. [Mallarmé, 'Other Poems and Sonnets' ('Autres poëmes et sonnets'), *Collected Poems*, p. 84.]

17. [Rimbaud, *Collected Poems*, p. 212.]

18. [*Republic* (595a), trans. Paul Shorey, in *The Collected Dialogues*, ed. Edith Hamilton and Huntington Cairns (Princeton: Princeton University Press, 1989), p. 819. Translation modified.]

19. [*Republic*, 607d, p. 832. Translation modified.]

20. [*Republic*, 607b, p. 832. Translation modified.]

21. [Rimbaud, *Collected Poems*, p. 336.]

22. [Stéphane Mallarmé, 'The Afternoon of a Faun', *Collected Poems*, p. 38.]

23. ['Vous, mathematicians, expirâtes', Mallarmé, *Igitur*, *Oeuvres Complètes*, p. 434.]

24. ['Philosophes, vous êtes de votre Occident', Rimbaud, 'The Impossible' ('L'impossible'), *Collected Poems*, p. 340.]

25. ['Là-bas, où que ce soit, nier l'indicible, qui ment', Mallarmé, 'Music and Letters' ('La musique et les lettres'), *Mallarmé in Prose*, p. 44. Translation modified.]

POSTFACE
ALEATORY RATIONALISM

Rimbaud employs a strange expression: 'les révoltes logiques', *'logical revolts'. Philosophy is something like a 'logical revolt'. Philosophy pits thought against injustice, against the defective state of the world and of life. Yet it pits thought against injustice in a movement which conserves and defends argument and reason, and which ultimately proposes a new logic. Mallarmé states: 'All thought begets a throw of the dice.' It seems to me that this enigmatic formula also designates philosophy, because philosophy proposes to think the universal – that which is true for all thinking – yet it does so on the basis of a commitment in which chance always plays a role, a commitment which is also a risk or a wager.*

Alain Badiou, 'Philosophy and the Desire of the Contemporary World'

This philosophy is in every respect a philosophy of the void: *not only a philosophy that* says *the void that pre-exists the atoms that fall within it, but a philosophy that* makes *the philosophical void in order to give itself existence: a philosophy that instead of starting off from the famous* 'philosophical problems' *('why is there something rather than nothing?')* begins by evacuating every philosophical problem, *and therefore by refusing to give itself any* 'object' *whatsoever ('philosophy has no object'), in order to begin from* nothing, *and from this infinitesimal and aleatory variation of the nothing which is the deviation of the fall.*

Louis Althusser, 'The Subterranean Current of the
Materialism of the Encounter'

1. In these pages, as elsewhere, Alain Badiou has steadfastly declared his allegiance to a tradition of philosophical rationalism among whose most illustrious representatives we can number Plato, Descartes, Spinoza, Leibniz and whose last and most problematic proponent is perhaps Hegel. Badiou is a systematic thinker, profoundly at odds with the passion for the limit and the mistrust of pure thought that typified much twentieth-century philosophy, be it phenomenological, hermeneutic, deconstructionist or therapeutic.

What's more, he lays claim to the exalted standard of philosophical rigour represented by his rationalist predecessors while dispensing with venerable models of methodological discipline such as Kant's transcendental critique, Hegel's dialectic, Husserl's phenomenological reduction, or Heidegger's existential analytic. So what novel philosophical method underlies Badiou's system?

At first sight, none. Readers of Badiou well-versed in the grand tradition of German philosophy that begins with Kant and ends with Heidegger, in which methodological scrupulousness is the *sine qua non* for serious philosophizing, will find the conspicuous absence of anything like a methodological propaedeutic in a book as ambitious as *Being and Event* (1988) deeply troubling. Yet this is more than just a glaring oversight on Badiou's part. For in his eyes, philosophy, like everything else, is a situation; it is neither unified nor perennial.[1] The conviction that the philosopher is in a position to begin by defining and mobilizing a *sui generis* philosophical method assumes that a subject of philosophy is already given in a more or less absolute sense, whether as a normative model or in the latent recesses of a reflexive capacity available to all.

Furthermore, it assumes that such a subject could articulate a method by appropriating its own intra-philosophical conditions; in other words, that method is something that I, as a subject of philosophy, always already possess, regardless of the discipline and training I may have to undergo in order to master it. Such a putative subject of philosophy would thus be *auto-positional* or *self-presupposing*. It would strive to appropriate its own conditions as given within a philosophical situation which is already 'naturally' its own and which has the unique feature of being able to encompass and reflect all other situations. The counterpart of this auto-positional appropriation is thus the (chimerical) notion of something like a global or absolute situation, a reflexive Whole of philosophy.

Following the terms laid out in meditations 8 and 9 of Badiou's *Being and Event*, we could argue that the logic of such an appropriation is that of the re-presentation, or 'state' of the philosophical situation. Method, to adopt Badiou's vocabulary, would thus be something like *the state of philosophy*. This intra-philosophical re-presentation of philosophy's conditions harbours two spontaneous, or rather prejudicial, intuitions. First, an intuition about what needs to be philosophized. The authority of philosophical tradition is encoded in the re-presentation of the philosophical situation and serves to legitimate an intuition about those phenomena that will always require 'philosophizing'. To paraphrase Deleuze, the tradition and teleology of *sophia* converge in a kind of trans-historical 'good sense' about what requires thought. Favoured examples of these natural concerns of philosophy include the possibility of objective knowledge, the mystery of human self-consciousness, the meaning of being, etc. Second, the auto-representation of philosophy mobilizes an intuition about *what it is like* to think philosophically (as opposed to scientifically or anthropologically or sociologically). Philosophy is transcendental critique, speculative dialectic, ontological questioning, deconstruction and so on. Thus, an intuition (rather than argument) about what needs to be philosophized is used to underwrite the characterization of the task of philosophy and the identification of the methodology best suited to that task. Accordingly, the intuition that cognitive judgement needs to be legitimated fuels the characterization of philosophical method as transcendental critique; the intuition that all consciousness is irreducibly intentional fuels the characterization of philosophical method as phenomenological reduction; the intuition that the meaning of being is at issue in human existence fuels the characterization of philosophical method as existential analytic of *Dasein*, and so on.

Badiou rejects these philosophical intuitions together with the methodologies they subtend because he refuses the gesture of auto-position through which the subject of philosophy re-presents the philosophical situation and appropriates those intra-philosophical conditions deemed necessary for philosophizing. His philosophy does not begin with a gesture of auto-position but with an axiomatic decision entailing that philosophy be *expropriated* of its conditions, deprived of the appeal to intuition – whether natural or transcendental – and irrevocably sundered from its foundation.[2] This decision is encapsulated in the axiom *the One is not*.[3] It has a theorematic counterpart, which has its basis in the agonistic history of mathematical logic and its paradoxes: *there is no Whole*. The non-being of the One and the inexistence of the Whole are the indispensable correlates of the rationalist decision to identify mathematics with ontology.[4] This is the decision that conditions Badiou's entire philosophical enterprise. Rather than isolating and securing the kind of philosophical intuition that would provide the foundation for a method, this decision immediately deprives philosophy of its customary arsenal of intuitions about what needs to be philosophized and rules out the possibility of accessing a paradigmatic model of philosophical method. It thus ungrounds philosophy by evacuating it of all previously available founding intuitions about the propriety of its content and the appropriateness of its method.

The simplicity of this axiomatic-theorematic conjunction (the One is not and there is no Whole) belies its devastating consequences for the usual premises that philosophy calls upon to shore up its ultimate sovereignty over the domain of thought. It is not just that philosophical thought no longer enjoys access to a fundamental *arché*, principle, or universal overview ('beings as a whole') – that would be platitudinous – but that it must now abjure any intuition that continues to assume the integral unity of the phenomenon with which philosophy is supposed to begin, regardless of how it may be characterized. Philosophy cannot presuppose a unitary instance of thought, a unitary relation of intentionality, or a unitary phenomenon like 'the world'. There is no such thing as what it is *like* to think. Philosophy, as a situation, can neither be founded on a unified subject nor reflected in a totality.

It is this subtraction of philosophy from any authentic destination or secure and eminent placement within the system of thought that also separates the 'decisionist' predilection for the axiom from the theme of beginning or the origin, from all the instances of more or less laborious parthenogenesis that punctuate the history of philosophy. Philosophy has no starting point, no home, be it ego or Earth, praxis or contemplation. Decision as affirmed within the parameters of what we shall refer to as Badiou's 'aleatory rationalism' is not grounded in some putative sovereignty since it is always a decision on an undecidable, on an event that philosophy itself does not and cannot give rise to.

This has noteworthy consequences as far as the question of philosophical method is concerned. For Badiou, the methodological pomp and circumstance so beloved of German philosophers from Kant to Habermas is an otiose extravagance still wedded to a teleological and fundamentally organicist model of systemic integrity; one that continues to presuppose a transitivity between systematic *consistency* and systemic *unity*. On the contrary, the rigour and consistency of Badiou's thought, from *Theory of the Subject*, through *Being and Event*, right up to the forthcoming *Logics of Worlds*, is not circumscribed in advance by a pre-delineated systemic unity linking philosophical subjectivity and reflexive totality. Hence the important amendments, revisions and retractions that Badiou has been willing to carry out, all the while reasserting his fundamental commitment to the basic axiomatic coordinates that have consistently shaped and oriented his thinking.[5] For Badiou, the best guarantor of philosophical precision is not the sort of ostentatious architectonic splendour generated by the premise of systemic unity, but rather a bare axiomatic-theorematic mode of argumentation suited to the mobile constraints of systematic consistency. Badiou's philosophy does not derive its cohesion from an underlying architectural blueprint but from a closely interconnected series of argumentative linkages between axioms and theorems; arguments sustained by the resources of mathematical thought as well as of poetic invention but devoid of any totalizing transcendental methodology.

Purged of the intuitions that bolstered its claim to methodological autonomy and shored up its previous self-identifications, whether as transcendental epistemology or fundamental ontology, philosophy asserts its effective independence by renouncing its self-grounding pretensions and abrogating its traditional claims to the theory of being and the theory of knowledge, the better to identify itself as theory of truth. If mathematics, according Badiou, has always been the theory of being, it now seems that cognitive science (or even neurobiology) is in the process of hegemonizing the theory of knowledge.

Here, as ever, the logic of subtraction provides the key to Badiou's approach. It is a question of subtracting philosophy's self-assertion from those modalities of definition that are a function of its statist representation as a discipline within the academy. Once under evental condition, philosophy need no longer conform to reactionary institutional interests bent on artificially perpetuating an arid and essentially anachronistic academic discourse. In asserting its own necessarily empty form as theory of truth, philosophy becomes free to engage with the most innovative manifestations of scientific, artistic and political thought. By emptying itself, philosophy identifies and formalizes its real conditions of possibility as extra-philosophical truths, without thereby re-appropriating them as 'projections' of a *sui generis* philosophical subject.

2. Far from relapsing into the kind of pre-critical metaphysical dogmatism that simply assumes a straightforward correspondence between thought and reality, Badiou radicalizes the critique of intellectual intuition – the cornerstone of Kantianism – by invalidating the authority of *every* form of philosophical intuition, whether transcendental, dialectical or formal-phenomenological. This is why he refuses the premise of a fundamental transitivity between the philosophical and the pre-philosophical; the idea that philosophical insight is already latent in pre-philosophical experience and that the philosopher's task consists in extracting the former from the latter in order to purify it. Though we might fruitfully seek instances of dialectical articulation or torsion in his work, this denial of intuition, presuppositions (objective or subjective), sensibility and everything that smacks of everyday perception and experience, makes Badiou's philosophy – like his politics,

we might add – a philosophy of separation. This separation is not to be understood as a simple abstraction; nor is mathematics the source of a new intuition, more securely grounded and powerful than that of philosophy. As Badiou asserts at the outset of *Being and Event*, mathematics, or ontology, is a *discourse*, and its privileged role in Badiou's attempt to formulate a genuinely atheistic contemporary philosophy derives from the fact that it has succeeded in thinking (or 'writing') *without the one:* set theory thinks (or writes) the multiple, but it does not have *a* concept of the multiple, *an* intuition of the multiple. Mathematics does not expropriate philosophy from its hold over ontology because of a privileged insight, or a superior method, but because of the deductive consistency and relentless inventiveness of its discourse.

Thus, Badiou reinvents rationalism after Critique. But his is a rationalism purged of any intellectual intuition of the One or the Whole, be it Plato's One-beyond-being, Descartes's capture of the infinite in the One of God, Spinoza's *facies totius universi*, Leibniz's ideal of *mathesis universalis* or Hegel's reflexive, self-articulating Whole. Rather than postulating the inexorable primacy of some figure of the One and the Whole, Badiou's post-Cantorian rationalism asserts an untotalizable ontological dissemination and the aleatory emergence of a plurality of truths. For it is the decision to identify mathematics with ontology that functions as the precondition for the evental theory of truth, splitting the subject of philosophy from within by forcibly expropriating it of its (imaginary) grip on its own constitutive conditions. *The conditions for the possibility of philosophy are no longer intra-philosophical.* This claim is altogether more novel than its familiar Marxist ring may suggest. Badiou's philosophy does not defer to the putatively extra-philosophical reality of history only to re-philosophize and re-idealize the latter by relentlessly dialecticizing its own relation to it. Philosophy purges itself of its imaginary self-sufficiency by subjecting itself to extra-philosophical conditions that are now themselves autonomous instances of thought with no need for a dialectical supplement ensuring their philosophical comprehension, mediation, or reflection.

Instead, in identifying its evental conditions of real possibility, philosophy formalizes those conditions. That is why the challenge for philosophy is to mobilize an empty form, or to deploy a non-experiential arsenal of procedures whose substantive content must be filled out by extra-philosophical truths. But since all truths are extra-philosophical, and since a subject is nothing but the bearer of an evental truth, there is no autonomous subject of philosophy for Badiou. Thus systematic philosophy is rendered a-subjective and heteronomous. This heteronomy – the conviction that philosophical thought is always spurred from outside; that it is radically dependent upon the existence of a real, extra-philosophical instance, whether event or procedure – is one instance of Badiou's basically materialist stance.[6] Yet strange as it may seem, this expropriation of philosophy increases its potency. The transitivity of philosophy, its desperate suture to psychology, anthropology, politics, science, is what imposes extraneous limitations upon the potentially subversive capacities of philosophical reason. As far as philosophy and its conditions are concerned, sovereignty or ubiquity can only lead to impotence.[7]

Philosophical thinking is thus internally fissured by the split between philosophy as empty or formal (metaontological) theory of truth and the substantive extra-philosophical truths that provide this empty philosophical form with the material it must seek to *compossibilize*. Whatever operational specificity philosophy possesses would seem to reside in this logic of compossibilization. Yet Badiou has yet to flesh it out beyond the rather vague indications provided in his *Manifesto for Philosophy*: 'It is a question of producing concepts and rules of thought, which may in one instance remain devoid of any explicit mention of [specific] names and acts, while in another instance they may be intimately tied to them, but in such a way as to ensure that through these concepts and rules our era will be representable as the era wherein *these instances of thought took place*, which had never taken place before and which will henceforth be freely available to everyone, even those that are ignorant of them, because a philosophy has constructed for everyone the common shelter for this taking place.'[8] Thus, if evental truths are now the material of philosophy, the task of compossibilization seems to consist in creating a conceptual space in which the 'illegal' inventions and truth procedures of 'our time' can demonstrate their shared fidelity to the disparate production of the generic and transmit the novelty of their for malizations. In other words, a 'space' (for want of a better word) in which subjects, always rare, can communicate in the absence of any pre-given horizon of consensus.

Nevertheless, the vagueness of Badiou's indications concerning compossibilization casts an ambiguous light on the status of his own philosophical project. For either Badiou's philosophy merely provides one possible instance of compossibilization among others, in which case it becomes incumbent upon him to delineate a 'novum organon' for philosophy in the shape of a logic of compossibility for truths; or his principled disavowal of philosophical method entails that his philosophy is sui generis, and hence exemplifies the logic of compossibilization as a singular unrepeatable instance. But if Badiou's philosophy is not only articulating an apparatus of capture for the truths of his own time and other times to come, but turns out to be the only instance of the compossibilization of truths which he thinks every philosophy should carry out, then surely this entails a severe limitation in its potency and rational transmissibility. In a move that seems suspiciously Hegelian, it's almost as if it is only from the standpoint of Badiou's doctrine that other philosophies can be recognized as what they were all along (despite their own pretension to 'fill out' truth or be the Truth of truth): ways of rendering compossible the truths arising from the generic procedures of their time.

Moreover, the way in which Badiou's own philosophy supposedly exemplifies the logic of compossibilization is not without inherent difficulties. For there is a stark disequilibrium in the constitutive conditions of Badiou's system: almost all the conceptual details proper to the theory of philosophy's eventual conditioning are entirely dependent upon its mathematical condition. The ontological inconsistency of eventual truth and the consequent characterization of philosophy as theory of truth is almost exclusively reliant upon the identification of set theory with ontology. In *Being and Event*, the impasse of the mathematical-ontological theory of presentation gives rise to a philosophical-metaontological account of how, via the decision that gives rise to a subject, that which is ontologically inconceivable or unpresentable – i.e. a set that belongs to itself, which is how Badiou defines an event (the 'ultra-one') – comes to supplement a situation by measuring the excess of representation over presentation.[9] This is the theory of the generic set and of truth as subtraction. But the metaontological formalization of truths is only possible if the discourse of being qua being has been handed over to set theory, *something which itself seems to be an eventual decision*. Does the theory of eventual decision proposed in the course of *Being and Event* retroactively ground the decision with which the book begins, the decision that mathematics is ontology, that the One is not, and that there is no Whole? Does it do so in the manner of the Hegelian positing of a presupposition? If it does, its virtuous circularity may be incompatible with the expropriation of dialectical method and the abjuring of systemic unity which we have tried to suggest is intrinsic to Badiou's system. For then the danger is that such virtuous circularity is won only at the cost of reintroducing the kind of dialectically coordinated systemic totality disavowed by Badiou's own aleatory rationalism. But perhaps we are overstating the difficulty. For it could be that the theory of the event merely *explains* rather than grounds the book's opening decision. In which case, conceptual consistency may be ensured without reintroducing systemic unity. Although we cannot hope to provide a satisfactory resolution of this issue within the confines of this Postface, our aim here as elsewhere throughout these remarks is simply to alert readers of Badiou to these sorts of difficulties.

3. As we now know, Badiou's metaontological decision that 'ontology is mathematics' stipulates that beings always appear in situation. Consequently, ontology itself is a situation, the situation of post-Cantorian set theory, whose singular privilege according to Badiou is to be the only situation in which there is presentation without re-presentation, i.e. the presentation of presentation.[10] This is to say that set theory effectuates a presentation of the multiple shorn of any predicative trait other than that of its pure multiplicity. Set theory is the theory of inconsistent multiples as such. This means that although set theory is a consistent presentation (since everything presented must consist, i.e. be counted-as-one, in the terminology of *Being and Event*), *what* is presented in set theory is nothing but pure inconsistency as such. For the originary set whose existence the theory declares, and from which all other sets are woven, is the empty set, which is simply the *mark* or inscription of the unpresentable, and is not to be mistaken for the presentation of the unpresentable (for Badiou the latter is impossible, on pain of mysticism). Thus set theory is the presentation of the multiple-without-oneness, which is to say, multiplicity-without-presence, for crucially, as Badiou emphasizes, 'presence is the precise contrary of presentation.'[11] That is why there can be no intuition or experience of being, only a coherent, formalizable discourse in which being itself is inscribed as pure inconsistent multiplicity.

Once again, the austerely anti-phenomenological tenor of Badiou's *meontology* (a theory of being as nothingness, an ontology of the void) cannot be overemphasized. As he puts it: 'We will oppose the rigour of subtraction to the temptation of presence, and being will be said to be only insofar as it cannot be postulated on the basis of any presence or experience.'[12] Consequently, the originary subtraction from presentation inscribed in set-theoretical discourse, and hence the fundamental distinction between the consistency of presentation and the retroactively posited inconsistency of that which will have been presented (or 'counted-as-one') – i.e. the void qua inconsistent multiplicity – should not be conflated with some post-Heideggerean version of the ontological difference. Although the notion of ontico-ontological difference is not entirely foreign to Badiou, he proposes a meontological materialism wherein if being is nothing, this is not because it is *more* than anything, some sort of unconceptualizable excess, but simply because it is *less* than anything. *L'étantité de l'étant* – literally, 'the entityness of the entity' – is merely its inconsistent emptiness, an emptiness that cannot be reduced to the consistency of absence understood as the mere opposite of presence. Inconsistency, which is perfectly codifiable, is the originary, indiscernible ontological 'stuff' or 'material', rather than the entity's adverbial coming-to-presence or the *way in which* it is spatiotemporally articulated. Meontological presentation operates quite independently of any notion of space and time, whether as a priori forms of intuition or ekstatico-horizonal phenomenalization. Badiou's meontology is so radically indifferent to difference that it refuses not only qualitative and categorial differences but even Heidegger's distinction between entities and their way of being. Consequently, the originary subtraction of the void's multiple inconsistency cannot be equated with being's withdrawal from presence in the bestowal of presencing: '[The] notion of "subtraction" is here opposed to the Heideggerean thesis of the withdrawal of being [. . .]. It is because it is foreclosed to presentation that being is, for man, bound to be sayable according to the imperative consequences of the most stringent of all conceivable laws: the law of formalizable and demonstrative inference.'[13]

Yet if ontology is a situation, and if being is not available to intuition or experience, what pertinence can the concept of 'being' have outside of the ontological situation? If being is not given, whether in intuition or experience, and if the concept of 'presentation' is a purely formal concept generated from set theory and hence exclusively pertaining to the deductive consistency of set theoretical discourse, rather than to 'experience', then what relevance do the concepts of 'being' and 'presentation' have when considered apart from that discourse? Why are there situations other than the ontological one? What is the relation between the ontological situation and non-ontological situations? On what basis does Badiou distinguish between different *kinds* of situation? The requirements of meontological univocity would seem to be perfectly satisfied by the mathematical situation alone. More precisely, Badiou's refusal to specify the conceptual and procedural (as opposed to merely evental) parameters for the *philosophical* situation within which *Being and Event* operates threatens to ruin that univocity by introducing an equivocal dimension of analogy through philosophy's metaontological re-presentation of ontology (set theory).

Badiou's recent work, culminating in the forthcoming *Logics of Worlds* (an excerpt from which we have previewed in this collection), is an attempt to deal with these and related objections by supplementing the purely formal concept of ontological presentation in *Being and Event* with a more substantive concept of ontological appearance. Being appears precisely because there is no whole. Thus being is always localized or being-there (existence). Yet, once again, difficulties arise because of Badiou's reluctance to specify the philosophical situation in anything other than evental terms. Philosophy identifies the link between the pure unbinding of being qua being (as prescribed by set theory) and the bound character of being in situation (as delineated through the resources of category theory). Philosophy's specificity would thereby seem to reside in its ability to identify the link between being and existence, and hence in effectuating the relation between the bound and the unbound – or the related and the non-related – by thinking the aleatory emergence of the subject of truth, such that the latter, in a position of 'torsion', undoes the related (knowable, classifiable) order (or language) of a situation. In this respect, the relation between bound and unbound, or related and non-related, is itself split: first, in terms of the ontological articulation of consistency and inconsistency; second, as the result of the suspension or disqualification of the system of relations that constitutes the situation which is transformed by the affirmation of an event. In other words, philosophy as a theoretical practice is defined by the manner in which it relates two subtractions: the ontological or axiomatic subtraction marked by the empty set and the evental subtraction which is the procedural substance of a truth-subject. Yet if philosophy is able to oversee these twin subtractions, is it not thereby accorded a function – first as meta-ontological, then as meta-procedural – every bit as totalizing, if not more so, than those figures of the Whole proposed by dialectics (whether idealist or materialist) and the Deleuzean ontology of the virtual?

4. What Badiou's rationalism retains from the Kantian/Heideggerian critique of metaphysics is the fundamental distinction between truth and knowledge. However, contra both Kant and Heidegger, Badiou insists that truth's extra-propositional character – its transcendence vis-à-vis knowledge – need not be consigned to non-conceptual intuition and the extra-conceptual and non-formalizable domains of morality or poetry. It can be precisely circumscribed using the resources of mathematical discourse. According to Badiou, truth's unknowable or indiscernible character remains rationally conceivable because the distinction between the determinate possibilities of knowing and the indeterminate potency of thinking has been rendered ontologically specifiable through the work of the mathematician Paul Cohen. But Badiou's ontology stipulates that the unknowable is never One; thus it is never an absolute, it is always situated, localized. Truth's transcendence is only ever relative, never absolute; it is the transcendence *from* this situation

through the unknowable *of* this situation. What is unknowable is only ever unknowable from within a situation, and the forcing of a truth (cf. 'Truth: Forcing and the Unnameable' in this collection) accounts for how what was unknowable within a given situation can be rendered knowable by transforming that situation's cognitive dimensions from the inside. Truths are always plural and discontinuous, never unitary and homogeneous. By the same token, deductive consistency is discontinuously sequential rather than homogeneously arborescent, and hence no longer vitiated root and branch by the emergence of inconsistency (this is the upshot of what Badiou calls 'the Cantor-Gödel-Cohen sequence'). Upsurges of inconsistency petition new decisions and give rise to new deductive sequences. 'Event' is simply Badiou's name for such upsurges. The axiomatic assertion of evental inconsistency – what Badiou calls 'deciding the undecidable' – is made in the absence of any pre-existing cognitive criteria for verifying that assertion. We affirm that something happened, even though we do not know how to prove or verify its occurrence. But the assertion itself will bring about the conditions for its own verification: in drawing the consequences of that assertion, we slowly transform the parameters of cognitive possibility governing the logic of the situation in such a way as to render what was previously unthinkable thinkable (the situation's generic truth) and what was previously unknowable knowable ('forcing' the generic supplement of the situation).

It is this precise articulation of the deductive force of mathematics and a Real instance of rupture which defines the specificity of Badiou's thought, setting it apart from the otherwise ambient concern with the themes of excess and exceptionality. Rather than leaving novelty to mutate dialectically into the structures of established fact or to remain ultimately indiscernible from states of affairs (an accusation levied at the concept of the virtual in Badiou's *Deleuze*), the ontological apparatus set in motion by Badiou is intended to purify the event to the point where its incomprehensibility from the point of view of the knowledge or state of the situation is rendered exorbitant. Instead of discerning novelty in the interstices of any phenomenon, Badiou opts for conceding almost everything to the indifferent order of ontology – to the pervasive normality of things as they are – so as to ensure that the sundering of normality be in turn given its due. Evental novelty is not ubiquitous but rare, and the measure of its rarity is provided by ontology's almost boundless capacity for rendering all phenomena thinkable as more or less unexceptional. Indeed, one of Badiou's most common polemical gambits, exhibited in his objections to Deleuze's Riemann (in this volume's

'One, Multiple, Multiplicities'), consists precisely in seeing a kind of harmless banality where other thinkers think they perceive the outer limits of thought.

But the event is precisely *not* what it is *possible* to think, at least not until its consequences have been drawn in a traversal of the situation and in the production of a truth, with all the consequences it entails. The event, as Real, is always in some sense impossible. And it is the great glory of mathematics that its history is marked by the decisions to force certain impossible entities into existence and intelligibility (be they imaginary numbers, infinitesimals, Mahlo cardinals or what have you). For Badiou, in complete contrast to classical rationalism or even the temporalized adventures of dialectics, everything is *not* thinkable here and now. Were it so, the capacity of being would be exhausted by the modality of the possible, and all novelty would have the status of an insignificant supplement, a simulacrum. Rather, what is unthinkable in a situation *now*, rather than what is absolutely unthinkable, can become thinkable. As we have seen, for Badiou there can be no such thing as an other of thought *tout court*, an unthinkable *sub specie aeternitatis*. The productive and groundless character of truths and subjects entails the wager that 'we will have been able to think what was previously unthinkable'. It also entails the purely adjectival character of rationality, the non-identity of reason as the principle for a possible, and thus implicitly actualized, space of possibilities. While we may axiomatically affirm the incompleteness of all situations, their lying at the edge of the void, and thus the ever-present chance that we may come to think and to be otherwise, there is no identity, not even a negative one, for the impossible-Real that aleatory rationalism tries to situate through the resources of set-theoretical ontology (and specifically, the axiom of foundation and the theorem of the point of excess).

In a sense, the whole point of the finely articulated apparatus of ontology is to reveal, through its paradoxes and points of undecidability, that the Real has a non-transcendental, situational specificity. Or rather, that precisely because it can only be subjectively attested in its effects, in the construction of a generic set, there is no such (one) thing as the Real, but rather non-denumerable instances of the determinate puncturing of different situations by the (empty, indifferent) truth of being. The multiplication of infinities ensures that there is no Real as absolutely Other, no unthinkable that would constitute the limit or transcendent object of *a* reason. Whence Badiou's manifest indifference to the turn to the sublime (which he plausibly regards as founded on a completely impoverished notion of infinity and a rather miserable humanism) and his palpable and combative disdain for the pathos of finitude – both of which are, after all, intimately connected intellectual phenomena. Although foreclosed from the standpoint of the constituted knowledge or language of the situation, the Real affirmed by Badiou's aleatory rationalism is not the counterpart of a thought marked by finitude, and it is not One, since it can only be retroactively attested, which is to say produced, for and through a determinate situation in the process of evental subjectivation.

Thus, deductive fidelity offers a paradigm of rationality which is no longer about validating cognitive necessity but about wagering on the aleatory and unverifiable in a way that entails a process of conceptual invention and cognitive discovery that will transfigure the structures of intelligibility within a given situation. Far from hypostasizing 'reason' as some sort of faculty or disposition naturally inherent in the human intellect, far from seeking to bolster the allegedly normative authority of 'rationality', Badiou's brand of rationalism subtracts 'reason' from the ambit of the psyche in a way that subverts the presumed fixity of cognitive structures and undermines the pseudo-transcendental bounds of linguistic sense. This is a rationalism without 'reason', one that has been radically de-psychologized. 'Rationality' is a pseudo-normative category mired in logicism at best, psychologism at worst. Axiomatic-theorematic reasoning provides a model of 'rationality' whose resemblance or lack thereof vis-à-vis human cognitive processes is ultimately irrelevant. Moreover, this aleatory rationalism is devoid of constitutive interests or intrinsic ends that would conjoin the moral and the epistemological. It is 'disinterested' in the sense that it declares the possibility of a 'formalised in-humanism'.[14] It is rare, discontinuous and inherently subversive, inasmuch as it does not shore up the authority of cognitive norms, but rather disqualifies them. Where dogmatic rationalism asserts the sovereignty of 'reason' qua cognitive faculty harbouring the ends of our activity (whether manual or intellectual) and guaranteeing our orderly dwelling in a predictable categorized world, Badiou's aleatory rationalism affirms the potency of *thought* as that which is defined precisely by the discontinuous invention of means for wagering on novelty and forcing the dysfunction of the categories that partition worlds into distinct domains that can be overseen, counted and controlled.

This focus on the extra-philosophical procedures that allow subjects to *avoid* the structures of knowledge and produce generic truths outside the norms of possibility suggests that, despite the emphasis on axiomatic decision as an inaugural separation from any religious theme of origin or beginning, aleatory rationalism – the thinking of the event – is best understood in terms of the *consequences* of affirmation; consequences that, counter to traditional philosophical intuition, involve the invention of new extra-philosophical methods which in turn will inflect the practice of philosophy itself, much as Lenin's theory of the party and Mallarmé's experiments with syntax have left their mark on that space of compossibility constituted by Badiou's thought. There is no sovereign subject of rationality, only rational subjects elicited by a decision on an event and caught up in the aleatory construction of singular universal truths. Consequently there is no thought outside of its dissemination in these procedures. What these procedures share, what renders them (retroactively) compossible is not their conformity to 'reason' but their production of generic sets, i.e. truths subtracted from the inevitably partial distributions of knowledge. Philosophy's arduous task consists in coordinating these perforations of the orders of knowledge. 'Thought' – if we can speak of such a thing independently of situated procedures – is not defined as a faculty, but as the contingent and transversal product of such a coordination.

5. The mainstream of contemporary 'Continental' philosophy continues to operate within the bounds of the critical interregnum: the (broadly) anti-metaphysical and post-rationalist problematic initiated by Kantian critique and radicalized by Heidegger's fundamental ontology. We should not allow this post-Kantian consensus – conformity to which fuels the current détente among 'Continental' philosophers – to occlude the peculiar repartition of modesty and ambition carried out by Badiou's philosophy. Confronted with the latter's seemingly irrepressible confidence in the affirmative capacities of philosophical formalization, the Kantian reflex – now crucially and insidiously supplemented by the para-political and meta-aesthetic ideology of the unrepresentable (so well diagnosed by Jacques Rancière) – is to castigate what it identifies as a peculiarly anachronistic version of 'fanaticism'. The recourse to set-theoretical ontology, mustering varieties of infinity as yet undreamt of by metaphysicians, seems to herald a baleful recrudescence of pre-critical dogmatism, a disastrous pretension, as Kant put it, 'to SEE the infinite'. Perhaps it is time to consider whether the particular image of philosophy endorsed by Badiou may or may not prove reducible to a kind of 'raving with reason'.

To begin with, and in light of the demarcations rehearsed above, such fanaticism could not without further ado be ascribed to philosophy, strictly speaking. We have already noted that the secularization of the infinite requires that philosophy expropriate its putative capacity to think the latter. Thus, in abandoning the project of critique (or rather, in never taking it up), Badiou's aleatory rationalism also abjures the putative pre-eminence of philosophy when it comes to delineating the very possibilities of thought. Far from constituting an instance of perilous philosophical hubris, the claim that 'we can begin purely and simply with the infinite' is a claim that rests on the inventions of mathematics. In other words, if the infinite can come first it is because philosophy has abdicated the autonomy of its intuition the better to defer to the cognitive innovations of mathematics and – in a way we shall not be able to investigate here – politics.[15] If anything then, philosophy is immodestly heteronomous, since its hubris does not arise from its own capacities but from the capacities of thought in its heterogeneous instances of production and subjectivation. The plurality of thought, or rather of those procedures that produce truths, a plurality concomitant with the denial that there is *a* subject of or for philosophy, also entails the impossibility of carrying out an immanent delineation of the limits of cognitive or subjective possibility.

Once immanence has been handed over to the actual and non-totalizable inconsistency of the set-theoretical multiple, and is therefore no longer immanence *to* a philosophical subject, the problematic of the limit (or even of what Badiou has sometimes referred to as 'the unnameable') is itself made relative to the situation under consideration. We have already mentioned that the subtraction of a unifying *arché* for thought makes the notion of an absolute limit vanish. Philosophy thus acknowledges the potency of thought, the fact that it has no absolute limit, by emptying itself of the appeal to an originary experience of thought. By disavowing traditional claims to privileged intuition and to a faculty of supra-disciplinary synthesis, Badiou's philosophy precludes any attempt to impose a priori limits on non-philosophical thought procedures (whence the relentless affirmation that mathematics *thinks*, science *thinks*, politics *thinks*, love *thinks*). We could even say that for Badiou philosophy evacuates transcendence by making nothing immanent *to* philosophy, and in particular by refusing to make thought, subjectivity and truth coextensive with philosophical practice.

In this regard, Badiou's philosophy cannot be seen as yet another in the sequence of hopeful subreptions or transgressions of the limits set by Kant or reset by Wittgenstein. Lest it be confused for some kind of *scientia dei* or *mathesis universalis*, for the mobile totalization promised by sundry varieties of dialectical thinking, or for the related realization of the latent content of philosophical practice in world-transforming praxis, it is imperative to reiterate once more the weight that must be accorded to the non-being of the One and the inexistence of the Whole. The sundering of the infinite (or, more precisely, of infinities) from capture in a unitary divinity, the absence of any pre-evental subject of cognition, and the mathematical affirmation that there is no (one) Universe, all clearly point toward the impossibility of reducing Badiou's standpoint to that of any classical variant of metaphysical rationalism. This systematic thought is emphatically not a theory of everything.

An examination of Badiou's relation to dialectics, a constant in his intellectual trajectory, can prove illuminating in this regard. In a recent essay, Badiou writes, with reference to Hegel: 'Not only, contrary to what Hamlet declares, is there nothing in the world which exceeds our philosophical capacity, but there is nothing in our philosophical capacity which could not come to be in the reality of the world.'[16] This confidence in the powers of reason displayed by dialectical thinking leads Badiou to see in it the culmination as well as the collapse of classical rationalism. A culmination in the sense that any transcendent or transcendental check on the extension of rationality is removed; a collapse insofar as the hyper-rationalism of dialectics is fuelled by its hostility to the eminent role of mathematical infinity within classical rationalism (see 'Philosophy and Mathematics: Infinity and the End of Romanticism' in this volume). Though we are sympathetic to Bruno Bosteels's claim that over and above the theorem concerning the inexistence of the Whole, Badiou's recent ontological work on the theme of appearance could be seen to herald a qualified return of the kind of dialectical thinking so prominent in the earlier *Theory of the Subject*, it nevertheless remains the case that the mathematical expropriation of a sui generis philosophical intuition or subjectivity entails that there is no philosophical capacity per se that would stand as a potentially determinable reservoir for dialectical realization.[17] The inconsistent is not the potential or the determinable and it is not 'in thought' as such. Rather than a capacity held by a totalizing reason, the modality of truth in Badiou is that of a retroactive possibility: only on the basis of a decision which no capacity guarantees and through the construction of a generic set that has no store of knowledge to refer to 'will it have been possible' to formulate the truth of a situation. Thus, while Badiou holds on to the dialectical refusal of any a priori constraint on thought, and on the subversive consequences of the realization of rationality, he abandons, in conformity with the motifs of expropriation and pluralization mentioned above, the notion that thought or philosophy can be unified or totalized as a capacity which would expand 'its' limits.

Why not then simply dissolve philosophy into the multiplicity of discourses and practices, rescind its delirious pretension to sovereignty, dilute it into an ornamental meditation on the crimes and shortcomings of rationality? Why not simply welcome the age of sophistry? In a sense, Badiou's opposition to these postmodern strategies is unjustified and indeed unjustifiable, at least from a transcendental as opposed to axiomatic standpoint. The commitment to the new, the exceptional and the generic is simply non-negotiable. As Badiou declares: 'The new is the just.' Equally, the Platonic injunction to separate truth from doxa, to cut through the dense and incoherent mass of opinions and the arbitrary norms that regulate the interactions of the polis is undoubtedly a primary requirement of Badiou's philosophizing, but certainly not one that could be 'legitimated'. For Badiou, to hold on to the category of truth, albeit in a guise that has been comprehensively recast, is to assert that philosophy's task is always one of supporting or dis-inhibiting whatever subversions and separations occur in the different domains of thought.

We may want to ask what renders such a conviction immune from Rortyan attempts to sap the confidence and foundations of philosophical practice. In a sense, nothing. The identification of philosophy with a kind of courage for truth, excess, and separation is a subjective conviction with absolutely no guarantee either in the domain of representable objectivity or in the psychological structure of a cognizing subject. Yet closer examination of the sophist's challenge reveals what is rationally objectionable about it. As Badiou has argued elsewhere (most prominently in the *Manifesto for Philosophy*), the inestimable worth of the sophist, from Protagoras to Lyotard, is his ability to alert the philosopher to the untenable nature of philosophical autocracy, to disabuse him of the futile and disastrous delusion of being the keeper of the Truth of truth. Moreover, the sophist's nagging rejoinders open philosophy up to the multifariousness of cases, thus emphasizing the challenge inherent in the aim of reducing the equivocal phenomenology of common sense to the mathematical indifference of a rational ontology. All this militates toward Badiou's call to spare the sophist, rather than to force his or her elimination.

But to respond to the challenge of modern sophistry by expropriating philosophical intuition permits the truly contemporary philosopher to recognize that the sophistical schema only seems to be in favour of dissemination and multiplicity. From the standpoint of an aleatory rationalism, it is essential to perceive how the sophist, while seeming to sing the praises of universal difference and exception and the inapplicability of any rational categorial schema, is still committed to the notion that the multiple can itself be characterized, that it can be given the quasi-transcendental lineaments of discourses, language games, embodiment, strategies, and so on. Though sophistry abandons the immanence of thought to philosophical intuitions of the kind still endorsed by critique and dialectics, it simply shifts the locus of unified transcendental legislation, to language in particular, thereby generating, beneath the gaudy apparel of discursive multiplicity, a new figure of the Whole and the One. Short of the resort to the unintuitable and the absolute alterity of some sublime instance, such postmodern thinking remains incapable, from Badiou's perspective, of thinking the determinate emergence of an exception and its systematic yet aleatory disfigurement of an established situation. Situated excess is here pitted against the *universal variability* which, in its amorphous constitution, remains a profoundly conservative image of thought since it precludes the subtractive specificity of a truth – that which renders truth at once 'illegitimate' (it is irreducible to the language governing a situation, bereft of any proof or guarantee in the domain of knowledge) and rational (it proceeds through a strict, albeit decisionistic, logic of consequences).

Most importantly, to affirm philosophy against sophistry is to reiterate the importance of localizing the practical break between thought (or truth) and language (or knowledge), something that can only be done, according to Badiou, so long as we are attentive to the rare instances in which a regime of discourse and intelligibility is suddenly beset by a dysfunction and transformed by a subject. Note here that one of the provocative consequences of such an approach is that for Badiou *there is no difference in kind between opinion and knowledge*, both being opposed by truth. This is not to say that there is any interest here in a *critique* of doxa, or in the establishment of a clear and distinct reservoir of knowledge to counter a common sense gone astray. Only real separations from doxa matter, those sequences in which the stability of a situation and its language are traversed, disqualified, and perhaps destroyed. In this regard, doxa is never the critical *object* either of philosophy or of a particular truth procedure, but rather the obstacle they circumvent and the material they transform. Needless to say, this means that Badiou's philosophy abandons one of the main concerns common to critique, dialectics and sophistry, not to mention numerous manifestations of philosophical materialism: the account of the genesis of doxa or the sources of representation. Separation, rather than constitution, is the core of aleatory rationalism.

6. Badiou's acosmism, with its undermining of totality, is adamantly *not* an intra-philosophical response to some sublime catastrophe of reason,

predicated upon the dubious isomorphism of philosophical totality and political 'totalitarianism'. It is the untamed infinities averred by mathematics and the boundless thought they announce which determine the attack on totality, not the thinker's feigned humility or guilt at his or her inexcusable hubris. We could even say that just as Badiou eschews the faculty of reason only to intensify the possibilities of rationalism, so he focuses on the irruptions of the universal by postulating the inexistence of *the* Universe (or the Whole of all wholes).

The obverse of this empowering evacuation or self-expropriation of philosophy, whose formalizing rationality is radically dependent on the contingency of events and truths over which it has no sway, is the refusal to provide any internal or immanent account for the genesis or possibility of philosophy itself (and the concomitant rejection of anything which is even distantly related to epistemology, including the discontinuous diagrams and narrations of Bachelard, Canguilhem or Foucault). According to Badiou, to display a concern with the genetic sources of philosophy would be once again to render extra-philosophical truth procedures (in science, politics, art, love) immanent to a more or less sovereign philosophical subject, one that would make a detour through their externality only in order, when all is said and done, to rediscover itself in the unfolding of its latent interiority. No such avenue is open to Badiou, who consequently seems to leave in abeyance the very question of the origin or beginning of philosophy, and, more broadly, the very problem of the genesis of the intellect as such. As Althusser once wrote: 'There is no obligatory beginning in philosophy, philosophy does not begin with a beginning that would also be an origin. Philosophy jumps onto a moving train . . .'[18]

Thus, while Badiou's philosophy is in great part preoccupied with generating a theory of the subject capable of thinking through the consequences of the truths of its time, it is bereft of a theory of (the emergence of) the *philosophical* subject. Indeed, it appears that one of the conditions for holding to the tenets of an aleatory rationalism is that of writing off as a dead end any reflection on philosophical subjectivation itself. This is of course a corollary of the definition of the event as undecidable and indiscernible from within the parameters of its situation. Aleatory rationalism is based precisely on the fact that there is no 'reason', in the sense of *ratio* or *Grund*, for events and the truths they give rise to. So while the type of philosophical subjectivity espoused by Badiou does seem to rest on the postulate which we could call that of 'the justice of the new' – on a kind of a priori and thus void fidelity to what happens insofar as it happens – the critical philosopher (or any of his epigones) will look with suspicion upon a philosophy so determinedly and doctrinally committed to saying next to nothing about the conditions for its own exercise. Where the seemingly momentous sundering of philosophy from ontology is concerned, we are offered the account of a *decision* which, although strategically persuasive, cannot lay claim to any guarantee or justification besides that of the consequences it may harbour with regard to the intensification or purification of thought, as well as the latter's capacity to separate instances of truth from the representational networks of doxa and knowledge. While philosophy's self-expropriation for the sake of the event may turn it into a kind of metaontology (albeit one whose exact situation is difficult to pin down), there is no Archimedean point – whether faculty, subject or divine reason – from which to judge the validity or construct the consistency of the metaontological decision: *mathesis* is no longer *universalis*; all *scientia* is now without a *deus*.

And yet one could argue that in spite of abdicating its powers of survey over thought, philosophy's articulation of the unbound multiplicity of mathematics and the practical production of generic truths turns it into a supplementary instance, a transcendent apparatus for generating the aleatory univocity of being and event in the guise of a rare and formalized truth.[19] This charge is perhaps exacerbated by Badiou's refusal to countenance any account of the genesis of the philosophical subject itself. Ultimately, what we are faced with is a veritable division within contemporary philosophy's materialist camp.[20] The status of materialism in Badiou's thought is not easy to adjudicate, and one would need to refer back to the lengthy treatment of it in Chapter IV of his *Theory of the subject* in order to shed some real light on this issue. But in very broad and preliminary terms, we could say that Badiou's materialism depends on: (1) a fidelity to the Lacanian notion of the Real as that which resists its symbolisation and capture in a thought of possibility; (2) a thinking of the event as immanent to the Real of a situation, that is, as being *in* a situation (presented) but not *of* a situation (represented); (3) a recasting of the praxis-centred tendency in materialism through the thesis that the truth of an event can only be produced, and retroactively attested, via the construction of a generic set; (4) a repudiation of any figure of matter as (the) One or (the) Whole, in short, of any doctrine of monism (Badiou's materialism is in this respect a variant on acosmism, and can be seen to derive from his strictly meontological use of the multiple); (5) a sharp and incontrovertible distinction, founded principally on point (1), which says that materialism is incompatible with naturalism, if by the latter we understand any attempt to account for the genesis of thought either in terms of some continuity with the natural sciences (neurophysiology, cognitive science, ethology) or in terms of a more metaphysical notion of *natura naturans.*

Badiou thus wishes to argue both that thought is not some ineffable, angelic 'stuff' over and above situations and that it cannot be circumscribed (for instance, within the human nervous system) in such a way as to set the stage for its reduction, explanation, and genesis. In a sense, the classical question of materialism is rescinded by Badiou to the extent that he does not permit of any operative distinction between the (material-) real and the ideal, displacing that traditional trope into the distinction between the real of the event and the knowledge, language or representation of the situation. The key difference between this aleatory rationalism – or what Badiou himself describes as his 'materialism of grace' – and a transcendental materialism of the Deleuzean variety is that while the latter wishes to set out the real conditions for the possibility of (the experience of) thought, the former leaves a fundamental heteronomy (which some might interpret as miraculous transcendence) in place.

We might even hazard the claim that in a rather paradoxical manner, Badiou's aleatory rationalism is a kind of historical materialism, in the precise, restricted sense that its claims regarding the real of the event as the basis of rare truths depends on a distinction – which Badiou maintains on set-theoretical grounds – between nature and history; a distinction which is profoundly inimical to any brand of naturalist materialism, whether of the ancient (Lucretius), modern (Spinoza) or post-Kantian variety (Deleuze and Guattari). Badiou's is ultimately an anti-naturalist materialism. It rests on the provocative proposition that nature, far from being the arena of savage becomings, is a domain of perfectly adjusted representation, of seamless normality, and that the event-history is the only site of the upsurge of inconsistent immanence.

But where does this leave not just materialism, but philosophy *tout court*? Badiou's aim is to provide philosophy with the resources for formalizing – as opposed to substantializing – extra-philosophical novelty. His abiding conviction is that holding true to the independent rationality and subversive irruption of non-philosophical subjects means effecting a radical separation of thought, not only from the entire apparatus of critique, but also from the kind of naturalism proposed by most self-avowed materialists. However, by simply writing off the question of *philosophical* subjectivity as a hindrance to the reckoning with extra-philosophical truths, Badiou may well be depriving himself of the means for shedding light on the very logic of compossibility that specifies philosophy's relation to its conditions, a logic that should also account for the manner in which Badiou's own doctrine, far from being an arbitrary dogmatism, is conditioned, particularly by mathematics. Can Badiou retain his linking of rational ontology to the subjective contingency of truths without elucidating the way in which evental historicity and the atemporal theorems on being combine to generate philosophical discourse?[21] Isn't philosophical formalization, which relies on the unique capacity with which mathematical discourse is supposedly endowed – the capacity to inscribe the Real in transmissible symbolisms and chains of deductive inference – itself temporalized by events in mathematics and by its own practice of compossibility, thus demanding a much fuller, and perhaps more 'critical', account of philosophical subjectivity? When all is said and done, Badiou's philosophy is simply a theory of truth, which is to say, of thought. But it is a theory which, while abounding in prescriptions about the style and ethos of philosophical practice, seems to be predicated on a deliberate refusal to formulate anything like a theory of philosophy or of philosophical subjectivity. Perhaps this refusal is the sine qua non for the revitalization of a senescent academic discipline. Alternately, the rejuvenation promised by Badiou's philosophy may require a full and explicit account of how a subject comes to philosophy (and vice versa), in order to open the logic of compossibilization to theoretical practices whose possibilities extend beyond the co-ordinates of Badiou's own relation to the extra-philosophical.

R.B., A.T.

London and Teheran, May 2004

Notes

1. A situation is minimally defined by Badiou as 'a multiple composed of an infinity of elements, each one of which is itself a multiple'. See the discussion in Peter Hallward's *Badiou* (Minneapolis: Minnesota University Press, 2003), pp. 93–4. To forestall any possible confusion, it is important to note that, as a metaontological postulate, this notion of situatedness is not that of an existential subject-in-situation or a Leibnizian-Nietzschean perspective on or from a world. Being-in-situation is simply the 'objective' correlate of the inexistence of a Whole of all wholes, or Universe, and of the relative or local nature of ontological consistency.

2. With this notion of expropriation, or rather self-expropriation, we have attempted in part to translate some of the key insights put forward by Oliver Feltham in his essay 'And Being and Event and . . .' in *Polygraph* 17 (2005), pp. 27–40. Feltham persuasively characterizes the relation between philosophy, mathematics and ontology in terms of a 'hetero-expulsion' of philosophy's claim

on ontology in favour of mathematics for the sake of a thinking of truth as praxis.

3. Although, as Badiou, following Lacan puts it, 'there is oneness', *il y a de l'un* – a crucial qualification pertaining to the distinction between the inconsistency of being qua being and the consistency of being qua appearance. We will have more to say about this below.

4. We write 'rationalist' rather than 'rational' advisedly, since for Badiou the domain of the decision and the axiom lies outside of any simple dichotomy between the 'rational', understood as that which is always already vouchsafed by a standard image of adequate cognition, and the 'irrational', understood as the act welling up from some obscure source, be it demonic, vital or unconscious. The only time Badiou uses the adjective 'rational' in any philosophically consequential way is to qualify ontology. 'Rational ontology' identifies the sequence of attempts to wed ontology to mathematics, and thereby to subject philosophy to the cutting edge of mathematical invention. Bar a few, somewhat marginalized exceptions (Desanti, Cavaillès, Lautman), it is a sequence which was terminated in philosophy by Hegel and was continued, more or less implicitly, within the work of mathematicians such as Cantor and Cohen. The expression 'rational ontology' in no way indicates a reference to some quality or ideal which could go by the name of 'rationality'. Or rather, the dissemination of ontology and the demotion of human cognition effectuated by rational ontology makes any unitary, non-eventual, definition of rationality impossible. It is worth noting that Badiou's one defence of rationality 'as such' comes in a plea for a philosophy that would be able to counter the idiotic fanaticisms and archaisms that mark the contemporary world. See 'Philosophy and Desire' (originally entitled 'Philosophy and the Desire of the Contemporary World'), in *Infinite Thought*, edited by Oliver Feltham and Justin Clemens (London: Continuum, 2003), p. 55, where he writes: 'Philosophy is required to make a pronouncement about contemporary rationality. We know that this rationality cannot be the repetition of classical rationalism, but we also know that we cannot do without it, if we do not want to find ourselves in a position of extreme intellectual weakness when faced with the threat of these reactive passions.'

5. Examples would include *Being and Event*'s critique of the notion of 'destruction', which is a fundamental category in *Theory of the Subject*; *Logics of Worlds*' critique of the account of eventual naming in *Being and Event*; Badiou's own recent decision to retract the theory of the unnameable outlined in texts such as 'On Subtraction', 'Truth: Forcing and the Unnameable' and the *Ethics*; and last but not least, the substantially revised theory of the event Badiou proposes in *Logics of Worlds*.

6. In Meditation 3 of *Being and Event* and 'Notes Toward a Thinking of Appearance' (this volume), Badiou identifies Zermelo and his 'axiom of separation' as the source for such a materialism within the lineage of rational ontology. For a long treatment of the question of materialism in Badiou's earlier work, see *Théorie du sujet* (Paris: Seuil, 1982), pp. 193–253, and Bruno Bosteels's forthcoming *Badiou and the Political* (Duke University Press).

7. Whence Badiou's insistence, in the wake of his turn away from the dialectics of destruction espoused in *Theory of the Subject*, on the exemplary status of Mallarmé's notion of *action restreinte*, restricted action. For the concept of suture see the *Manifesto for Philosophy* and Alberto Toscano, 'To Have Done with the End of Philosophy', *Pli: The Warwick Journal of Philosophy* 9 (2000), pp. 223–4.

8. *Manifeste pour la philosophie* (Paris: Seuil, 1989), p. 69.

9. Badiou characterizes Cantor's theorem, in which the quantitative excess of the state of a situation (representation) over a situation (presentation) is shown to be undecidable, as 'the impasse or the real point of ontology'. This theorem, along with the related Cohen-Easton theorem, which establishes 'the complete errancy of excess', will provide the basis for Badiou's theory of the event. See *L'être et l'événement* (Paris: Seuil, 1988), p. 559.

10. *L'être et l'événement*, Meditations 1–6, pp. 31–117, in particular pp. 35–6.

11. *L'être et l'événement*, p. 35.

12. *L'être et l'événement*, p. 35.

13. *L'être et l'événement*, p. 35.

14. Alain Badiou, *The Century* (forthcoming).

15. This point is made by Nina Power in 'What is Generic Humanity? Badiou and Feuerbach', *Subject Matters: A Journal of Communication and the Self* 2, forthcoming.

16. 'Metaphysics and the Critique of Metaphysics', trans. Alberto Toscano, *Pli: The Warwick Journal of Philosophy* 10 (2000), pp. 189–90.

17. This is not to say that there is no problem of capacity or potentiality in Badiou's thought. However, it is a problem that arises in the context of his characterizations of the relationship between thought and 'generic humanity' rather than in his vision of philosophical activity per se. See Nina Power and Alberto Toscano, '"Think, Pig!": An Introduction to Badiou's Beckett', in Alain Badiou, *On Beckett*, ed. Nina Power and Alberto Toscano (Manchester: Clinamen Press, 2003).

18. Louis Althusser, 'Le courant souterrain du matérialisme de la rencontre', *Écrits philosophiques et politiques, Tome I*, ed. François Matheron (Paris: IMEC, 1995), p. 576. We have chosen to dub Badiou's project an 'aleatory rationalism' precisely in order to foreground what, in the final analysis, distinguishes it from the tradition sketched by Althusser in that late fragment. Although focused on chance as the real basis for any production of truth, Badiou's philosophy maintains the rationalist allegiance to mathematization so as to circumscribe and separate the event and its consequences from the ordinary course of the world. As we have tried to suggest, Badiou invokes Cantor, Zermelo and Cohen (among others) in an attempt to overturn Althusser's late verdict, to wit that all rationalism must be teleological, essentialist and committed to a notion of the origin. What prevents aleatory rationalism from being the mere acknowledgment (*constat*, a term emphasised by Althusser)

of the deviations of matter, and turns it into an intervention, is the manner in which it articulates a rational, set-theoretical ontology and a theory of the subject, which is exactly what Badiou, in all his writings on Althusser, criticises his old mentor for failing to do. Without a theory of the subject, according to Badiou, materialism collapses into a description of material events and fails to grasp the difference between real novelty and mere change, or, more importantly, the difference between a truth and a catastrophe, be it political or topological.

19. This is the crux of the rather elliptical verdict on Badiou's *Being and Event* voiced by Deleuze and Guattari in their *What is Philosophy?* (London: Verso, 1994), pp. 151–3, where they identify three interlinked instances of transcendence: (1) the evental site; (2) the nondescript multiplicity [*multiplicité quelconque*], which they juxtapose to their theory of the two multiplicities (intensive and extensive); (3) philosophy itself. They appear to argue that it is the first two that combine to make philosophy into an activity of survey: 'philosophy thus seems to float in an empty transcendence, as the unconditioned concept that finds the totality of its generic conditions in the functions (science, poetry, politics, and love). Is this not the return, in the guise of the multiple, to an old conception of the higher philosophy?' Although we are willing to concede the possibility that Badiou has reinvented a certain eminence for philosophy, Deleuze and Guattari's verdict misses the crucial point: the generic procedures cannot be totalized and do not, as such, 'fill out' philosophy. They are not functions because they do not depend on 'slowing down' the infinite into a space of coordinates. Furthermore, the axiomatic character of the set-theoretical thinking of the multiple is based precisely on the possibility of eschewing any concept of it, whether unconditioned or not.

20. This division has been amply and ably treated by Éric Alliez in *De l'impossibilité de la phénoménologie* (Paris: Vrin, 1995).

21. 'Atemporal' here refers to ontology in its 'current state'. Although its situational character entails that mathematics is itself punctuated and transformed by its own events, and therefore endowed with a kind of historicity, the axioms and theorems that make up the discourse on being are not themselves temporally conditioned. In other words, according to Badiou, the periodisation of mathematical truths is just as historical as that of politics or art, but mathematical truths are eternal, as are those of politics and art.

INDEX OF CONCEPTS

INDEX OF NAMES

Index of Names

Jung, Carl 127

Kant, Immanuel xii, xiv, xv, 8–10, 15,
    18, 24, 68, 129, 141–8, 171–3, 177,
    180, 190, 192–4, 208–9, 221
Kierkegaard, Soren xiv, xv
Kleene, Stephen Cole 181
Koyré, Alexandre 198–9
Kronecker, Leopold 68

Lacan, Jacques 19, 51, 107, 114, 116,
    125–36, 137, 139, 149, 162, 192, 245
Lagneau, Jules xiv
Lagrange, Comte Joseph de 11, 19, 111
Lardreau, Guy 72
Lautman, Albert 104, 254 n.1
Lautréamont, Comte de 8, 11–13, 15,
    16–17
Lazarus, Sylvain 163
Leblanc, Georgette 212
Lenin, Vladimir Ilyich 138–9
Leibniz, G. W. xiv, 24, 44, 68, 120, 181,
    183
Levy, Azriel 4, 5
Lucretius xv, 45, 46, 51, 87–8, 90, 108,
    186
Lyotard, Jean-François 157

MacLane, Saunders 182
Mallarmé, Stéphane 21, 44, 118, 122,
    158, 184, 243, 244–7,
    249, 251
Maeterlinck, Maurice 203, 207, 212,
    215
Malebranche, Nicolas xv
Mankiewicz, Joseph 212
Mao, Zedong 15
Marx, Karl xiv, 139
Meillasoux, Quentin 17, 206
Merleau-Ponty, Maurice xiv
Messiaen, Olivier 203

Neumann, John von 66, 68
Nietzsche, Friedrich xiv, 11, 12, 15, 28,
    37, 72, 73, 108, 126, 256 n.4

Oldenburg, Henry 91

Paris, Jeff 110
Parmenides xv, 44, 54, 84, 208
Pascal, Blaise 104
Peano, Guiseppe 68, 69
Perrault, Charles 203
Pessoa, Fernando 18, 21
Plato xiv, xv, 11, 13–14, 16–18, 27,
    30–2, 35–8, 41, 43, 45, 48–9, 51,
    53–5, 58, 61–2, 63, 84, 103, 155, 175,
    180, 185–6, 208–9, 248–9, 250–1
Poincaré, Jules Henri 177
Putnam, Hilary 53

Ricoeur, Paul 15, 135
Riemann, Bernhard 75, 79–80, 83
Rilke, Rainer Maria 19
Rimbaud, Arthur 11, 18, 156, 243,
    247–9, 251
Rousseau, Jean-Jacques xv, 104
Russell, Bertrand 69, 186–7

Saint-Just, Louis Antoine Léon de 155
Sartre, Jean-Paul xiv, 83
Schelling, Friedrich xv, 231
Schopenhauer, Arthur xiv
Schuller, George Hermann 91
Spinoza, Baruch xii, xv, 8, 15,
    16–17, 24, 72, 73, 83, 87–99,
    231, 256 n.4
Straub, Jean-Marie 83

Tarski, Alfred 181
Thales 9, 24
Thucydides 158
Tschirnhaus, Ehrenfried Walther
    von 91

Wagner, Richard 18
Whitehead, Alfred North 256–7 n.4
Wittgenstein, Ludwig 16, 25–6, 51, 58,
    68, 69, 108, 244

Zermelo, Ernst 50, 56, 188